TOGETHER *with* GOD

TOGETHER *with* GOD
PSALMS

DAVE BRANON
EDITOR

Discovery House.
from Our Daily Bread Ministries

TOGETHER *with* GOD

In this lifetime, it may not be possible to adequately plumb the depths of the book of Psalms. The length of it is imposing on its own, but then as we begin to dig into its truths and teachings, we become further convinced that we could never mine all of its treasures.

Yet we need to start digging. This book, which John Calvin called "an anatomy of all parts of the soul," reveals to us an unending array of insights into the mind of God and in the ways of humankind. It continually challenges us to pursue wisdom and to seek God.

The songs and poetry that comprise the Psalms teach us to pray, encourage us to trust, and invite us to dine at the table of God's endless goodness. No wonder C. S. Lewis said, "The most valuable thing the Psalms do for me is to express the same delight in God which made David dance."

In these pages, we invite you to dance along with Lewis and with David as each day of the year an exciting new and God-directed truth is opened up to you in these devotional articles. More than thirty *Our Daily Bread* writers have examined the Psalms and have attempted to unearth valuable truths from its pages. It is our prayer that these articles will breathe a new excitement into your life of faith as you, together with God, celebrate His unsurpassing goodness, faithfulness, and majesty.

Dave Branon, editor and *Our Daily Bread* writer

Let's Get Growing!

PSALM 1

But grow in the grace and knowledge of our Lord and Savior Jesus Christ.
To him be glory both now and forever! Amen.
2 PETER 3:18

Several years ago my interest in flowers had our home resembling a nursery. There's something about the presence of growing plants that I find enjoyable. As I daily inspected their progress, I gained from my little green friends a new appreciation of the joy and necessity of the wonderful process of growth.

As Christians, we are a little like plants. We should put down our roots, break up through the earth, spread out our branches, and burst into blossom. But what if such a thriving condition isn't always evident in our lives? Sometimes the bland routine of our daily activities causes us to just hang on and merely exist rather than move steadily toward maturity and fruitfulness.

If we do find ourselves at a spiritual standstill, we must allow Jesus the "Sun of Righteousness" (Malachi 4:2) to warm our hearts anew with His love. We must send our roots deep into the Word of God by meditating on it day and night (Psalm 1:2). Then we will be like a fruitful tree planted by rivers of living water, and our branches will extend outward in an ever-increasing influence and witness (v. 3). They will be filled with blossoms that reflect the beauty of righteous living.

Let's get growing!

MART DEHAAN

When growth stops, decay begins.

Puddle Ducks and Divers

PSALM 1

*Blessed is the one . . . whose delight is in the law of the LORD,
and who meditates on his law day and night.*

PSALM 1:1–2

To know God, we must grow in our knowledge of the Bible. Through its pages we learn not only facts about Him but we also learn how to know Him personally. That happens as we read God's Word to gain information about God and as we plumb its depths by meditating on what we read.

When I began to paint duck decoys, I learned that there are two kinds of ducks: puddle ducks and divers. Puddle ducks, such as mallards and redheads, simply paddle around the edge of marshes and ponds and feed in the shallow water. They eat only what they can reach from the surface. Diver ducks, however, are able to dive to surprising depths in a lake to feed from the plants at its bottom. Mergansers and canvasbacks are typical of this group, some of which can dive to depths of one hundred fifty feet for their food!

As we think of how we read the Bible, maybe we are like these two kinds of birds. Perhaps, like puddle ducks, we stay near the surface, satisfied with the nourishment found in the shallows. Or maybe we are like the divers. Following the example of the psalmist, we plunge deeply into the Word through study, reflection, and meditation "day and night."

Sure, it's okay sometimes to be puddle ducks as we enjoy casual Bible reading. But think of what we can gain by becoming a diver—by going deeper into our study of God's holy Word.

DAVID EGNER

Treasures of truth from God's Word lie deep beneath the surface.

Madame Curie

PSALM 1

Blessed are those whose ways are blameless,
who walk according to the law of the Lord.
PSALM 119:1

Madame Marie Curie holds her place in history as a pioneer in the study of radioactivity. In 1903, she was the first woman to win the Nobel Prize, capturing the honor in physics. Then, in 1911, she received a second Nobel Prize, this one in chemistry.

Such a wonderful contribution did not come without tremendous sacrifice. Madame Curie died of leukemia caused by prolonged exposure to radioactive materials. Even today, scholars who wish to read her handwritten journals and lab papers must wear protective clothing because these materials are still radioactive.

No one today would approach radioactive material without protection. But many seem unconcerned about exposure to the dangers of sin. Psalm 1 warns us against sinful attitudes, speech, and behavior (vv. 1, 4–6).

Obedience to God's law is a spiritual safeguard from sin and its deadly consequences. The psalmist also wrote to the Lord, saying, "I have hidden your word in my heart that I might not sin against you" (119:11).

Madame Curie didn't know about the serious health dangers of exposure to radioactivity. But God has given us ample warning about the dangers of sin. Let's apply daily what we read in His life-giving Book.

DENNIS FISHER

The Bible will tell you what is wrong before you have done it!
—Dwight Moody

What Makes God Laugh?

PSALM 2

The One enthroned in heaven laughs; the Lord scoffs at them.
PSALM 2:4

I was washing my car as the late evening sun was preparing to kiss the earth good night. Glancing up, I impulsively pointed the hose at the sun as if to extinguish its flames. Then the absurdity of my action hit me. I laughed. Here's how it might look as a news headline:

MAN TRIES TO DOUSE SUN WITH GARDEN HOSE

Then I thought of God's laugh in Psalm 2. Wicked nations were plotting to overthrow God's Anointed, thus ultimately opposing the Almighty himself. But He sits in the heavens, calm and unthreatened. Man's boldest efforts to oppose such awesome power are ludicrous. The Almighty doesn't even rise from His throne; He just laughs in derision.

But is this a heartless or cruel laughter? No! His same infinite greatness that mocks man's defiance also marks His sympathy with man in his lost condition. He's the same God who takes no pleasure in the death of the wicked (Ezekiel 33:11) and who wept over Jerusalem (Matthew 23:37–39). He is great in judgment but also in compassion (Exodus 34:6–7).

God's laughter reminds us that Christ will ultimately triumph over evil. Any defiance of Him and His will is futile. What a comfort it is for us to submit to the Lord Jesus and take refuge in Him!

DENNIS DEHAAN

Humankind's limited potential accents God's limitless power.

The Ultimate Bodyguard

PSALM 3

But you, LORD, are a shield around me, . . .
I will not fear though tens of thousands assail me on every side.
PSALM 3:3, 6

Usually, bodyguards are employed to protect only wealthy or prominent people. Most of us can only imagine what it would be like to walk around with someone at our side who commands the immediate respect of anyone who might harm us.

For some of us, our thoughts may be similar to those of the littlest guy in the second grade. He likes to imagine that former heavyweight boxer Mike Tyson is his bodyguard. Just as the school bully is about to unleash his latest round of push, shove, and trip, up walks Mike, wondering what's going on. There is something reassuring about having the protection of someone who could take on the whole second grade if he wanted to.

There's a huge difference between pretending to have a very strong person protecting us and actually knowing we have protection. One person who had that was David, king of Israel. He knew what it was like to be troubled, hated, and filled with self-doubt. But he also knew what it was like to put himself in the care and protection of One who could take on the whole world if He wanted to.

Father, help us to experience that same kind of confidence. Help us to see that 10,000 enemies cannot touch us as long as you want us safe.

MART DEHAAN

God is always stronger than your strongest foe.

Begin the Day with Hope

PSALM 3

I lie down and sleep; I wake again, because the LORD sustains me.
I will not fear though tens of thousands assail me on every side.

PSALM 3:5–6

Do you ever awaken in the morning to discover feelings of dread clouding your soul? If so, you know that dark, depressing thoughts can quickly overwhelm us. I had a wonderful Christian friend, for instance, who generally had a healthy outlook on life. Yet she became so distressed that she made a feeble attempt to commit suicide as a cry for help.

If anyone had reason to feel like that, it was David when he composed Psalm 3. He and a small band of followers had been driven from the palace in Jerusalem because of a rebellion staged by his son Absalom. They had spent the first night fording the Jordan River, had made camp the next day, and had retired on the second night with the problem still unresolved. Even so, David was able to lie down and go to sleep. When he awoke in the morning, the thought of the great odds against him came to mind (v. 1), but he didn't entertain it long. Instead, he looked upward in faith to God, backwards in gratitude for His mercies, and forward in expectation of His mighty deliverance. He could enter the new day with hope.

Some mornings we do wake up to a very difficult day. When this happens, we can either give in to despair or follow the example of David. Faith, gratitude, and expectation will enable us to face the most trying day with strong confidence in God.

HERB VANDER LUGT

If the best things are not possible,
make the best of the things that are possible.

What's in a Smile?

PSALM 4

A happy heart makes the face cheerful, but heartache crushes the spirit.
PROVERBS 15:13

Changes of the heart can show up on the face. But can changing our expression also help to change our heart? According to an article in *The New York Times,* the act of smiling can contribute to pleasant feelings. Writer Daniel Goleman says there is a relationship between facial expression and resulting mood. He cites experiments in which researchers found that pronouncing the word *cheese* prompted a smile and pleasant feelings, while pronouncing the word *few* tended to create another expression, resulting in negative emotions.

Smiling isn't the only thing we can do to change the way we feel. In Psalm 4, we find many actions that troubled people can take. When distress grips our soul, we can ask the Lord for relief and mercy (v. 1). We can take comfort in knowing we are among those who are favored by Him, remembering that He hears us when we call (v. 3). We can acknowledge our feelings and be quiet before Him (v. 4). We can do what is right (v. 5) and trust in Him to give us overflowing gladness (v. 7). And we can rest in the assurance of His peace and safety (v. 8).

Father, help us in our low moments to look up to you. And may we find in you the peace and inner gladness that will put a smile on our face.

MART DEHAAN

A heart touched by grace brings joy to the face.

Early Defense System

PSALM 5:1–8

Hear my cry for help, my King and my God, for to you I pray.
PSALM 5:2

Every believer in Christ is involved in spiritual warfare every day. We cannot afford, therefore, to enter the day complacently.

In an article for the *San Francisco Chronicle*, Herb Caen wrote, "Every morning in Africa, a gazelle wakes up. It knows it must run faster than the fastest lion or it will be killed. Every morning a lion wakes up. It knows it must outrun the slowest gazelle or it will starve to death. It doesn't matter whether you're a lion or a gazelle; when the sun comes up, you'd better be running."

Charles Spurgeon wrote many years ago, "If you are not seeking the Lord, the devil is seeking you." Therefore, it's best to have a strategy ahead of time so we can escape the attacks of the enemy of our soul. We must seek the Lord early and rely on His help, keenly aware that "the devil prowls around like a roaring lion looking for someone to devour" (1 Peter 5:8).

In Psalm 5 we read that David came to God early in the morning and asked Him for His protection and help (see verses 1–3). For him this was a regular practice.

Let's not move into any new day without being aware of our urgent need for the Lord. Being prepared is the best way to be ready for Satan's attack.

DAVID EGNER

**Start each day with your armor in place
and your marching orders in hand.**

A Surprise Package

PSALM 5

In the morning, Lord, you hear my voice;
in the morning I lay my requests before you and wait expectantly.
PSALM 5:3

Are you a morning person? Some of us aren't. Maybe for you, waking up and getting out of bed is a daily ordeal. But after you're fully alert, what's your mood? Do you have a spirit of thankfulness despite problems or afflictions you may have? Do you face the hours that lie ahead with confidence and expectancy?

I was challenged by the epitaph engraved on a tombstone in The Mackinac Island Cemetery in northern Michigan. Marking the grave of Virginia Verdier Allen, who died at the age of 57, are these words:

SHE NEVER LOST HER SENSE OF WONDER
APPROACHING EACH DAY
AS A SURPRISE PACKAGE
TO BE OPENED WITH ENCHANTMENT

Admittedly, life for even the most dedicated of God's people may be marked by difficulty. But the Lord wants us to bring our cares to Him. The psalmist had the right idea when he said to God, "To you I pray. In the morning, Lord, you hear my voice; in the morning I lay my requests before you and wait expectantly" (Psalm 5:2–3).

When we start each day with prayer, we'll be able to say with the psalmist, "This is the day the Lord has made; we will rejoice and be glad in it" (118:24 NKJV). We can open this "surprise package" with a heart of anticipation for God's goodness and direction.

VERNON GROUNDS

Each day is a gift to be opened with prayer.

God Is Listening

PSALM 5

I, by your great love, can come into your house;
in reverence I bow down toward your holy temple.

PSALM 5:7

The day before Billy Graham was to be interviewed on *The Today Show*, his director of public relations, Larry Ross, requested a private room for Graham to pray in before the interview. But when Mr. Graham arrived at the studio, his assistant informed Ross that Mr. Graham didn't need the room. He said, "Mr. Graham started praying when he got up this morning, he prayed while eating breakfast, he prayed on the way over in the car, and he'll probably be praying all the way through the interview," Ross later said. "That was a great lesson for me to learn as a young man."

Prayerfulness is not an event; it is a way of being in relationship with God. This kind of intimate relationship is developed when God's people view prayerfulness as a way of life. The Psalms encourage us to begin each day by lifting our voice to the Lord (5:3); to bow down to the Lord in reverence (v. 7), to fill our day with conversations with God (55:17); and in the face of accusations and slander, to give ourselves totally to prayer (109:4). We develop prayer as a way of life because we desire to be with God (42:1–4; 84:1–2; 130:5–6).

Prayer is our way of connecting with God in all life's circumstances. God is always listening. We can talk to Him any time throughout the day.

MARVIN WILLIAMS

In prayer, God hears more than your words—
He listens to your heart.

A Matter of Trust

PSALM 5

Let all who take refuge in you be glad;
let them ever sing for joy. Spread your protection over them,
that those who love your name may rejoice in you.

PSALM 5:11

A news item from Australia told the story of Pascale Honore, a paraplegic woman who, after eighteen years in a wheelchair, took up surfing. How?

Ty Swan, a young surfer, straps her to his back with duct tape. After getting the balance perfect, Ty paddles out into the ocean so they can catch a wave, and Pascale can experience the exhilaration of surfing. This requires a tremendous amount of trust; so many things could go wrong. Yet her confidence in Ty is enough to enable her to enjoy a dream come true, in spite of the danger.

Life is like that for the follower of Christ. We live in a dangerous world that is filled with unpredictable challenges and unseen perils. Yet we have joy because we know Someone who is strong enough to carry us through the churning waves of life, which threaten to overwhelm us. The psalmist wrote, "Let all who take refuge in you be glad; let them ever sing for joy. Spread your protection over them, that those who love your name may rejoice in you" (5:11).

In the face of life's great dangers and challenges, we can know a joy borne out of our trust in God. His strength is more than enough!

BILL CROWDER

Our faith is stretched when we exchange
our weakness for God's strength.

When You're Down

PSALM 6

Away from me, all you who do evil, for the LORD has heard my weeping.
PSALM 6:8

Sometimes it doesn't take much to get us down, does it? Even on the sunniest day, an unkind remark from a friend, bad news from the auto mechanic, or even a misbehaving child can put a cloud of gloom over everything, making simple tasks a struggle. You know you should be joyful in God's goodness, but everything seems to be against you.

David must have been feeling that way when he wrote Psalm 6. He felt faint and sickly (v. 2), troubled (v. 3), forsaken (v. 4), weary (v. 6), and sorrowful (v. 7). But he knew what to do when he was down. He looked up and trusted God to take care of him and to see him through.

When we look up and begin to focus on God, something good begins to happen. We get the attention off ourselves, and we gain a new appreciation for Him. Next time you're down, try looking up to God. He is sovereign (Psalm 47:8); He loves you (1 John 4:9, 10); He considers you special (Matthew 6:26); He has a purpose for your trials (James 1:2–4).

Life can seem unbearable at times. But don't let circumstances keep you down. Meditate on God's goodness to you, and talk to Him. Knowing that He loves you and "accepts [your] prayer" (Psalm 6:9) will give you strength to help you get up when you're down.

DAVE BRANON

Things looking down? Try looking up!

Tell It Straight

PSALM 6

*Let us then approach God's throne of grace with confidence,
so that we may receive mercy and find grace to help us in our time of need.*
HEBREWS 4:16

Have you ever found it tough to pray? That can happen when we're reluctant to tell God how we're really feeling. We might even stop abruptly in mid-sentence, fearful of being disrespectful of our heavenly Father.

A trip through the book of Psalms can help us pray more openly. There we can overhear David's conversations with God and realize that he was not afraid to be completely honest with the Lord. David cried out: "LORD, do not rebuke me in your anger" (Psalm 6:1). "Have mercy on me, LORD, for I am faint" (6:2). "Why, LORD, do you stand far off?" (10:1). "Do not turn a deaf ear to me" (28:1). "Contend, LORD, with those who contend with me" (35:1). "Hear my prayer, O God" (54:2). "Listen to my prayer, O God, do not ignore my plea" (55:1).

Think about David's approach. He was saying to God: "Help me!" "Listen to me!" "Don't be mad at me!" "Where are you?" David boldly went to God and told Him what was on his mind. Of course, God expects us to come to Him with a clean heart, and we need to approach Him with reverence—but we don't have to be afraid to tell God what we're thinking and feeling.

Next time you talk with your heavenly Father—tell it straight. He'll listen, and He'll understand.

DAVE BRANON

Prayer is an open line to heaven.

Danger Below

PSALM 7:11–17

Whoever digs a hole and scoops it out falls into the pit they have made.
PSALM 7:15

Residents of some communities in Michigan's Upper Peninsula are living with a hidden danger. In years past, thriving towns—places like Negaunee, Iron River, and Marquette—grew up around the great iron mines that fueled the economy. These mines are huge caverns carved beneath the surface of the earth so the ore could be taken out. Each cavern is several stories deep and is supported by huge timbers anchored in the ground.

But now, reports *The Detroit News*, many of these timbers have rotted. If they ever gave way, the mines would collapse and everything above or near them would be swallowed up by the gigantic holes that would form. The citizens of those former mining towns must therefore be on constant watch for the danger below.

David wrote about dangers of a different kind. He said the time would come when the wicked would fall into their own pit because of their ungodly ways. Oh, it may not happen right away. On the surface, everything may seem to be going well with people who disregard God. But the principle cannot be avoided: Anyone who continually disobeys the Lord is headed for a fall.

How important, then, to live by the principles of God's Word. It's the only way to escape the disastrous results of sin and to avoid the "danger below."

DAVID EGNER

Sin undermines.

Passengers on a Speck of Dust

PSALM 8

What is man that You are mindful of him,
and the son of man that You visit him?
PSALM 8:4 (NKJV)

A highly acclaimed astronomer was giving an address on recent discoveries about the vast workings of our universe. The information was amazing!

When the astronomer fielded questions, someone asked, "Professor, after all you have told us about the complexity of our universe, do you think a God great enough to make such a world could be concerned about us mortals?" After careful thought, the professor answered, "It depends on how great your God is!"

Planet earth is a mere speck of dust traveling through the vast expanses of space. And we, its passengers, might well be viewed as less noticeable than the tiny, almost invisible insects that we unwittingly trample underfoot. But God is not like man. His power is so great that He sees us. He knows us. He cares for us. He seeks us. He meets our need. Yes, this all-powerful God loves us.

The Christian faith affirms that the God who created and sustains the universe is great enough to know you, the creature He has made. He is great enough to care about you personally.

When I think how small and helpless we are in God's expansive and awesome creation, I'm thankful that His love is as great as His power.

RICHARD DEHAAN

God loves His children not because of who they are
but because of who He is.

Rocks and Robots

PSALM 8

When I consider Your heavens, the work of Your fingers,
the moon and the stars, which You have ordained, what is man that
You are mindful of him, and the son of man that You visit him?

PSALM 8:3–4 (NKJV)

During a walk through the picturesque Garden of the Gods in Colorado Springs, our attention was diverted from the huge, majestic, sandstone rocks toward two people wearing homemade robot suits. The park was filled with summer tourists who immediately began taking pictures of the robots while their children gathered round to touch them and talk to them. Folks who had come to admire the silent beauty of God's creation were now watching people in cardboard costumes sprayed with silver paint.

It reminded me of my quiet time. How often I sit down to seek the Lord through Bible reading and prayer, only to be drawn away by the newspaper, an unpaid bill, or a list of things to be done. The psalmist had better focus when he wrote: "O LORD, our Lord, how excellent is Your name in all the earth, who have set Your glory above the heavens! . . . what is man that You are mindful of him?" (Psalm 8:1, 3–4 NKJV).

While contemplating the Lord and meditating on His creation, the psalmist's self-important attitude shifted to one of humble appreciation for God's goodness. It can be true of us too—if we can keep the robots and the rocks in proper perspective.

DAVID MCCASLAND

It's good to worship God in nature if it leads us
to worship the God of nature.

Waiting for an Answer

PSALM 9:1–10

*Those who know your name trust in you, for you, LORD,
have never forsaken those who seek you.*

PSALM 9:10

When our daughter was fifteen, she ran away. She was gone more than three weeks. Those were the longest three weeks of our lives. We looked everywhere for her and sought help from law enforcement and friends. During those desperate days, my wife and I learned the importance of waiting on God in prayer. We had come to the end of our strength and resources. We had to rely on God.

It was on a Father's Day that we found her. We were in a restaurant parking lot, on our way to dinner, when the phone rang. A waitress at another restaurant had spotted her. Our daughter was only three blocks away. We soon had her home, safe and sound.

We have to wait on God when we pray. We may not know how or when He will answer, but we can put our hearts constantly before Him in prayer. Sometimes the answers to our prayers don't come when we would hope. Things may even go from bad to worse. But we have to keep persevering, keep believing, and keep asking.

Waiting is never easy, but the end result, whatever it is, will be worth it. David put it this way: "Those who know your name trust in you, for you, LORD, have never forsaken those who seek you" (Psalm 9:10).

Keep seeking. Keep trusting. Keep asking. Keep praying.

JAMES BANKS

Time spent in prayer is always time well spent.

God Is Watching!

PSALM 10

But you, God, see the trouble of the afflicted; you consider their grief and take it in hand. The victims commit themselves to you; you are the helper of the fatherless.

PSALM 10:14

As I scanned my local newspaper online, I noticed that it carried its usual daily share of bad news. Financial woes. Foreign policy concerns. Domestic squabbles. Nothing out of the ordinary.

Then I moved to the next page and looked into the beautiful face of a smiling teenager. But she will never smile again on earth. An honor student home from college for the weekend, she decided to go jogging with her dog. The dog came home. She never did. Searchers found her body several days later. Murdered.

The story stopped me cold. Not again, I thought. Not another innocent victim. Not another family left to grieve the senseless loss of a precious daughter. Not more dashed hopes and shattered dreams. Why do the young keep dying at the hands of ruthless killers?

I found the answer in Psalm 10. The wicked person acts horribly because "in all his thoughts there is no room for God" (v. 4). "From ambush he murders the innocent" (v. 8), thinking, "God will never notice" (v. 11). Murder and violence result when people don't think God sees or cares what they do. But God does, and He will avenge the murder of the innocent (vv. 14–15).

Yes, God is still on the throne. Evil men may think they're getting away with murder, but we can be assured that God's justice will prevail.

DAVE BRANON

**The harvest of judgment is sure as soon as
the seed of sin is sown.**

The Inevitable God

PSALM 10

*The LORD is King for ever and ever;
the nations will perish from his land.*

PSALM 10:16

It happened again! In 1982, a mountain in Mexico that had lain dormant since the fourteenth century suddenly came alive. It erupted with so much power that it became the world's largest active volcano at the time. The 3,700-foot-high giant El Chichon had been quiet for hundreds of years before its explosive reawakening. The people near the mountain had lived in complacency, never anticipating such drastic changes.

El Chichon's eruption can represent all the unforeseen and unplanned for changes in history that have occurred since David wrote Psalm 10. They remind us of the shattered security and pride of ungodly men and women in generations past who thought their evil ways would never catch up with them. They were preoccupied with the present and resisted the lessons of history. Yet, like the "wicked" referred to in today's Scripture (v. 2), they had to face the fact that sooner or later they would have to answer to God.

Maybe you think God is inactive, and that the present is reinforced with concrete and steel. But that's just the way it seems. Time always catches up with man. Every sinner will someday face his own kind of exploding mountain. The once seemingly stable foundations of life will then give way to God's power and judgment. God remains the inevitable God.

MART DEHAAN

**God is the great inescapable One—
He must be embraced now in grace or faced later in judgment.**

Head for the Hills?

PSALM 11

When the foundations are being destroyed,
what can the righteous do?

PSALM 11:3

If you're waiting for good to win out over evil in society, you may be in for a long wait. Things appear to be going from bad to worse. As we look around us today, we see the crumbling of one cherished value after another. Here's a partial list of the evils growing in today's world: sexual immorality, terror, crime, dishonesty, disregard for Christian values. We could easily feel that we have nowhere to turn—that we must escape.

Psalm 11 was written at a time when Israel may have felt that escape was the only answer. The people feared the attacks of the enemy and sensed that the foundations of justice were crumbling. That's why they said to David, "Flee like a bird to your mountain" (v. 1).

But escape is not the answer. We must refocus our thinking. If we look only at the evil in our world, we're likely to despair and seek to drop out. God, however, is still on His throne. He is keeping His eye on things. He will have the last word. That's what we must keep in view.

No matter what the world says, God's order is being maintained. He still hates the wicked and the violent (v. 5). He will bring about justice (v. 6). He still loves those who do what is right (v. 7).

So don't head for the hills. Trust God and keep doing what's right.

DAVE BRANON

When the world around you is crumbling,
God is the rock on which you can stand.

Flawless Words

PSALM 12

And the words of the LORD are flawless,
like silver purified in a crucible like gold refined seven times.
PSALM 12:6

You may have had a co-worker say to you, "I need to borrow some money so I can go out for lunch. I'll pay you back after my next paycheck." But two months and several hints later, you still don't have your money back.

Or maybe a friend has told you, "Thanks for letting me use your car. I'll have it back early enough for you to get to church on time tonight." But you end up waiting and then hurrying into church a half-hour late.

Or a husband or wife has said, "I promise, dear, we'll talk about it tonight." But it never happens, and the issue that is harming the marriage keeps growing.

People give their word, but sometimes we can't rely on what they tell us. After we get burned a few times, we begin to feel that we can't trust anybody.

David, who wrote Psalm 12, felt the same way. We don't know the specific situations that prompted his words, but he felt surrounded by untrustworthy people. He lamented, "Everyone lies" (v. 2).

Everyone, that is, except God. His words are pure and flawless, like silver that has been through a refiner's fire seven times (v. 6). We can believe God. His promises stand. He cannot lie.

DAVID EGNER

God never made a promise that was too good to be true.
—Dwight Moody

Spiritual Slump

PSALM 13

How long, LORD? Will you forget me forever?
How long will you hide your face from me?

PSALM 13:1

Athletes hate slumps. They'll try anything to get out of those times when they can't hit the baseball or make a free throw or catch a pass. Baseball players change bats. Basketball players change shoes. Football players change their routine. They'll do whatever they can to find success.

Christians should hate slumps too. We should try anything to get out of those dry spells when we can't seem to pray past the ceiling or when reading the Bible seems more frustrating than it is helpful.

A spiritual slump can make us feel forsaken by God. We struggle with troubling thoughts. Our hearts become sorrowful. We're sure that we're fighting a losing battle.

That was the position David found himself in as he described his situation in Psalm 13:1–2. His spiritual slump came, it seems, from a delayed response to his request for help. Yet David knew how to work his way out of the slump. First, he appealed to God (vv. 3–4), the true source of spiritual refreshment in dry times. Second, he trusted God (v. 5), the only One who knows the way out. Third, he sang God's praises (v. 6), recognizing how important worship is.

In a slump? Plead with God, trust Him, and praise His name. Then get back in the game!

DAVE BRANON

To tackle life's problems, trust God's promises.

Not Abandoned

PSALM 13

How long must I wrestle with my thoughts and day after day
have sorrow in my heart?

PSALM 13:2

As Karissa Smith was browsing in a local library with her babbling four-month-old daughter, an older man rudely told her to quiet her baby or he would. Smith responded, "I am very sorry for whatever in your life caused you to be so disturbed by a happy baby, but I will not tell my baby to shut up, and I will not let you do so either." The man put his head down and apologized, and then he told her the story of how his son died of Sudden Infant Death Syndrome over fifty years earlier. He had repressed his grief and anger all those years.

In Psalm 13, David expressed his grief. He addressed God with raw and honest language: "How long, LORD? Will you forget me forever? How long will you hide your face from me? How long must I wrestle with my thoughts and day after day have sorrow in my heart?" (vv. 1–2). These questions reflected fears of abandonment. David's language of distress gave way to a plea for help and reaffirmation of his faith in God's love for him (vv. 3–6). Confidence and firm resolve came alongside the cry of distress.

We all go through dark nights of the soul when we wonder if God has abandoned us. As with David, our aching can give way to joy when we approach God honestly, plead for help, and reaffirm our trust in a God whose love for us will never waver or change.

MARVIN WILLIAMS

God will never leave us nor forsake us.

I Am Not Forgotten

PSALM 13

We wait in hope for the Lord; he is our help and our shield.
PSALM 33:20

Waiting is hard at any time; but when days, weeks, or even months pass and our prayers seem to go unanswered, it's easy to feel God has forgotten us. Perhaps we can struggle through the day with its distractions, but at night it's doubly difficult to deal with our anxious thoughts. Worries loom large, and the dark hours seem endless. Utter weariness makes it look impossible to face the new day.

The psalmist grew weary as he waited (Psalm 13:1). He felt abandoned—as if his enemies were gaining the upper hand (v. 2). When we're waiting for God to resolve a difficult situation or to answer often-repeated prayers, it's easy to get discouraged.

Satan whispers that God has forgotten us and that things will never change. We may be tempted to give in to despair. Why bother to read the Bible or to pray? Why make the effort to worship with fellow believers in Christ? But we need our spiritual lifelines the most when we're waiting. They help to hold us steady in the flow of God's love and to become sensitive to His Spirit.

The psalmist had a remedy. He focused on everything he knew about God's love, reminding himself of past blessings and deliberately praising God, who would not forget him. So can we.

MARION STROUD

God is worth waiting for; His time is always best.

Christian "Atheists"

PSALM 14

*The fool says in his heart, "There is no God." They are corrupt,
their deeds are vile; there is no one who does good.*

PSALM 14:1

When we hear of atheists who blatantly deny the existence of God, we may think of the words of Psalm 14:1. This verse underscores the foolishness of not recognizing the reality of the God of the Bible.

Foolish, too, are people who profess to believe in God but who live as though He does not really exist. They go right on with their sinful practices. They ignore the God who sees, hears, and knows everything they do, and who will hold them responsible for their deeds. They pay little attention to God's written Word. And they pray only when they're in deep trouble and see no way out.

There is another group of people who can act foolishly. It's made up of Christians who fail to appropriate everything God has made available to them. They try to live the Christian life in their own strength. They do not take advantage of being temples of God—that the Holy Spirit dwells within them (see 1 Corinthians 6:19–20). They do not seek God's guidance for the decisions of life. They do not enjoy the spiritual riches that became theirs when they received Christ as Savior (Ephesians 1:3).

To deny the existence of God is foolish indeed. But to believe in Him yet fail to enjoy His gracious provision is foolish as well. Let's not be Christians who live like atheists.

RICHARD DEHAAN

A Christian cannot be an atheist, but he can live like one.

Pointing Fingers

PSALM 14

*All have turned away, all have become corrupt;
there is no one who does good, not even one.*

PSALM 14:3

An employee in the bill-collection department of a large store gave me an insight into human nature. He told me that he repeatedly gets the following response from customers who are delinquent in paying their bills: "I know you must have others who owe a lot more than I do. Get off my back, will you!"

The employee then told me, "They miss the point entirely. Sure, there are a lot of others who owe more. But somehow I have to tell them in a nice way, 'Look, what somebody else owes isn't the issue. Our records say that your account is overdue!'"

The tendency of sinful man has always been to shift attention from himself by pointing the finger at others. Religious people excuse their inconsistencies by referring to the "lost people" around them. And the "lost people" try to sidestep the issue by talking about the hypocrisies of the religious. But God is not fooled by finger-pointers.

When someone else appears to be a greater sinner than we are, it's just an illusion. The sooner we realize that no one owes more to God than we do, the more likely we are to receive His free forgiveness. He extends His pardon only to those who humbly acknowledge that they are hopelessly in debt.

MART DEHAAN

One sin rationalized becomes two.

Rock-Solid Integrity

PSALM 15

LORD, who may dwell in your sacred tent?
Who may live on your holy mountain?
The one whose walk is blameless, who does what is righteous,
who speaks the truth from their heart.

PSALM 15:1, 2

In the first verse Psalm 15, David asked what kind of person could live in God's holy presence. He answers his own question in verse two by saying it is one "whose walk is blameless"—a person of integrity. Some commentators say that the rest of the psalm describes in practical terms how such a person lives.

A young man I know about meets the psalmist's definition of integrity. Mike was a college graduate with a degree in construction management and was trying to get started with a good company. He was delighted, therefore, when a local firm hired him. He enthusiastically went to work— eager to please his new employers. It wasn't long, however, before his supervisor was asking him to make misleading statements to customers about materials and costs. After a brief inner struggle, he shared his dilemma with his wife. Mike and Alice prayed, asking the Lord what he should do. The next day Mike told his boss he would not lie to customers and suppliers. That Friday he was laid off. He knew why. He also knew he would never be called back.

Do we have the kind of rock-solid integrity that can stand the test of living honestly day by day? David said that if we do, we will "never be shaken" (15:5).

DAVID EGNER

Only by living on the level can anyone
rise to the highest plane.

What Did You Say?

PSALM 15

The one whose walk is blameless, who does what is righteous . . .
Whoever does these things will never be shaken.
PSALM 15:2, 5

At Santa Clara University in California, a researcher surveyed 1,500 business managers in a study that revealed what workers value most in a supervisor. Employees said they respect a leader who shows competence, has the ability to inspire workers, and is skillful in providing direction.

But there was a fourth quality they admired even more—integrity. Above all else, workers wanted a manager whose word was good, one who was known for honesty, and one they could trust.

While this finding holds special significance for Christian managers, it also says something to everyone who claims to be a follower of Jesus. Integrity should characterize all believers, no matter what their position may be.

According to Psalm 15, truth is at the heart of every word and deed of a godly person. Since the God of the Bible always keeps His word, it follows that a godly person will be known as one who does what he says he will do.

We all need to be more careful about our integrity. Do those around us admire us for our honesty? Does the Lord see us faithfully doing what we said we would do—even when it hurts? (Psalm 15:4).

MART DeHAAN

Only by being on the level can we rise in the eyes of others.

Doing What's Right

PSALM 15

Who lends money to the poor without interest;
who does not accept a bribe against the innocent.
Whoever does these things will never be shaken.

PSALM 15:5

Bruce Weinstein is known as "The Ethics Guy." His books and seminars challenge people to make choices based on principle rather than convenience or self-interest. In his business workshops, he often asks the participants, "Why should we be ethical?" He says that most responses center on the benefits of honesty and morality—avoiding punishment and having a clear conscience. While acknowledging that there are long-term benefits, Weinstein emphasizes doing the right thing because it's the right thing to do.

Psalm 15 gives a vivid picture of the person whose conduct grows out of fellowship with the living God. The question "LORD, who may dwell in your sacred tent?" (v. 1) is answered with examples from everyday living: "He whose walk is blameless, who does what is righteous, who speaks the truth from their heart" (v. 2). It goes on to describe honest relationships with neighbors and friends (vv. 3–4), along with integrity in business and financial matters (v. 5). The psalm ends with the words, "Whoever does these things will never be shaken" (v. 5).

Ethical living is more than a concept discussed in seminars. It's a powerful means of demonstrating the presence of Christ in our lives. Doing what is right is always the right thing to do.

DAVID MCCASLAND

There is no legacy as rich as integrity.

Can You Face the Challenge?

PSALM 16

I keep my eyes always on the LORD.
With him at my right hand, I will not be shaken.

PSALM 16:8

If an athlete talks about "psyching up" for a game, he's referring to the process of getting himself into the right mental attitude. One college football player, for instance, said he spent up to three hours doing this: "I think about the good plays I could make. In my mind I jump around and ward off blockers and tackle the quarterback for a loss."

Some golf pros do much the same thing getting ready for a tournament. They imagine themselves making a perfect drive that drops the ball a few inches from the flag.

This type of mental preparation is also useful for the challenges of Christian living. It's a way of preparing spiritually for specific needs and then visualizing yourself making the kind of godly response the situation calls for.

If you're a husband and father, maybe you'll see yourself coming home after a long day at the office. Your kids' bikes and toys are scattered across the driveway. Your wife is preoccupied helping your daughter with her homework, and you get an e-mail reminder of a special church board meeting that night.

Okay, sit back and relax. Set the Lord before you. Picture Him at your right hand, keeping you from responding poorly. Imagine Jesus walking with you, and claim the power of the Holy Spirit. Then you'll be ready to go home, not merely "psyched up," but anticipating the Lord's help. That's how to meet the challenges of the day.

MART DEHAAN

God has you in His plans: do you have Him in yours?

Feeling Chained

PSALM 16:1–11

I am not saying this because I am in need,
for I have learned to be content whatever the circumstances.

PHILIPPIANS 4:11

Boethius lived in sixth-century Italy and served the royal court as a highly skilled politician. Unfortunately, he fell into disfavor with the king. He was accused of treason and imprisoned. While awaiting execution, he asked for writing materials so he could compose his reflections. Later, these essays became an enduring spiritual classic on consolation.

As Boethius sat in prison, pondering his bleak prospects, his faith in Christ infused his perspective: "Nothing is miserable but what is thought so, and contrariwise, every estate is happy if he that bears it be content." He understood that our view of changing circumstances and contentment is a personal choice.

The apostle Paul reinforced the idea that the way we view our circumstances is more important than the circumstances themselves. While he too was in prison, he wrote: "I have learned to be content whatever the circumstances" (Philippians 4:11). Both men could be content because they drew their ultimate satisfaction from God, who never changes.

Do you feel chained to difficult circumstances? God can give you contentment. Lasting satisfaction can be found only with Him, as Psalm 16:11 explains: "you will fill me with joy in your presence, with eternal pleasures at your right hand."

DENNIS FISHER

When all you have is God, you have all you need.

Grandpa Snucked Out

PSALM 16

Therefore my heart is glad and my tongue rejoices;
my body also will rest secure.

PSALM 16:9

My cousin Ken fought a courageous four-year battle with cancer. In his final days, his wife, three children, and several grandchildren were in and out of his room, spending time with him and sharing special goodbyes. When everyone was out of the room for a moment, he slipped into eternity. After the family realized that he was gone, one young granddaughter sweetly remarked, "Grandpa snucked out." One moment the Lord was with Ken here on earth; the next moment Ken's spirit was with the Lord in heaven.

Psalm 16 was a favorite psalm of Ken's, and he requested it to be read at his memorial service. He agreed with the psalmist David, who said that there was no treasure more valuable than a personal relationship with God (vv. 2, 5). With the Lord as his refuge, David also knew that the grave does not rob believers of life. He said, "You will not abandon me to the realm of the dead" (v. 10). Neither Ken nor anyone else who knows Jesus as Savior will be abandoned in death.

Because of Jesus's own death and resurrection, we too will rise one day (Acts 2:25–28; 1 Corinthians 15:20–22). And we will find in heaven "eternal pleasures" (Psalm 16:11 NKJV).

ANNE CETAS

God is our treasure now, and being with Him
in heaven will bring pleasures forever.

Thinking about Heaven

PSALM 16

You make known to me the path of life;
you will fill me with joy in your presence,
with eternal pleasures at your right hand.

PSALM 16:11

In his classic devotional book titled *The Saint's Everlasting Rest*, English Puritan pastor and author Richard Baxter (1615–1691) wrote:

"Why are not our hearts continually set on heaven? Why dwell we not there in constant contemplation? . . . Bend thy soul to study eternity, busy thyself about the life to come, habituate thyself to such contemplations, and let not those thoughts be seldom and cursory, but bathe thyself in heaven's delights."

That's sound advice. We as believers in Jesus Christ need to spend some time thinking about where we will spend eternity. We're going to a place prepared especially for us (John 14:2). We'll be with God, where we'll enjoy "eternal pleasures" (Psalm 16:11). Isn't that worth contemplating?

Baxter goes on to point out four benefits of thinking about heaven: It protects us from temptation because it keeps the heart focused on what pleases God. It maintains the vigor of the Christian life. It provides medicine for our afflictions, cheering our spirits and easing our suffering. And it makes us an encouragement to other believers.

With this in mind, we ask as Baxter did, "Why are not our hearts continually set on heaven?"

DAVID EGNER

Those who have their hearts fixed on heaven
will hold loosely the things of earth.

God's Special Care

PSALM 17:1–9

Keep me as the apple of your eye; hide me in the shadow of your wings.
PSALM 17:8

The human eye is truly remarkable. The Lord has marvelously designed it so that the eyelashes and the eyebrows keep foreign matter out of the eye. And if a tiny particle of grit irritates the eye, the tear glands and eyelids go to work to wash it out.

Likewise in the spiritual realm, our heavenly Father gives special care to His own, for they are spoken of as "the apple of his eye," which refers to the pupil. We read, "Whoever touches you touches the apple of his eye" (Zechariah 2:8). And Deuteronomy 32:10 says, "He guarded him as the apple of his eye."

These passages refer to Israel, but they are equally true of all who belong to God through faith in Christ. He marvelously guards us by His grace and keeps us through all of the trying experiences of our pilgrimage from earth to glory. And when we are besieged by the enemy, He comes swiftly to our defense.

The pupil of the eye needs special care because through it light enters the eye. It cannot protect itself, but it completely depends on the lashes, the brows, the lids, and the tear glands. So too we must rely on Christ. His tender care and loving concern will shield us from the assault of the enemy.

Remember, Christian, you are as dear to God as "the apple of his eye."

PAUL VAN GORDER

**Our lives are never more secure than when
they are shielded by God.**

When the Ground Shakes

PSALM 18:1–6

*The LORD is my rock, my fortress and my deliverer;
my God is my rock, in whom I take refuge.*

PSALM 18:2

Several days after a devastating earthquake in the San Francisco area, a young boy was seen rocking and swaying on the school playground. His principal asked him if he was okay, and the boy nodded yes and said, "I am moving like the earth, so if there's another earthquake I won't feel it." He wanted to prepare himself for another shaking of the ground.

Sometimes after a traumatic event, we brace ourselves for what might be coming next. If we've had a phone call that brought bad news, every time the phone rings we feel panicky and wonder, *What has happened now*?

The "ground was shaking" for the psalmist David after King Saul tried to kill him (1 Samuel 19:10). He ran and hid. He thought death was next and told his friend Jonathan, "There is only a step between me and death" (20:3). He wrote, "The cords of death entangle me; the torrents of destruction overwhelmed me" (Psalm 18:4).

David cried to the Lord in his distress (v. 6) and found that He was a stabilizer, One he could trust would always be with him. He said, "The LORD is my rock, my fortress and my deliverer; my God is my rock, in whom I take refuge; . . . my stronghold" (v. 2). The Lord will be that for us also when the ground shakes under us.

ANNE CETAS

To survive the storms of life, be anchored to the Rock of Ages.

Before the Phone

PSALM 18:1–6

In my distress I called to the LORD;
I cried to my God for help. From his temple he heard my voice;
my cry came before him, into his ears.

PSALM 18:6

As a mom of young children, I'm sometimes susceptible to panic. My first reaction is to call my mom on the phone and ask her what to do with my son's allergy or my daughter's sudden cough.

Mom is a great resource, but when I read the Psalms, I'm reminded of how often we need the kind of help no mortal can give. In Psalm 18 David was in great danger. Afraid, close to death, and in anguish, he called on the Lord.

David could say, "I love you, LORD" because he understood God was a fortress, a rock, and a deliverer (vv. 1–2). God was his shield, his salvation, and his stronghold. Maybe we cannot understand David's praise because we have not experienced God's help. It may be that we reach for the phone before going to God for advice and help.

Surely God puts people in our lives to give us help and comfort. But let's also remember to pray. God will hear us. As David sang, "From his temple he heard my voice; my cry came before him, into his ears" (v. 6). When we go to God, we join David's song and enjoy Him as our rock, our fortress, and our deliverer.

Next time you reach for the phone, remember also to pray.

KEILA OCHOA

Prayer is the bridge between panic and peace.

Upward Escape

PSALM 18:25–36

He makes my feet like the feet of a deer;
he causes me to stand on the heights.

PSALM 18:33

The bighorn sheep in Colorado's Rocky Mountain National Park will often allow visitors to approach them from below and take close-up photos. But don't try to get above them, or the entire herd will run away. The bighorns' escape route from predators is always upward. On level ground a bobcat or cougar can easily overtake the wild sheep, but scrambling up a boulder-strewn slope, the bighorns will get away every time.

Years ago I heard a speaker say, "No matter what danger you face from trouble or temptation, don't let it get between you and God." As Christians, our escape route is always upward toward the Lord, never downward into sin or self-pity.

The psalmist's words remind us how to keep difficulty on the downhill side: "My voice You shall hear in the morning, O LORD; in the morning I will direct *it* to You, and I will look up." (Psalm 5:3 NKJV). Then, in a beautiful word picture, David described how God answered his prayer for help: "He makes my feet like the feet of a deer; he causes me to stand on the heights" (18:33).

The example of the bighorns and the words of the psalmist teach us to keep spiritual danger on the downhill side, with a wide-open upward path between ourselves and God.

DAVID MCCASLAND

You can be sure of your footing when you walk close to Jesus.

Our Great God

PSALM 19:1–4

The heavens declare the glory of God;
the skies proclaim the work of his hands.

PSALM 19:1

Who can contemplate the magnificence of the universe without acknowledging the greatness of God? His handiwork can be seen in the intricacies of this complex world. Consider these facts about the precise design of our amazing planet.

The distance of the earth from the sun, approximately ninety-three million miles, is just right to sustain life.

The 23½-degree tilt of the earth on its axis ensures seasonal changes, without which much of the earth would be a desert.

The balance of oxygen (twenty-one percent) and nitrogen (seventy-eight percent) in the air we breathe is perfect for supporting life.

An ozone layer in the atmosphere shelters our planet from deadly ultraviolet rays from the sun.

Yes, evidences of remarkable design exist throughout God's creation—speaking of a God of order, design, and greatness.

Even more amazing is the fact that God has taken a personal interest in us. The psalmist expressed his astonishment by saying, "When I consider Your heavens, the work of Your fingers, . . . what is man that You are mindful of him?" (Psalm 8:3–4 NJKV). God cared so much that He sent His only Son to die for us. The great Creator became our Savior. How great is our God!

PAUL VAN GORDER

The wonders of the universe compel us to worship our wonderful God.

A Message to All

PSALM 19:1–14

Day after day [the heavens] pour forth speech;
night after night they reveal knowledge.
PSALM 19:2

A United States Army general speaking in Japan told a story with the punch line, "Show me. I'm from Missouri." His translator knew the audience wouldn't understand, so he said in Japanese, "The general has made a joke, and I'll be in trouble if you don't laugh." The people obligingly laughed. But because some things don't translate well, the general had failed to communicate.

There is a message, however, that is always clear. It crosses the barriers of language and culture to communicate plainly with every person on the face of this earth.

In Psalm 19, speaking of God's glorious creation, David says of the heavens: "their voice goes out into all the earth, their words to the ends of the world" (v. 4).

No matter where we are or no matter what language we speak, the message is unmistakably clear: God is glorious!

In Borneo or Belgium, in hut or high-rise, God's creation reveals His power and glory. No one can miss it. And to us He has entrusted the message of His love—the good news of salvation in Jesus Christ. God's message in the heavens paves the way for His messengers on earth to complete the story for those who haven't heard it.

Are you ready to speak to someone who has seen the stars and longs to know the One who made them?

DAVID MCCASLAND

All creation is an outstretched finger pointing toward God.

It's Still Relevant

PSALM 19:7–11

For you have been born again, not of perishable seed,
but of imperishable, through the living and enduring word of God.
1 PETER 1:23

It's estimated that every year more than a million new books are published worldwide. What a torrent of print! Yet one volume, the Bible, stands out above all the others.

How do we explain the appeal of this ancient book? The answer is simple. It is God's Word, given in human language, and it tells us about our Creator and His purposes for the world. But it also gives us the most accurate understanding of mankind's perplexing nature and why we behave the way we do.

Harvard professor and Pulitzer Prize winner Robert Coles has interviewed hundreds of people in many different societies. When asked what he had learned from his research on human nature, Dr. Coles pointed to the Bible on his desk and said, "Nothing I have discovered about the makeup of human beings contradicts in any way what I learn from the Hebrew prophets . . . and from Jesus and the lives of those He touched."

The writings of others and our own experience can teach us much about why we behave as we do. But only the Bible tells us that our sinful heart is the heart of our problem and that we can be changed from within by trusting Jesus.

Yes, the Bible is still relevant. Are you growing in your love for this ancient book?

VERNON GROUNDS

The Bible is a mirror that lets us see
ourselves as God sees us.

The Greatest Treasure

PSALM 19:7–11

I rejoice in following your statutes as one rejoices in great riches.
PSALM 119:14

What is the world's greatest treasure? Some people might say it's all the gold stored in Fort Knox. Others might suggest it's the Sistine Chapel in Rome. Still others would think of the fabulous wealth once displayed in the czarist palaces of Russia. The answer that I hope would come to your mind is the Bible, God's Word.

At the coronation of England's Queen Elizabeth II in 1953, Geoffrey Fisher, the Archbishop of Canterbury, presented her with a Bible and said, "Our gracious Queen: To keep your Majesty ever mindful of the Law and the Gospel of God as the Rule for the whole life and government of Christian Princes, we present you with this Book, the most valuable thing that this world affords."

If the world were somehow robbed of all the splendid things we call treasures, that would be an incalculable loss. Suppose, though, the world were somehow stripped of the Bible and every trace of its influence. What a barren, blighted desert this planet would be!

Yes, the Bible is our greatest treasure, worth far more than gold (Psalm 19:10). It is our "Rule for the whole life." Praise God for giving us this magnificent treasure!

VERNON GROUNDS

**The rich treasures of God's Word
are waiting to be discovered.**

The Most Influential

PSALM 19:7–14

The precepts of the LORD are right, giving joy to the heart.
The commands of the LORD are radiant, giving light to the eyes.

PSALM 19:8

Many of us own a copy of the Bible. Some of us may have many copies in different versions and even different languages. This ancient book, written originally in Hebrew and Greek, with small portions in Aramaic, is still "the most influential book in history" according to most lists compiled on that topic.

In one survey, 79.8 percent of the people said that the Bible was the most influential. Other books, such as Charles Darwin's *The Origin of Species* and George Orwell's *1984* were favored by percentages in the single digits. The Bible was the overwhelming winner among influential books.

Applauding the Bible's influence is one thing. Reading it and living by its precepts is something far different. The words of God's book, which are "more precious than gold . . ." and "sweeter than honey" (Psalm 19:10) should draw us into the Bible's pages as we read and contemplate its message.

Is this book decisively influencing our lives? Is our relationship to the Bible one of obedience? After all, this book is immeasurably more than a collection of human writings. It is God's authoritative Word.

VERNON GROUNDS

If a Christian is careless in Bible reading,
he will care less about Christian living.

Singing at Night

PSALM 20

God my Maker . . . gives songs in the night.
JOB 35:10

There are two little birds that are beautiful pictures of the spirit of song. One is the skylark. It awakens early in the morning and greets the rising monarch of the day with music. Its whole being seems to burst forth in song.

The other bird is the nightingale. This dark-colored little bird hides away in the bushes and doesn't sing much in the daytime. But when evening comes, it trills forth with its beautiful, tender, moving night song.

In the spiritual realm, as in the world of nature, the singers of the day are more numerous than the singers of the night. But surely we can glorify God the most by singing in spite of the dark.

It is not hard to praise the Lord when everything is going well, when we have our health, when the family is happy, and when we have a good job. But what happens when trials come? When our health is gone, our money is spent, relationships are broken, or tragedy strikes, the reality of our faith is tested. Only those who are wholeheartedly committed to Christ can have a song in the night.

Some of the sweetest Christians I have ever met were God's patient sufferers on their beds or in their wheelchairs who had learned to sing in the dark.

M. R. DeHaan

**If you keep in tune with Christ,
you can sing even in the dark.**

Misplaced Trust

PSALM 20

Some trust in chariots and some in horses,
but we trust in the name of the LORD our God.

PSALM 20:7

I like watching birds, an activity I developed while growing up in a forest village in Ghana—where there were many different species of birds.

In the city suburb where I now live, I recently observed the behavior of some crows that interested me. Flying toward a tree that had shed most of its leaves, the crows decided to take a rest. But instead of settling on the sturdy branches, they lighted on the dry and weak limbs that quickly gave way. They flapped their way out of danger—only to repeat the useless effort. Apparently their bird-sense didn't tell them that the solid branches were more trustworthy and secure resting places.

How about us? Where do we place our trust? David observes in Psalm 20:7: "Some trust in chariots and some in horses, but we trust in the name of the LORD our God." Chariots and horses represent material and human assets. While these represent things that are useful in daily life, they don't give us security in times of trouble. If we place our trust in things or possessions or wealth, we will find that they eventually give way beneath us, as the branches gave way beneath the crows.

Those who trust in their chariots and horses can be "brought to their knees and fall," but those who trust in God will "rise up and stand firm" (v. 8).

LAWRENCE DARMANI

In a world of change, we can trust our unchanging God.

Getting What We Want

PSALM 21:1–7

Take delight in the LORD, and he will give you the desires of your heart.
PSALM 37:4

A certain airline pilot had a peculiar habit. Whenever he took off from his hometown of Minneapolis, he would ask the copilot to take the controls. Then he would stare intently out the window for a few moments.

Finally the copilot's curiosity got the best of him, so he asked, "What do you always look at down there?"

"See that boy fishing on that riverbank?" the pilot asked. "I used to fish from that same spot when I was a kid. Whenever a plane flew over, I would watch it until it disappeared and wish that I could be the pilot." With a sigh he added, "Now I wish I could be back down there fishing."

It's natural to spend time thinking about where we'd like to be or what we'd like to have. But we must evaluate our desires to make sure they are consistent with what God says will truly satisfy.

King David found satisfaction by putting first things first. His joy was rooted in the strength of the Lord and the salvation He provided (Psalm 21:1–2). It was because David sought the Lord that God gave him the desires of his heart (37:4).

When our desires conform to God's will, we're not likely to waste time wishing for things that can't satisfy. Real joy comes not in getting what we want, but in wanting to be close to God.

DAVID EGNER

**Contentment comes when we realize God
has everything we need.**

The Value of Prophecy

PSALM 22:1-8

For prophecy never had its origin in the human will,
but prophets, though human,
spoke from God as they were carried along by the Holy Spirit.

2 PETER 1:21

Some people believe that the Bible is merely a haphazard collection of ancient writings. But we have every reason to believe it is God's inspired Word. For example, the Bible contains prophecies that have been fulfilled. Centuries before specific events took place, the writers of Scripture predicted their occurrence, and in the course of time those events came to pass exactly as forecast.

No matter how farsighted we may be, we cannot foretell the future with any precision. Indeed, our best guesses often turn out to be wrong. Here are some examples:

"Airplanes are interesting toys but of no military value." Who said that? A renowned professor of military strategy. "Stocks have reached what looks like a permanently high plateau." This pronouncement was made by a distinguished economist just before the financial crash of 1929.

The Bible, however, is replete with dramatic examples of fulfilled prophecy. Isaiah 52:13–53:12 and Psalm 22:1–18 record details about the crucifixion of Christ hundreds of years before this cruel form of execution was ever practiced.

When we pick up the Bible, we can rest assured that we are holding in our hands the one authoritative divine revelation of truth—a claim verified by fulfilled prophecy.

VERNON GROUNDS

You can trust the Bible—God always keeps His word.

Hope for Worriers

PSALM 23

The Lord is my shepherd, I lack nothing.
PSALM 23:1

Everyone worries occasionally, but I was once a "professional worrier." My daily preoccupation was mulling over my worries, one by one.

Then one day I had to face an uncomfortable medical test, and I was frantic with fear. Finally, I decided that during the test I would focus on the first five words of Psalm 23: "The Lord is my shepherd." This exercise in meditation not only calmed me but I also gained several fresh insights. Later, as I slowly meditated through the entire psalm, the Lord gave me more insights. Eventually I was able to tell others publicly at conferences what the Lord had taught me.

If you're a worrier, there's hope for you too! Rick Warren, author of *The Purpose Driven Life*, wrote: "When you think about a problem over and over in your mind, that's called *worry*. When you think about God's Word over and over in your mind, that's *meditation*. If you know how to worry, you already know how to meditate!"

The more we meditate on God's Word, the less we need to worry. In Psalm 23, David meditated on his great Shepherd instead of worrying. Later, God chose him to be the shepherd of His people (Psalm 78:70–72). God uses those who can honestly say, "The Lord is my shepherd."

JOANIE YODER

**The more we think about God's Word,
the less we'll think about our worries.**

God Said That

PSALM 23

Even though I walk through the darkest valley, I will fear no evil,
for you are with me; your rod and your staff, they comfort me.
PSALM 23:4

When my eight-year-old grandson Jacob visited me in the hospital, he came with his own custom-made "Get Well" card. It was an 8-1/2" x 11" piece of stiff white paper folded in half. On the front he had written, "Hope you feel better soon." On the inside, in large block letters, was this message:

I WILL BE WITH YOU
WHEREVER YOU GO.

There was no Scripture reference, so Jacob added these words: "God said that." He wanted to be sure I didn't expect him to be at my side during my entire hospital stay.

That added note conveyed an unintended and deeper truth that brought a smile to my face and comfort to my heart. A hospital can be a lonely place. It's a world of unfamiliar faces, first-time medical procedures, and uncertain diagnoses. But it's in just such a setting that God can quiet an anxious heart and give assurance that He'll go with you down every hall, through every new door, into any unknown future—yes, even through "the darkest valley" (Psalm 23:4).

Maybe you have had an unexpected setback or loss. Your future is unknown. Trusting Jesus as your Savior and Lord, you can be sure of this: He will go with you wherever you go. You can believe it. God said that!

DENNIS DEHAAN

No danger can come so near the Christian that God is not nearer.

The Fear of Dying

PSALM 23

Yea, though I walk through the valley of the shadow of death,
I will fear no evil; for You are with me;
Your rod and Your staff, they comfort me.

PSALM 23:4 (NKJV)

In his book *The Mystery of Marriage*, Mike Mason said, "[Death] builds by slow degrees of awareness like the unfolding of a murder mystery in which we ourselves turn out to be the victim."

Yes, death is a mystery. A veiled, relentless threat. It is the essence of separation and sadness. This makes *death* a repulsive word to many people. For them, to speak of death is to discuss life's most unfathomable reality. The word paralyzes them. They see death as a dark, foreboding, abysmal, incomprehensible gulf.

There's a danger in that kind of thinking. Author and pastor Henry van Dyke (1852–1933) observed, "Some people are so afraid to die that they never begin to live." The fear of dying deprives many people of happiness and contentment.

Psalm 23 makes it clear that this doesn't have to be true for God's followers. If you're a child of God and are afraid of dying, consider these reassuring facts: God is right beside you (v. 4). He will comfort you (v. 4). He provides for you in spite of your enemies (v. 5). He makes goodness and mercy follow you (v. 6). He will receive you at death into His house (v. 6).

Don't be ashamed to admit you're afraid of dying. But then ask God to replace your fear with the confidence He alone can give.

DAVE BRANON

Those who fear God need not fear death.

A Dose of Psalm 23

PSALM 23

Blessed is the one . . . whose delight is in the law of the LORD,
and who meditates on his law day and night.

PSALM 1:1–2

The way a Christian thinks determines the way he or she lives. The Bible tells us that instead of worrying we should concentrate on things that are true, noble, right, pure, lovely, and admirable (Philippians 4:6–8).

The truths of Scripture provide excellent content to fill the mind. And for comfort and mental support, perhaps there is no better passage than Psalm 23. One pastor suggested the following prescription for those who came to him with fear and anxiety: "Take a dose of Psalm 23 six times a day for two weeks! Read it even before you get out of bed in the morning. Go slowly over the verses, interspersing them with prayer. Repeat the dosage after breakfast and lunch, again before and after dinner, and finally upon going to bed at night. Read it thoughtfully and go over the passage word by word." This remedy was simple, yet many didn't take him seriously and follow his instructions. One man read the passage quickly six times before work and complained that it did him no good. That would be like taking in one swallow all the medicine a doctor might prescribe for a month.

The beautiful words of Psalm 23 present a pattern of thinking that can transform our minds. They can change our attitudes and strengthen our faith. So why not try a dose of Psalm 23 six times a day for the next two weeks. You'll be pleased with the results!

HENRY BOSCH

He that will not command his thoughts
will soon lose command of his actions.

God's World

PSALM 24

The earth is the Lord's, and everything in it,
the world, and all who live in it.

PSALM 24:1

I knew my son would enjoy receiving a map of the world for his birthday. After some shopping, I found a colorful chart of the continents, and it included illustrations in every region. A birdwing butterfly hovered over Papua, New Guinea. Mountains cascaded through Chile. A diamond adorned South Africa. I was delighted, but I wondered about the label at the bottom of the map: *Our World.*

In one sense, the earth is our world because we live in it. We're allowed to drink its water, mine its gold, and fish its seas—but only because God has given us the go-ahead (Genesis 1:28–30). Really, it's *God's World.* "The earth is the Lord's, and everything in it, the world, and all who live in it" (Psalm 24:1). It amazes me that God has entrusted His incredible creation to mere humans. He knew that some of us would mistreat it, deny He made it, and claim it as ours. Still, He allows us to call it home and sustains it through His Son (Colossians 1:16–17).

Today, take a moment to enjoy life in God's world. Savor the taste of some fruit. Eavesdrop on a bird and listen to its song. Revel in a sunset. Let the world you inhabit inspire you to worship the One who owns it.

JENNIFER BENSON SCHULDT

The beauty of creation gives us reasons to sing God's praise.

Clean Hands

PSALM 24

Who may ascend the mountain of the LORD?
Who may stand in his holy place?
The one who has clean hands and a pure heart,
who does not trust in an idol or swear by a false god.

PSALM 24:3–4

It seems that wherever you go these days, you see signs encouraging people to wash their hands. With the constant threat of germs and viruses spreading disease throughout the general public, health officials continually remind us that unwashed hands form the single greatest agent for the spread of germs. So, in addition to the signs calling for vigilant hand-washing, public places will often provide hand sanitizers to help take care of germs and bacteria.

David also spoke of the importance of "clean hands," but for a dramatically different reason. He said that clean hands are one key to being able to enter into God's presence for worship: "Who may ascend the mountain of the LORD? Who may stand in his holy place?" he asked. And the answer? "The one who has clean hands and a pure heart" (Psalm 24:3–4). Here "clean hands" is not a reference to personal hygiene but a metaphor for our spiritual condition—being cleansed from sin (1 John 1:9). It speaks of a life committed to what is right and godly—enabling us to stand blameless before our Lord in the privilege of worship.

As His life is lived out in our lives, He can help us to do what's right so that our hands are clean and our hearts are ready to give worship to our great God.

BILL CROWDER

The road to worship begins with gratefulness
for the cleansing of God.

Back on the Farm

PSALM 24

*For this is what the high and exalted One says—he who lives forever,
whose name is holy: "I live in a high and holy place, but also with the one
who is contrite and lowly in spirit, to revive the spirit of the lowly
and to revive the heart of the contrite."*

ISAIAH 57:15

As a five-year-old keeping the cows out of my father's fields, I was in awe of
the sounds and sights of a North Dakota summer day. Only the occasional
mooing of a cow or the whistling of a meadowlark broke the soft stillness.
Shimmering heat waves danced across the prairie while a cautious coyote
skulked nearby. Hungry hawks circled overhead as snow-white clouds la-
zily floated in the sky.

My parents taught me that far above the idyllic Dakota scene was a
personal God, great and holy beyond all imagining. I felt small and vulnerable. But my parents also taught me that God loved me so much He
sent Jesus to die for me, so I felt love for Him.

Children can sense those kinds of essential truths long before they
understand terms like God's transcendence (His immeasurable difference
from us) and His immanence (His nearness). I know the words now, but I
still find it helpful to recapture that innocent wonder by imagining myself
back on the farm as a child.

We can't relive our childhood, nor should we want to. But we can recall
the wonder of our early days when the world was big and wonderful in
our eyes. Then, with a childlike sense of awe, reflect on the majesty of the
"High and Lofty One."

HERB VANDER LUGT

**The Creator hides secrets from sages,
yet He can be known by children.**

Riding Out the Waves

PSALM 25

Guide me in your truth and teach me,
for you are God my Savior, and my hope is in you all day long.

PSALM 25:5

What can ride ocean currents for years before finally washing ashore and springing to life? According to *National Geographic Kids* magazine, it is a nut, native to South America and the West Indies. Some people call them "sea hearts."

These two-inch, chestnut-colored nuts are hardy, heart-shaped seeds that grow on high-climbing vines. They often fall into rivers and float out to sea. There they may ride the currents for years before coming to shore and sprouting into a plant.

This life-bearing, time-enduring, wave-riding seed reminds me of a basic spiritual principle. God's plans may include extended times of waiting for Him to act on our behalf. This was true of Noah, who endured ridicule while spending one hundred twenty years building a ship; of Abraham, who waited for the fulfillment of God's promise that he would have a son in his old age; and of David, God's anointed, who chose to wait for God's timing rather than take the life of envious Saul.

Sea hearts can't choose to be patient, but we can. Nothing is harder or better for us than waiting on the Lord. That one truth alone answers a multitude of otherwise unanswerable questions. By waiting on the Lord we can have peace, and our faith will grow even while we are riding out the waves.

MART DEHAAN

God may stretch your patience to enlarge your soul.

Always with You

PSALM 25:4–10

*I am with you and will watch over you wherever you go,
and I will bring you back to this land. I will not leave you
until I have done what I have promised you.*

GENESIS 28:15

The highway that winds around the southern shore of Lake Michigan can be treacherous in the winter. One weekend as we were driving back to Grand Rapids from Chicago, a buildup of snow and ice slowed traffic, caused numerous accidents, and almost doubled our drive time. We were relieved as we eased off the expressway onto our final road. It was then that my husband said out loud, "Thanks, Lord. I think I can take it from here."

Just as he finished saying those words, our car spun around one hundred eighty degrees. As we came to a stop, hearts pounding, we could just imagine God saying: "Are you sure?"

Why do we sometimes try to go it alone in life when at every moment we have access to God? He said: "I am with you and will watch over you wherever you go" (Genesis 28:15). And He assures us: "Never will I leave you; never will I forsake you" (Hebrews 13:5).

Scottish mathematician and theologian Thomas Chalmers (1780–1847) wrote: "When I walk by the wayside, He is along with me. When I enter into company, amid all my forgetfulness of Him, He never forgets me. . . . Go where I will, He tends me, and watches me, and cares for me."

What a comfort to know that God is always with us—we don't need to go through life alone!

CINDY HESS KASPER

God's presence brings great comfort.

God of New Beginnings

PSALM 25:1-12

He gives us more grace. That is why Scripture says:
"God opposes the proud but shows favor to the humble."

JAMES 4:6

How did you learn to skate?" someone asked the winner of a competition. "By getting up every time I fell down," was the reply.

The Christian life is also a series of new beginnings, of falling down and getting up again. When we stumble, we often think, "I've failed again. I might as well give up." But God is the God of new beginnings. He not only forgives our sins but He also uses our failures to make us wiser.

Sometimes our pride can cause us to resist starting again. In Psalm 25, David showed a heart of humility by praying for forgiveness. He asked the Lord to forgive the sins of his youth (v. 7), and he rejoiced that God teaches sinners (v. 8), guides and instructs the humble (v. 9), and teaches His ways to those who fear Him (v. 12).

John Newton (1725–1807), the composer of "Amazing Grace," expressed a similar perspective: "Though I am not what I ought to be, nor what I wish to be, nor yet what I hope to be, I can truly say I am not what I once was . . . . By the grace of God I am what I am!"

Do you feel like a failure? Do you need a new start? Go to the Lord in humility, and He'll show you that He's the God of new beginnings.

JOANIE YODER

Failure is never final for those who begin again with God.

Take Time to Wait

PSALM 25:1–9

*Guide me in your truth and teach me, for you are God
my Savior, and my hope is in you all day long.*

PSALM 25:5

To get the most from our devotional times, we must learn to wait upon God. If we spend sufficient time studying the Bible, meditating, and praying, we will know we have been in His presence. Only then can we experience added power and holiness throughout the day.

H. A. Ironside told of visiting a godly Irishman, Andrew Frazer, who had come to southern California to recover from a serious illness. Though quite weak, he opened his worn Bible and began expounding the deep truths of God in a way that Ironside had never heard before. Ironside was so moved by Frazer's words that he asked him, "Where did you get these things? Could you tell me where I could find a book that would open them up to me? Did you learn them in some seminary or college?" The sickly man gave an answer that Ironside said he would never forget. "My dear young man, I learned these things on my knees on the mud floor of a little sod cottage in the north of Ireland. There with my open Bible before me I used to kneel for hours at a time and ask the Spirit of God to reveal Christ to my soul and to open the Word to my heart."

Let's learn to dwell with God and feel His love and sense His power. We would know Him better and understand His Word more clearly if we would be less hurried in His presence. Let's take time to get to know Him.

PAUL VAN GORDER

**If prayer and meditation unlock the gates of day,
the hours that follow will be filled with blessing.**

The Rugged Road

PSALM 25:4–11

Stand at the crossroads and look; ask for the ancient paths, ask where the good way is, and walk in it, and you will find rest for your souls.

JEREMIAH 6:16

A fishing buddy of mine told me about an alpine lake located high on the north flank of Jughandle Mountain here in Idaho. Rumor had it that large cutthroat trout lurked up there. My friend got a pencil and scrap of napkin and drew a map for me. Several weeks later I gassed up my truck and set out to follow his directions.

His map put me on one of the worst roads I've ever driven! It was an old logging road that had been bulldozed through the forest and never regraded. Washouts, fallen timber, deep ruts, and large rocks battered my spine and bent the undercarriage of my truck. It took half a morning to reach my destination, and when I finally arrived I asked myself, "Why would a *friend* send me up a road like this?"

But the lake was magnificent and the fish were indeed large and scrappy! My friend had put me on the right road—one I would have chosen myself and patiently endured had I known what I knew at the end.

There is a faithful saying: "All the ways of the LORD are loving and faithful toward those who keep the demands of his covenant" (Psalm 25:10). Some of God's paths for us are rough and rugged, others tedious and boring, but all are filled with His love and faithfulness. When we come to the end of our journey and know what we then will know, we will say, "God's path was best for me."

DAVID ROPER

Our path may have obstacles, but God will lead us.

Calling Myself

PSALM 26

Vindicate me, LORD, for I have led a blameless life;
I have trusted in the LORD and have not faltered.

PSALM 26:1

As I was moving my laptop, cell phone, and assorted books and papers from one room to another, the "regular" phone rang. I hurriedly set down my stuff and rushed to answer the call before the answering machine kicked in. "Hello," I said. No reply. I said hello again when I heard rustling, but still no response. So I hung up and went back to my stuff on the floor. When I picked up my cell phone I realized that I had accidentally speed-dialed my home phone number!

I laughed at myself, but then wondered: How often are my prayers more like calling myself than calling on God?

For example, when I am falsely accused, I plead with God for vindication. I want my name cleared and the guilty person held accountable for the harm done to my reputation. But then I get impatient with God and try to vindicate myself. I may as well be praying to myself.

Vindication does not come from self-defensive arguments; it stems from integrity (Psalm 26:1). It requires that I allow God to examine my mind and heart (v. 2) and that I walk in His truth (v. 3). This, of course, requires patient waiting (25:21).

When we call on God, He will help us—but in His perfect time and in His perfect way.

JULIE ACKERMAN LINK

The purpose of prayer is not to get what we want,
but to become what God wants.

"Always Do Right"

PSALM 26

Test me, Lord, and try me, examine my heart and my mind.
PSALM 26:2

Mark Twain took delight in exposing the follies of human behavior. He once said, "Always do right. This will gratify some people and astonish the rest."

People are often surprised when someone does what is right. That's why it was national news a few years ago when a high school basketball coach "turned in" his state championship team after he discovered that he had unknowingly used an ineligible player. He and his players had achieved the dream of every coach and every prep athlete—one that carries with it a lifetime of cherished memories. But they gave it all back—the trophy, the glory, the pride. They gave it back so they could keep something much more important—their integrity. Amazing!

Doing what's right is not a new idea. David realized what it took to walk in integrity. He knew that to do right he would have to steer clear of hypocrites, evildoers, and the wicked (Psalm 26:4–5). Integrity was worth more than anything they could offer.

What will doing right cost you? Some worldly entertainment? Some money at tax time? Some travel time on the highway because you obey the speed limit? Are any of these things worth more than honoring the Lord with your integrity?

DAVE BRANON

**They who do not live up to their ideals
soon find that they have lost them.**

Communicating Integrity

PSALM 26

I lead a blameless life; deliver me and be merciful to me.
PSALM 26:11

One side of Harry Elders' business card had a photo of his smiling face. On the other side was his motto: "Integrity Can Be Communicated."

For half a century, Harry worked as a narrator and actor in radio and TV. One of his favorite ongoing projects was *Unshackled*, a Chicago-based radio show dramatizing conversions to Christ. But whether he was narrating a film about foreign missions or a promotional video for a bank, his integrity permeated everything he did. There was no conflict between his walk and his talk. When you hired Harry, you got all of him—virtue, kindness, and principle.

After Harry died, a local newspaper had a column of tribute titled: "A voice of integrity is silenced, but its messages will live on."

People like Harry remind us of what David wrote in Psalm 26. Right living begins and ends with integrity: "I have walked in my integrity" (v. 1 NKJV), and "I will walk in my integrity" (v. 11 NKJV). In between these statements he wrote, "Test me, LORD, and try me; examine my heart and my mind" (v. 2). David's desire was to be pure before the Lord so he could worship Him and tell of all His wondrous works (vv. 6–7).

Integrity can be communicated—when we are true to the Lord everywhere, all the time.

DAVID MCCASLAND

There is no legacy as rich as integrity.

He Understands

PSALM 27:1–8

The LORD is my light and my salvation—whom shall I fear?
The LORD is the stronghold of my life—of whom shall I be afraid?
PSALM 27:1

Some young children have trouble falling asleep at night. While there may be many reasons for this, my daughter explained one of them as I turned to leave her bedroom one evening. "I'm afraid of the dark," she said. I tried to relieve her fear, but I left a nightlight on so she could be sure that her room was monster-free.

I didn't think much more about my daughter's fear until a few weeks later when my husband went on an overnight business trip. After I settled into bed, the dark seemed to press in around me. I heard a tiny noise and jumped up to investigate. It turned out to be nothing, but I finally understood my daughter's fear when I experienced it myself.

Jesus understands our fears and problems because He lived on the earth as a human and endured the same types of trouble we face. "He was despised and rejected by mankind, a man of suffering, and familiar with pain" (Isaiah 53:3). When we describe our struggles to Him, He doesn't brush us aside, minimize our feelings, or tell us to snap out of it—He relates to our distress. Somehow, knowing that He understands can dispel the loneliness that often accompanies suffering. In our darkest times, He is our light and our salvation.

JENNIFER BENSON SCHULDT

Jesus is our light in the darkest night.

On the Rock

PSALM 27:1–6

He lifted me out of the slimy pit, out of the mud and mire;
he set my feet on a rock and gave me a firm place to stand.

PSALM 40:2

A dear Christian lady was close to death when her minister came to visit her. He softly asked, "Sister, are you sinking?" She looked at him in disbelief and said nothing. Again, he said, "Sister, are you sinking?" She still could not believe that he would ask such a question. Summoning all her remaining strength, she raised herself up a little in her bed and said, "Sinking? Sinking? Did you ever know a person to sink through a rock? If I had been standing on the sand I might sink; but, thank God, I am on the Rock of Ages, and there is no sinking there."

The psalmist David knew what it meant to go through deep distress. Take a look at some of the dangers listed in Psalm 27: the wicked came upon him, a host was encamped against him, war was raging against him, and he was in the midst of great trouble. Yet he could say with confidence, "[God] will hide me in the shelter of his sacred tent and set me high upon a rock" (v. 5).

Are you facing something frightening in your life? If you have trusted Jesus as your Savior, you have been placed on a solid foundation. You can't sink through the Rock.

PAUL VAN GORDER

Christians may tremble on the Rock of Ages,
but the Rock will never tremble under them.

A Heart for Prayer

PSALM 27:7-14

My heart says of you, "Seek his face!" Your face, Lord, I will seek.
PSALM 27:8

While traveling on an airplane with her four- and two-year-old daughters, a young mom worked at keeping them busy so they wouldn't disturb others. When the pilot's voice came over the intercom for an announcement, Catherine, the younger girl, paused from her activities and put her head down. When the pilot finished, she whispered, "Amen." Perhaps because there had been a recent natural disaster, she thought the pilot was praying.

Like that little girl, I want a heart that turns my thoughts toward prayer quickly. I think it would be fair to say that the psalmist David had that kind of heart. We get hints of that in Psalm 27 as he speaks of facing difficult foes (v. 2). He said, "Your face, Lord, I will seek" (v. 8). Some say that David was remembering the time he was fleeing from Saul (1 Samuel 21:10) or from his son Absalom (2 Samuel 15:13–14) when he wrote this psalm. Prayer and dependence on God were in the forefront of David's thinking, and he found Him to be his sanctuary (Psalm 27:4–5).

We need a sanctuary as well. Perhaps reading or praying this psalm and others could help us to develop that closeness to our Father-God. As God becomes our sanctuary, we'll more readily turn our hearts toward Him in prayer.

ANNE CETAS

In prayer, God can still our hearts and quiet our minds.

No Thanks

PSALM 28

That my heart may sing your praises and not be silent.
LORD my God, I will praise you forever.
PSALM 30:12

While I was teaching at a Christian college, a talented young man pushed his way into my life. He needed one more course to graduate, so he decided that I should give him an independent study in writing. He would be everlastingly grateful if I would just do this—even though it required extra work on my part. The college dean agreed to the idea because of the young man's abilities.

What a headache this turned out to be! The student skipped appointments, missed deadlines, and rejected my evaluations of his writing. He even turned in the last assignment just hours before graduation.

After all that was done for him, you'd think he would have been grateful. But he didn't express one word of thanks on graduation day nor in all the years since.

I don't ever want to be that kind of person. I would rather be like David. When he was in deep trouble, he called out to the Lord for help (Psalm 28:1–2). Afterward, he remembered to give God thanks for delivering him (vv. 6–7). In fact, David's heart of gratitude toward the Lord is evident throughout the book of Psalms.

Like David, may we unceasingly express our thanks to God for His goodness.

DAVID EGNER

When you count your blessings, it adds up to thankfulness.

A Double Promise

PSALM 29

The LORD gives strength to his people;
the LORD blesses his people with peace.

PSALM 29:11

Psalm 29 has been called the "stormy psalm." It describes turbulent waters, rolling thunders, roaring fires, and the crashing cedars of Lebanon.

Then come verses 10–11. They are like a rainbow in the cloud, a calm in the storm—offering strength and peace to God's people. Its truth can become a reality in life's great crises.

In 1555, an English clergyman named Nicholas Ridley was burned at the stake over a religious conflict. On the night before Ridley's execution, his brother offered to remain with him in the prison chamber to be of assistance and comfort. Nicholas declined the offer and replied that he meant to go to bed and sleep as quietly as ever he did in his life. Because he knew the peace of God, he could rest in the strength of the everlasting arms of his Lord to meet his need. So can we!

God gives us strength for those times when we are weak and fearful. He provides it for each day and for every difficulty. God also gives us peace that guards the door of our heart in the midst of great peril and trials. As Paul said in Philippians 4:7, it's a peace that goes beyond our ability to understand it.

Are you facing a difficulty—divorce, the loss of a loved one, a severe physical or emotional crisis? Turn it over to God. You'll have many trying days, but He'll give you the strength to go on and His peace to comfort your soul. Claim the double promise of Psalm 29:11 as your own.

PAUL VAN GORDER

The secret of peace is to give all your anxieties to God.

What Really Matters

PSALM 30

You, LORD, brought me up from the realm of the dead;
you spared me from going down to the pit. Sing the praises of the LORD,
you his faithful people; praise his holy name.

PSALM 30:3–4

As a deadly tornado ripped through Will County, Illinois, a young father sat cradling his infant child, born just three weeks before. When the fierce, howling winds finally subsided and calm had returned, the man's house was gone—and so was his baby. But, according to news reports, the father found his child in a field near his house—and he was alive and well! And so was the rest of his family.

When asked by a reporter if he was angry he had lost his house and everything he owned, he replied, "No, I just thank God I have my baby and my family. Some people don't have that. Nothing else is important."

Often it takes times of tragedy to remind us what really matters in life. When things are going well, we can easily get preoccupied with what we own. We become tied to so many nonessential, unimportant things. We tend to grow overly concerned about countless trappings of modern life. But when life is reduced to the essentials, as it was in the Illinois tornado, we recall again that life itself is enough reason to praise God.

Let's praise God today for life and for the people He has given us to share life with. That's what really matters.

DAVE BRANON

Nothing can fill the place in our heart that was intended for God.

Ready to Go

PSALM 30

For his anger lasts only a moment, but his favor lasts a lifetime;
weeping may stay for the night, but rejoicing comes in the morning.
PSALM 30:5

Life in heaven is far better than anything earth can offer, yet we do our best to avoid dying. If we get sick, we pray for recovery. The psalmist was no different. He began Psalm 30 by praising God for saving him from death (vv. 1–4). Then he declared that his distress was only temporary and that God's favor would be everlasting (v. 5). God allowed the illness to humble him and to give him a new perspective on life. He saw more clearly than ever that eternal blessedness far outweighs present distress. Closing his song, he rejoiced in the prospect of praising God throughout eternity. God had prepared him so he could die in peace.

When my mother was in her early sixties, the doctor told her she would soon die from heart failure. She was despondent. She loved life and didn't want to leave her family. We prayed for her recovery, and God graciously answered by giving her twelve more years. Shortly before she died, I asked her, "Mom, do you still dread dying?" With a smile she replied, "No, I'm ready."

We don't need to feel guilty about not wanting to die and go to heaven. God made us that way. We need to keep walking with Him, doing His will, and trusting Him to meet our needs. When we are called home to heaven, by God's grace we'll be ready to go.

HERB VANDER LUGT

Death is the last chapter on time, but the first chapter on eternity.

Always Winter

PSALM 30:4–12

For his anger lasts only a moment, but his favor lasts a lifetime;
weeping may stay for the night, but rejoicing comes in the morning.
PSALM 30:5

Unlike some of my family—who can't wait to go downhill skiing—I don't look forward to winter. When the first snowflake falls, I immediately start calculating how many months of Michigan winter are left.

Imagine C. S. Lewis's fictional world of Narnia, where for a hundred years it was always winter. Cold, wet snow—with no hope of springtime ever arriving to wipe away the memories of icy temperatures and piles of white stuff. But worst of all, in Narnia, Christmas never came. Always winter and never Christmas! To me, the best part of winter is the anticipation, excitement, and wonder of Christmas. Life is bleak when you have nothing to look forward to.

There are some whose souls are locked in winter. The hardness of life has frozen their hearts. Disappointed with life, they find that each day is filled with despair. "Weeping may stay for the night," the psalmist tells us, "but rejoicing comes in the morning" (Psalm 30:5). In the darkest times of our lives, God longs to turn our "wailing into dancing" (v. 11).

David wrote, "When anxiety was great within me, your consolation brought me joy" (Psalm 94:19). If you cry out to God in the midst of your "winter," you can experience the joy of the Christ of Christmas today.

CINDY HESS KASPER

Jesus can turn your sorrow into dancing.

God Is Alive!

PSALM 30

My heart may sing your praises and not be silent.
LORD my God, I will praise you forever.

PSALM 30:12

The great sixteenth-century theologian Martin Luther once experienced a long period of worry and despondency. One day his wife dressed in black mourning clothes.

"Who has died?" asked Luther.

"God," said his wife.

"God!" said Luther, horrified. "How can you say such a thing?"

She replied, "I'm only saying what you are living."

Through his wife's words and actions, Luther realized that he indeed was living as if God were no longer alive and watching over them in love. He changed his outlook from gloom to gratitude.

Occasionally we too live as if God were dead. When we are discouraged, we can turn to the Psalms. Some of the writers faced bleak times, but they had one habit in common that encouraged them: giving thanks to God. For example, David wrote, "You have turned my wailing into dancing; . . . LORD my God, I will praise you forever" (30:11–12).

Meeting every situation with thanksgiving isn't a denial of trouble. It helps us see those situations from God's perspective—as opportunities to discover His power and love. Every time you express gratitude to God in a difficult situation, you're declaring, "God is alive!"

JOANIE YODER

Instead of complaining about the thorns on roses,
be thankful for the roses among the thorns.

David's Hiding Place

PSALM 31:1-16

*Turn your ear to me, come quickly to my rescue; be my rock of refuge,
a strong fortress to save me. Since you are my rock and my fortress,
for the sake of your name lead and guide me.*

PSALM 31:2-3

Protection comes in many forms. A rabbit dives for his hole. A squirrel clings to the backside of a branch. A deer runs for the dense cover of a swamp. A two-year-old runs for daddy's pant leg. A teenager looks for the security of friends. A marine digs in under cover of friendly guns. But what does a Christian do? Where does a believer hide when surrounded by danger?

The psalmist David has the answer. When he wrote Psalm 31, things were not going well for him. He was hurting; he was tired; he was weak. His mind was distressed, his heart was broken, his enemies were chasing him, and his friends had let him down.

He was in a vulnerable position—but he was not defenseless. David had a refuge. He knew that God is the best possible source of safety and that the wisest defense strategy is to have a right relationship with Him. Just as a small child might find confidence in using his older brother's name when threatened by a bully, David called upon the name of God. Because he was living in fellowship with Him, he hid himself in God's security.

Are we as wise? Are we as quick to seek that same security? God can be trusted. He who was a sure hiding place for David is also the One we should cling to for our protection.

MART DEHAAN

**The Christian finds safety not in the absence of danger
but in the presence of God.**

God's Tender Care

PSALM 31:1–14

I will be glad and rejoice in your love,
for you saw my affliction and knew the anguish of my soul.
PSALM 31:7

During a time of grief, C. S. Lewis observed that his neighbors walked across the street to avoid him when they saw him approaching.

David too knew a time of grief when he said, "I am the utter contempt of my neighbors . . . . I am forgotten as though I were dead" (Psalm 31:11–12).

Perhaps you've known times when friends seem to forget you in your sorrow. They fail to call or write or promise to pray.

But those are the times when we can sense God's tenderness most deeply. When the days are long and lonely and no one seems to care, He seeks us out and surrounds us with lovingkindness. Our sorrow, far from burdening Him, draws out His tender compassion. He knows the troubles of our soul (v. 7). And He cares. Thus we can commit our spirit into His hand (v. 5), as our Lord Jesus did when all forsook Him and fled.

Poet Frank Graeff asks, "Does Jesus care when my heart is pained too deeply for mirth and song; as the burdens press, and the cares distress, and the way grows weary and long?" The answer? Yes! He invites us to give our burdens and cares to Him, because He cares for us (1 Peter 5:7).

Trust God to care for you today.

DAVID ROPER

We can never get beyond the circle of God's care.

Tissue Boxes

PSALM 31:9–18

But I trust in you, Lord; I say,
"You are my God." My times are in your hands.

Psalm 31:14–15

As I sat in the surgical waiting room, I had time to think. I had been here recently, when we received the jarring news that my only brother, much too young, was "brain dead." And so on this day, waiting for news about my wife who was undergoing a serious surgical procedure, I listened for the quiet voice of God.

Suddenly, news! The surgeon wanted to see me. I went to a secluded room to wait. There, on the table, sat two tissue boxes, conspicuously available. They weren't for the sniffles. They were for cold, hard phrases like "brain dead" and "nothing we can do."

In such times of grief or uncertainty, the honesty of the psalms helps. Psalm 31 was the heart-cry of David, who wrote, "My life is consumed by anguish" (v. 10). Compounding that grief was the pain of abandonment by his friends and neighbors (v. 11). But David had the bedrock of faith in the one true God. "I trust in you, Lord; . . . My times are in your hands" (vv. 14–15). His lament concludes with resounding encouragement and hope. "Be strong and take heart, all you who hope in the Lord" (v. 24).

This time, the surgeon gave us good news: My wife could expect a full and complete recovery. We were relieved and grateful! But even if she hadn't been "okay," our times still remain in God's capable hands.

TIM GUSTAFSON

When we put our problems in God's hands,
He puts His peace in our hearts.

Coping with Fear

PSALM 31:14–24

I trust in you, Lord; I say, "You are my God."
PSALM 31:14

Many people are afraid of flying. The thought of being airborne fills them with anxiety. For that reason the American Phobic Society recommends these techniques for coping with the fear of flying:

- Avoid sugar and caffeine before and during a flight.
- Lean back at takeoff; let your muscles go limp.
- Rate your anxiety on a scale from 1 to 10. Think positive thoughts; note how much your fear decreases.
- Breathe deeply; close your eyes; stretch your arms.
- Wear a rubber band on your wrist and snap it to break unpleasant thoughts.

These are five good suggestions. But I have a sixth that works with all kinds of fear. In fact, it's the most important of all: Put your trust in God.

That's what David did in Psalm 31. A conspiracy had arisen against him. His friends had abandoned him. His reign appeared to be over. Death seemed certain. But he made a choice and declared, "I trust in you, Lord; I say, 'You are my God'" (v. 14).

When you're afraid, it may help to breathe deeply or snap rubber bands. But don't leave out the best way to cope with the fear of flying—or any other fear. Follow David's example and put your trust in God.

DAVID EGNER

Faith is God's antidote for fear.

The Hand

PSALM 31:1–16

You open your hand and satisfy the desires of every living thing.
PSALM 145:16

Satisfaction! It's all right there in God's hand. If He would only leave it open so we could fill ourselves and delight ourselves with all His riches. But so often it seems closed. In fact, it sometimes seems to signal more trouble than help.

If the family dog could think, he would probably have a similar complaint about his master's hand. He would resent the fact that it has other uses than to fill his dish or scratch his back. He would stay awake nights worrying because occasionally it fills a tub with water and plunges the unwilling, thrashing, shaking animal into a solution of suds. Then there's another discomfort. It occurs during the trials of obedience training. The hand is held out and a military-like order is heard: "Sit!" Seconds seem like hours. What cruelty! Then it happens. The hand turns. He hears, "Good dog! That's my pup. Come here. Have a treat!" Now it's a welcoming hand.

The discipline that our pet learns through waiting and temporary discomfort we too must learn through hardship. Behind God's hand is His loving heart. Behind His actions are design, order, love, and perfect timing. Controlling that sovereign hand is One who is in the process of teaching His little ones to look at Him, wait on Him, trust Him, love Him, and find their satisfaction in Him. He alone is able to satisfy "the desires of every living thing."

MART DeHAAN

Those who see God's hand in everything can best leave everything in God's hand.

Cut Off?

PSALM 31:14–24

In my alarm I said, "I am cut off from your sight!"
PSALM 31:22

During Antarctica's nine-month winter, the continent is engulfed in darkness and the temperature sinks to -115º F (-82º C). Flights are halted from late February to November, leaving workers at scattered research stations isolated and virtually cut off from outside help. Yet occasionally, daring rescue missions will penetrate the polar winter and airlift people with serious medical conditions to safety.

We all feel helpless and cut off at times. It may seem that not even God can hear or answer our cries for help. The psalmist David said to the Lord in a time of trouble, "I am cut off from your sight!" (Psalm 31:22). But David discovered that he had not been forgotten, and he rejoiced, "You heard my cry for mercy when I called to you for help" (v. 22).

What circumstances make you feel helpless or hopeless today? Poor health, broken relationships, a family member in great need? In Jesus Christ, God has pierced the dark winter of our world in a daring rescue through His redeeming love. He is therefore able to reach us and calm our fears in the most desperate circumstances.

We are never cut off from the mighty power and sustaining peace of God.

DAVID MCCASLAND

God's help is only a prayer away.

Just in Time

PSALM 31

Yet you heard my cry for mercy when I called to you for help.
PSALM 31:22

It was his wedding day, and the groom was in trouble. A storm had dumped three inches of rain in less than three hours on Louisville, Kentucky. The husband-to-be was heading for the church when his car stalled in high water at an intersection and wouldn't start again. Becoming frantic, he waved fifty-dollar bills at passing cars, hoping someone would give him a ride. When a driver finally did stop—to ask for directions—it was just in time.

The bridegroom arrived at the church, drenched, shoeless, and carrying his tuxedo in a plastic bag. Twenty minutes later he walked down the aisle, his hair still wet.

The experience of this groom reminds me of King David's life. In moments of alarm, David felt as though the heavens had turned against him (Psalm 31:22). Circumstances seemed out of control. He felt invisible to others and as forgotten as someone who had already died (v. 12). Yet his darkest hours invariably became the occasion for praise to God (vv. 19, 23). Time after time, tests of faith were followed by proofs of the Lord's presence and unending care.

As Christians, we too can expect trials on the road to heaven. But we can have confidence in God's ability to provide exactly what we need—just in time.

MART DEHAAN

**God's dawn of deliverance often comes
when the hour of trial is darkest.**

Covering Sinkholes

PSALM 32:1–5

*Blessed is the one whose transgressions are forgiven,
whose sins are covered.*

PSALM 32:1

In late May 2010, tropical storm Agatha hit Central America, producing torrential rains and landslides. Once it finished its course, a two-hundred-foot-deep sinkhole opened in downtown Guatemala City. This sinkhole caused the ground to collapse suddenly, sucking land, electrical poles, and a three-story building into the depths of the earth.

Though sinkholes can be devastating, the most universal and damaging sinkhole is the one that happens in the human heart. King David was an example of this.

The surface of David's life looked stable; however, his interior life rested on a fragile foundation. After his sins of adultery and murder, David thought he had successfully hidden his treacherous acts (2 Samuel 11–12). However, God's intense conviction after Nathan's confrontation caused him to realize that denying the presence of sin in his life weakened the foundation of his spiritual life. To prevent this spiritual sinkhole from worsening, David acknowledged his sin to God in repentance (Psalm 32:5). As a result, God covered David's sin and gave him the joy of forgiveness.

We too will experience God's grace when we confess our sins to Him. He will completely forgive us and cover our spiritual sinkholes.

MARVIN WILLIAMS

When we uncover our sins in repentance God will cover them.

Too Heavy

PSALM 32:1–6; MATTHEW 11:28–30

*"Come to me, all you who are weary and burdened,
and I will give you rest."*

MATTHEW 11:28

As I started up my car in the dark hours of early morning, I noticed a seat-belt light on the dashboard. I checked my door, opening and pulling it shut again. I tugged on my seatbelt to test it. But the sensor light still beamed. Then, in slow realization, I reached over and lifted my purse a few inches above the passenger seat. The light clicked off.

Apparently, a cell phone, three rolls of quarters, a hardcover book, and my lunch stuffed in my very large purse had equaled the weight of a small passenger, thus setting off the sensor!

While I can easily empty out a handbag, other weights are not so easy to shed. Those burdens of life involve a heaviness of spirit.

Whether the burden that weighs us down is one of guilt such as the one that consumed David's thoughts (Psalm 32:1–6), the fear Peter experienced (Matthew 26:20–35), or the doubt Thomas carried (John 20:24–29), Jesus has invited us to bring them all to Him: "Come to me, all you who weary and burdened, and I will give you rest" (Matthew 11:28).

We are not built to bear burdens alone. When we cast them on the One who wants to bear our burdens (Psalm 68:19; 1 Peter 5:7), He replaces them with forgiveness, healing, and restoration. No burden is too heavy for Him.

CINDY HESS KASPER

Burden God with what burdens you.

Dusty Leaves

PSALM 32:1–7

I acknowledged my sin to you and did not cover up my iniquity.
I said, "I will confess my transgressions to the LORD."
And you forgave the guilt of my sin.

PSALM 32:5

The rubber plant I bought for my wife Dorothy added a touch of life to our home. But one morning its leaves were drooping as if in a state of dejection. I wondered what happened.

When I came home for lunch that noon, the plant was completely transformed. It looked as hearty as it did the day I bought it. Its leaves were extended outward once again. When I asked Dorothy about it, she told me of reading a household hint on how to keep plants looking fresh. It stated that dust accumulating on the leaves can actually prevent the light from getting to them. So she wiped them off regularly. The result was amazing.

As we live in this world, tiny "particles" of sin can easily build up in our lives. Resentments, sharp words, impure thoughts, or selfish attitudes all take their toll on our spiritual vitality. Unless they are confessed right away, they begin to form a layer of "dust" that prevents us from experiencing the light of God's grace in our hearts. Those around us will sense that something is wrong.

If the accumulation of unconfessed sin has gathered on your soul, do as David did—confess it to the Lord (Psalm 32:5). Wipe off the "dusty leaves" of your life and enjoy again the glorious sunshine of God's love.

DENNIS DEHAAN

Confession of sin lets the light of God's forgiveness shine through.

Instincts

PSALM 32

I will instruct you and teach you in the way you should go;
I will counsel you with my loving eye on you.

PSALM 32:8

Flying into a storm is a dangerous experience. The temptation is to fly by your instincts, or, as aviators say, "by the seat of your pants." But as any pilot will tell you, that's a prescription for disaster. If you rely on your feelings and instincts, you become disoriented, thinking the plane is going up when it's actually going down. Thankfully, the instrument panel is set to magnetic north and can be trusted every time. Letting your instruments guide you, even when it feels like they're wrong, helps ensure safety in the storm.

We all face storms that threaten to confuse and disorient us. It may be a call from the doctor's office, a friend who has betrayed you, or a shattered dream. Those are the times to be especially careful. When you are blinded by life's disappointments, don't trust your instincts. Flying by the seat of your pants in the storms of life can lead to despair, confusion, and vengeful responses that make matters worse. God wants to guide you, and His Word is packed with wisdom and insights for living. His "Word is a lamp for my feet, a light on my path" (Psalm 119:105). Where He leads is always right!

Go to your Bible, and trust God to guide you. He promises, "I will instruct you and teach you in the way you should go" (Psalm 32:8).

JOE STOWELL

The closer we walk with God, the clearer we see His guidance.

As Stubborn as Prunes

PSALM 32:8–11

Do not be like the horse or the mule,
which have no understanding but must be controlled
by bit and bridle or they will not come to you.
PSALM 32:9

At a Colorado ranch where I once worked, we had a mule named Prunes. He was big, strong, and intelligent. He was also the ringleader of a small band of horses that regularly escaped from the corral.

One evening we hid near the barn to see how they got out. Just before dark, Prunes approached the gate, flipped up the latch with his nose, and then knocked his head against the lever. The gate swung open, and Prunes gave a satisfied snort as he and his friends trotted off to freedom.

Prunes was smart, but he was also stubborn; only a strong, skilled rider could control him. Perhaps the psalmist had known an animal like that when he wrote: "Do not be like the horse or the mule, which have no understanding but must be controlled by bit and bridle or they will not come to you" (Psalm 32:9).

The Lord longs to lead His children in a much different way: "I will instruct you and teach you in the way you should go; I will counsel you with my loving eye on you" (v. 8). While it takes a bit and bridle to direct a stubborn mule, just a glance from the Lord should be enough to keep an obedient, cooperative Christian on the right trail.

Which will it be for us today?

DAVID MCCASLAND

To avoid going wrong, follow God's leading.

Let's Sing

PSALM 33:1-11

Sing joyfully to the LORD, you righteous;
it is fitting for the upright to praise him. . . .
Sing to him a new song.

PSALM 33:1, 3

Singing has always played a vital role in the worship of God. The psalms were sung in the temple, often in the form of beautiful antiphons; that is, responses between a soloist and the choir, then between the choir and the worshipers. Jesus and His disciples sang a hymn after He had instituted the Lord's Supper (Matthew 26:30). Paul encouraged believers to address one another with "psalms and hymns and songs from the Spirit" (Ephesians 5:19).

Why should we sing? Is it only to prepare worshipers for the sermon? To say this would imply that singing is just a gimmick. Paul would have frowned upon such an idea because he was convinced that the gospel alone, truthfully proclaimed, is "the power of God that brings salvation" (Romans 1:16). No, we sing because it is a great way to express our adoration and proclaim our faith. Through song we praise God and edify one another.

The writer of Psalm 33 called upon the worshiping Israelites to sing praise to God for His powerful word, His unfailing counsels, and His continual concern for His people.

Let's join enthusiastically with others in praising Him through song. The Lord is pleased with any melody of praise that comes from the heart.

HERB VANDER LUGT

Each new day gives us new reasons to sing God's praise.

A New Song

PSALM 33:1–5

Praise the LORD with the harp;
make music to him on the ten-stringed lyre.
Sing to him a new song; play skillfully, and shout for joy.

PSALM 33:2–3

I was walking in the park one morning, listening to a tape by the Brooklyn Tabernacle Choir. I had my ancient Walkman clipped to my belt and my headphones clamped over my ears, tuned in to another world. The music was joyous! Oblivious to my surroundings, I began to sing and dance.

Then I spied my neighbor, leaning against a tree with a bemused look on her face. She couldn't hear my music, but she was delighted by my behavior. I wish she could have heard my song.

I thought afterward of the new song God has placed in our hearts, a song we hear from another world. It tells us that God loves us and always will, and that He has "rescued us from the dominion of darkness" (Colossians 1:13) and has "seated us with him in the heavenly realms in Christ Jesus" (Ephesians 2:6). Someday He'll take us to be with Him forever.

In the meantime He has given us eternally useful things to do. Grace now and glory ahead! Is this not a reason to sing?

Next time you're down in the dumps, think about God's goodness. Tune in to the music of heaven and sing a new song with the angels. It may set your feet to dancing and cause great wonderment in those around you. Perhaps they'll want to hear the music too.

DAVID ROPER

God's work in our life puts a new song in our heart.

His Goodness

PSALM 33:1–11

The LORD loves righteousness and justice;
the earth is full of his unfailing love.
PSALM 33:5

One Saturday my life came perilously close to being permanently altered. My brother and my nephew stopped by to pick up a desk. After loading it on the truck, they chatted for a few minutes and then drove off. I went into the house while my husband Jay pulled our car into the garage. Moments later I heard a loud crash, so I raced out to the garage. Jay was staring at the overhead garage door, which had suddenly slammed down. If the spring had broken a few minutes earlier, someone would have been hit by the two-hundred-pound door—and would have been seriously injured, or even killed.

It was not simply a matter of luck or coincidence that no one was hurt in that garage. God's protective hand was there—one more reminder of His goodness.

I sometimes long for a dramatic display of God's glory and power to show that He is with me. But He wants me to see Him in His little displays of goodness, which He demonstrates every day in hundreds of acts of mercy and compassion—just as He did in my garage that Saturday.

The psalmist reminds us that "the earth is full of [God's] unfailing love" (33:5). May God open our eyes to His many acts of goodness so we'll never doubt His presence and His love.

JULIE ACKERMAN LINK

If you know that God's hand is in everything,
you can leave everything in God's hand.

When God Speaks

PSALM 33:1–12

For he spoke, and it came to be; he commanded, and it stood firm.
PSALM 33:9

Recognize any of these statements? "I'm going to lose weight." "I'm going to start reading my Bible every morning." "I'm going to quit this or that bad habit." We all make statements like these—strong declarations of what we want to happen. But saying something and making sure it occurs are not the same. It takes effort and dedication, and even then what we want to happen may not take place.

Not so with God. According to Psalm 33, when He speaks, what He says comes into being. For instance, verse 6 says, "By the word of the LORD the heavens were made, their starry host by the breath of his mouth." God spoke, and the world came into existence. What a testimony of God's greatness! It should remind us of the infinite difference between the Creator and His creatures. When we speak, we voice our wishes; when God speaks, He creates reality.

This magnificent truth inspires us to put into action the commands of Psalm 33:1–3, "Sing joyfully to the LORD," "Praise the LORD," and "Sing to him a new song." His words bring forth worlds, and our words need to bring forth His praise.

Today, we should do more than just say, "I'm going to praise the Lord." Let's do it with our lives and with our words.

DAVE BRANON

God's great power generates our grateful praise.

Free from Fear

PSALM 34:1–10

I sought the LORD, and he answered me;
he delivered me from all my fears.

PSALM 34:4

Fear sneaks into my heart without permission. It paints a picture of help-lessness and hopelessness. It steals my peace and my concentration. What am I fearful about? I'm concerned about the safety of my family or the health of loved ones. I panic at the loss of a job or a broken relationship. Fear turns my focus inward and reveals a heart that sometimes finds it hard to trust.

When these fears and worries strike, how good it is to read David's prayer in Psalm 34: "I sought the LORD, and he answered me; he delivered me from all my fears" (v. 4). And how does God deliver us from our fears? When we "look to him" (v. 5), when we focus on Him, our fears fade; we trust Him to be in control. Then David mentions a different type of fear—not a fear that paralyzes, but a deep respect and awe of the One who surrounds us and delivers us (v. 7). We can take refuge in Him because He is good (v. 8).

This awe of His goodness helps put our fears into perspective. When we remember who God is and how much He loves us, we can relax into His peace. "Those who fear him lack nothing" (v. 9), concludes David. How wonderful to discover that in the fear of the Lord we can be delivered from our fears.

KEILA OCHOA

Ask God to free you from your fears.

Reflections on Windows

PSALM 34:1–10

Open my eyes that I may see wonderful things in your law.
PSALM 119:18

Much of the scenery I saw during our vacation in Alaska was through the windows of moving vehicles. I was thankful for glass that allowed me to see the beauty while remaining warm and dry. But the windows also presented a challenge. When it rained, water drops on the outside obscured the view. When the temperature changed, condensation caused fog to develop on the inside.

Those challenges help me understand why it is impossible for us to see life the way God intended it. Sin obscures the beauty of life that God wants us to enjoy. Sometimes sin is inside—our selfishness creates a fog that makes us see ourselves as more important than we are and causes us to forget about others' interests. Sometimes sin is outside. The injustice of others causes our tears to fall like rain, preventing us from seeing the goodness of God. Sin of any kind keeps us from seeing the wonder and glory of life as God designed it.

For now, even though "we see things imperfectly, like puzzling reflections in a mirror" (1 Corinthians 13:12 NLT), we see enough to know that God is good (Psalm 34:8). The many wonderful things God has revealed encourage us to forsake sin and to work on ways to minimize its consequences in the world.

JULIE ACKERMAN LINK

The only way to see life clearly is to focus on Christ.

Taste and Say

PSALM 34

Taste and see that the LORD is good;
blessed is the one who takes refuge in him.
PSALM 34:8

Do you believe God is good, even when life isn't? A woman named Mary did, and I gasped with amazement the day I heard her pastor share her story at her funeral. She, being dead, yet speaks!

Mary had been a widow, very poor, and totally housebound because of her ailments in old age. But like the psalmist, she had learned to praise God amid her hardships. Over the years she had come to savor with deep gratitude every good thing He sent her way.

Her pastor said he occasionally would visit her at home. Because of her crippling pain, it took her a long time to inch her way to the door to let him in. So he would call on his phone and tell her that he was on his way and the time he would get there. Mary would then begin the slow, arduous journey to the door, reaching it about the time he arrived. Without fail, he could count on her greeting him with these triumphant words: "God is good!"

I've observed that those who speak most often about God's goodness are usually those with the most trials. They choose to focus on the Lord's mercy and grace rather than on their troubles, and in so doing they taste His goodness.

Mary not only challenges us to taste and see, but to taste and say that the Lord is good—even when life isn't.

JOANIE YODER

Those who bless God in their trials
will be blessed by God through their trials.

God Hears Your Cry

PSALM 34:1–8

The righteous cry out, and the LORD hears them;
he delivers them from all their troubles.

PSALM 34:17

Someone once asked a lifeguard this question: "How can you tell if some-one needs help when dozens of bathers on the beach or in the water are all combining their voices in a hubbub of noise?" He replied, "No matter how great the sounds of confusion may be, there has never been a time when I couldn't distinguish a cry of distress above them all. I could always tell when there was an actual emergency."

That's sounds like our heavenly Father. In all the confusion that sur-rounds us, He never fails to hear the soul that cries out to Him for help amid the storms of life.

The psalmist David discovered that in his hour of trouble he could call on the Lord and be confident of receiving help. This was a great comfort to him. In Psalm 34 he told of his trials before praising God for His loving deliverance.

You may be sure that in your times of anguish and distress God is watch-ing over you. He sees you as if you were His only child in the whole world, and He offers relief or the strength to endure.

If you are encountering troubles today, cry out to the Lord. Then praise Him for the help He brings to you.

HENRY BOSCH

God takes heed to your every need.

Seeing the Unseen

PSALM 34:47

The angel of the LORD encamps around those who fear him,
and he delivers them.

PSALM 34:7

In a materialistic world like ours, we are tempted to conclude that the only real things are those we experience with our five senses. Yet "there are things we cannot see: things behind our backs or far away and all things in the dark," said C. S. Lewis.

There is another realm of reality, just as actual, just as factual, just as substantial as anything we see, hear, touch, taste, or smell in this world. It exists all around us—not out there "somewhere," but "here." There are legions of angels helping us, for which the world has no countermeasures (Hebrews 1:14). The psalmist David referred to them as a force of thousands of thousands of chariots (Psalm 68:17). We cannot see God nor His angels with our natural eyes. But they are there, whether we see them or not. I believe the world is filled with them.

Faith is the means by which we are able to "see" this invisible world. That is belief's true function. Faith is to the spiritual realm what the five senses are to the natural realm. The writer of Hebrews says that faith is "the assurance about what we do not see" (Hebrews 11:1). By faith we recognize the existence of the spiritual world and learn to depend on the Lord for His help in our daily life. Our goal, then, as one Christian writer once said, is to "grow eyes" to see the unseen.

DAVID ROPER

Faith sees things that are out of sight.

The Way to Happiness

PSALM 34:1–14

*The lions may grow weak and hungry,
but those who seek the LORD lack no good thing.*

PSALM 34:10

Pathways that seem to be marked "This Way to Happiness" are all over the landscape of our culture. Some people travel the money path. Others follow the way of entertainment. Still others head down the route of power or self-gratification.

The problem with those roads is that they are all dead-ends that lead to frustration. The only way to true happiness is the course God has clearly outlined in His Word.

God's route to joy is found in Psalm 34. In just fourteen verses, David charts a course that, when followed, leads to all the advantages we need in this world—advantages that can be ours no matter if we are rich or poor, healthy or sick, famous or unknown. The way to happiness is marked by these signs:

- Praising God: "I will glory in the LORD" (v. 2).
- Seeking God: "I sought the LORD, and he answered me" (v. 4).
- Fearing God: "Fear the LORD, you his holy people!" (v. 9).
- Living for God: "Turn from evil and do good" (v. 14).

Happiness comes from going God's way. Traveling other paths will take you on a long journey to nowhere.

DAVE BRANON

To find true happiness, trust and obey God's directions.

The Hiding Place

PSALM 34:4–8

Taste and see that the LORD is good;
blessed is the one who takes refuge in him.
PSALM 34:8

In the misery that is so often a part of this world, there is only one sure refuge: God himself. "He shields all who take refuge in him" (Psalm 18:30).

To "take refuge in" means "to hide in" or "to hide with." It suggests a secret place of concealment—a "hidey-hole," as we used to say back in Texas.

When we're exhausted by our efforts, when we're bewildered by our problems, when we're wounded by our friends, when we're surrounded by our foes, we can hide ourselves in God. There is no safety in this world. If we were to find safety here, we would never know the joy of God's love and protection. We would miss the happiness for which we were made.

The only safe place is God himself. When storm clouds gather and calamities loom, we must run into His presence in prayer and remain there (Psalm 57:1).

Nineteenth-century Scottish author George MacDonald said, "That man is perfect in faith who can come to God in the utter dearth of his feelings and desires, without a glow or an aspiration, with the weight of low thoughts, failures, neglects, and wandering forgetfulness, and say to Him, 'Thou art my refuge.'"

How safe and blessed we are!

DAVID ROPER

Safety is not found in the absence of danger
but in the presence of God.

Safe Forever

PSALM 34:8–22

"I have told you these things, so that in me you may have peace. In this world you will have trouble. But take heart! I have overcome the world."
JOHN 16:33

Amy Beth was out in her neighborhood taking her dog for a walk when she saw a young man run into a nearby alley. A car followed. The young man grabbed a huge piece of wood from a dumpster and started swinging at the car. Amy Beth froze. She was caught in a gang fight.

Suddenly, the young driver of the car tried to get away by accelerating backwards. He slammed into Amy Beth. She landed on the trunk and was thrown into the street. Amazingly, she wasn't seriously hurt.

Later, she tried to make sense of her experience and attempted to turn it around to make it seem good. She came to this conclusion: "Bad things happen—tragic and horrible things. Good things happen—amazing and miraculous things. And all this happens randomly to us. But it is not random to the God who cradles our aching hearts. He knows. . . . Suffering will come. But God is . . . larger than the events that seem to contradict God's goodness."

We will experience sickness, accidents, sorrow, and death. But we are not on our own. God is in control. "The righteous person may have many troubles, but the LORD delivers him from them all" (Psalm 34:19). We can be confident that one day we will be safe with Him forever.

ANNE CETAS

God is always in control behind the scenes.

Just You and God

PSALM 35:1-10

Contend, LORD, with those who contend with me;
fight against those who fight against me.

PSALM 35:1

My friend Ron wasn't having a good week. His new job had thrust him in the midst of some people who were foul-mouthed, rude, and obnoxious. Ron is one tough guy, but after two months of working in that environment, he wasn't sure he could tolerate any more ungodly, uncouth behavior.

Ron is by no means alone. Perhaps you too are in an environment that is not friendly to godliness—either at work, at home, or elsewhere. If so, what can you do? Here are some suggestions that may help you survive and even thrive:

Concentrate on God's goodness and depend on it. Our circumstances do not change the truth that the Lord is good all the time (Nahum 1:7).

Stay true to your convictions. Daniel refused to give in when he was surrounded by the ungodly (Daniel 1).

Immerse yourself in the Bible. Listen to God in His Word. It will encourage you (Psalm 119:49–50).

Do good for those who oppose you. Return good for evil (Matthew 5:44).

Trust God to be your companion. He will never leave you. And He won't forsake you (Hebrews 13:5).

When it's just you and God, that's enough.

DAVE BRANON

With God behind you and His arms beneath you,
you can face whatever is before you.

The Salt Lick

PSALM 35:22–28

May those who delight in my vindication shout for joy and gladness; may they always say, "The Lord be exalted, who delights in the well-being of his servant."
PSALM 35:27

One spring I put a salt block in the bushes a few yards behind my mountain home. I was hoping to draw in a small herd of deer that grazed at a distance. Each morning I slowly opened the window shades, hoping to see deer gathered around the lick; each morning I was disappointed. I didn't think the herd would ever find the salt.

Then one morning as I drew the shades, to my utter delight I spied a magnificent, young buck. He was licking the block, oblivious to my presence. I stood there for a long time watching him and savoring my joy.

My wife Carolyn reminded me later in the day that God takes a similar joy in me. The psalmist said that the Lord "delights in the well-being of his servant" (Psalm 35:27). He takes joy from bringing good to me and in seeing me bask in His blessings.

English preacher John Owen (1616–1683) said, "The souls of the saints are the garden of Jesus Christ, . . . a garden for delight; He rejoices in them."

God longs to be good to us and to satisfy our deepest longings with His love. We are His heart's delight.

DAVID ROPER

God takes delight in us—how can we help but delight in Him!

Welcome Wings

PSALM 36:5–9

How priceless is your unfailing love, O God!
People take refuge in the shadow of your wings.

PSALM 36:7

One spring a pair of blue jays built a nest in the persimmon tree in our backyard. I enjoyed watching the mother bird as she sat patiently on her eggs. In a matter of days, I noticed a new development as I peered from beneath the eaves of the carport. The father would fly in, the mother would perch on the side of that little home, and four little mouths would gap open above the edge of the nest.

To get a better look, I would edge closer to the tree. Then I would stand very still and watch the mother. When I got too close, however, she would spread her wings over her little brood. Her head would cautiously protrude as she looked first to one side and then to the other. She was always on guard, protecting her little ones by sheltering them with her wings.

This beautiful picture of protection reminds me of David's words in Psalm 36:7. When he said that we can find safety "in the shadow of [God's] wings," he may have been referring to the words of his ancestor Boaz (Ruth 2:12). Boaz had said to Ruth, "May the LORD repay you for what you have done. May you be richly rewarded by the LORD, the God of Israel, under whose wings you have come to take refuge."

That's a promise we all need. Life is filled with dangers, both physical and spiritual. Yet we can rest securely because we are covered by God's omnipotent protection. What better refuge could we have than to live in the shadow of His wings!

PAUL VAN GORDER

For the Christian, sometimes darkness is
but the shadow of God's wing.

Abundant Supply

PSALM 36:5–12

They feast on the abundance of your house;
you give them drink from your river of delights.

PSALM 36:8

We have a hummingbird feeder in the garden, and we love to see the little birds come and drink from its sugary water. Recently, however, we went on a short trip and forgot to replenish its contents. When we came back, it was completely dry. *Poor birds!* I thought. *Because of my forgetfulness, they haven't had any nourishment.* Then I was reminded that I am not the one who feeds them: God is.

Sometimes we may feel that all of the demands of life have depleted our strength and there is no one to replenish it. But others don't feed our souls: God does.

In Psalm 36 we read about God's lovingkindness. It describes those who put their trust in Him and are abundantly satisfied. God gives them water from His "river of delights" (v. 8). He is the fountain of life!

We can go to God every day for the supply of our needs. As Charles Spurgeon wrote, "The springs of my faith and all my graces; the springs of my life and all my pleasures; the springs of my activity and all its right doings; the springs of my hope, and all its heavenly anticipations, all lie in thee, my Lord."

Let us be filled with His abundant supply. His fountain will never run dry.

KEILA OCHOA

God's love is abundant.

The World We Live In

PSALM 37:1–7

Do not fret because of evildoers.
PSALM 37:1 (NKJV)

As the Lord's return draws near, godlessness is increasing. Standards that have stood for decades are falling all around us. Crime, lawlessness, and disrespect all seem to be growing.

If that's the way you've been looking at things recently, the psalmist David has good news for you. There is hope! There is a positive way to look at life.

Here are David's recommendations for facing a world marked by "evildoers," whose day in the sun is as fleeting as grass in the desert (Psalm 37:1–2).

- *Trust God* (v. 3). The alternative is to trust people with the future, and that doesn't seem to be working out so well.
- *Do good things* (v. 3). The more good we do, the less chance evil has to succeed.
- *Delight in the Lord* (v. 4). Take delight in God and His will, and He promises to provide what you need.
- *Commit your way to God* (v. 5). He will bless your efforts.
- *Wait patiently for the Lord* (v. 7). He will prevail.

The more we immerse ourselves in God, His Word, and His promises, the less we will fret over the troubles of this world. Sure, it's a tough world we live in, but with God we can be victorious!

DAVE BRANON

To make it in a tough world, keep in touch with God.

Frustrating Promises

PSALM 37:1–24

Take delight in the LORD, and he will give you the desires of your heart.
PSALM 37:4

Do any Bible promises frustrate you? Some people say that Psalm 37:4 is a guarantee that you'll get whatever you want—a spouse, a job, money. This has made me wonder at times: *Why don't I have what I want?*

When a promise frustrates us because it seems that God is not fulfilling it, maybe it's because we don't understand what the verse really means. Here are three suggestions to help, using Psalm 37 as an example:

Consider the context. Psalm 37 is telling us not to worry or be envious of the wicked. Our focus is not to be on what they have, nor on what they seem to be getting away with (vv. 12–13). Instead, we are commanded to trust and delight in the Lord (vv. 3–4).

Consider other verses. We're taught in 1 John 5:14 that our requests need to be according to God's will for us. Other Scriptures on the same topic can give us a balance.

Consult a Bible commentary. In *The Treasury of David*, Charles Spurgeon says this about verse 4: "[Those] who delight in God desire or ask for nothing but what will please God." Doing a little deeper study can help us understand frustrating Bible verses like this one.

As we learn to delight in the Lord, His desires will become our own—and He will grant them.

ANNE CETAS

You can't break God's promises by leaning on them.

Getting What You Want

PSALM 37:1-6

Commit your way to the LORD; trust in him and he will do this.
PSALM 37:5

Our family of six needed more room. The little house that seemed so spacious when there were just two of us was bursting at the seams. So we began looking for a bigger house. Right away we found just the one with enough room for everyone. Excitedly, we put in a bid, and it was accepted. All that stood in our way was selling our house. We waited. And waited. And waited. After two months, the owners of the house we wanted could wait no more. They sold it to someone else.

This kind of thing happens to all of us. For good reasons we want something. We pray about it, asking God's guidance. But then comes an answer that is not what we asked for. We don't get that home. Or that job. Or that child. Or that mate. Unfulfilled desires. But why don't we get the "desires of [our] heart" (Psalm 37:4)?

Psalm 37 helps us take a spiritual inventory so we don't disqualify ourselves for God's best by fretting (v. 1), envying (v. 1), not trusting God (v. 3), or not doing good (v. 3). But there's more. We must delight ourselves in the Lord and commit our way to Him (vv. 4–5) so His desire becomes more important than our desires.

Instead of wanting a certain house or job or answer, we must learn to be content with what God provides. As we take delight in Him and commit our way to Him, our desires will increasingly match His. Then we'll get what He wants—and we'll be thrilled with it.

DAVE BRANON

God gives His very best to those who leave the choice to Him.

Keep Going!

PSALM 37:34–40

*Do not fret because of those who are evil or be envious of those who do wrong; . . . Hope in the L*ORD *and keep his way. He will exalt you to inherit the land; when the wicked are destroyed, you will see it.*

PSALM 37:1, 34

This notice appeared in the window of a coat store in Nottingham, England:

> We have been established for over 100 years and have been pleasing and displeasing customers ever since. We have made money and lost money, suffered the effects of government control and bad payers. We have been cussed and discussed, messed about, lied to, held up, robbed, and swindled. The only reason we stay in business is to see what happens next.

The store owner knew that life was full of difficulties. But he was determined to survive, even if only to hope for the best and "see what happens next."

Christ's followers have a much better reason to endure tough times as they live for Him. The Lord has assured us in His Word that better times are ahead. The psalmist reminded us that in spite of the prosperity of the wicked, the righteous will be vindicated.

Certainly, we will become discouraged at times. David did. Elijah did. So did Moses and Solomon. But the follower of Christ has every reason not to give up but to wait on God.

What a waste it would be to give up! Instead, keep going! Keep looking for what the Lord has planned for you today, tomorrow, forever!

MART DEHAAN

There are no hopeless situations, only people who have lost hope.

How to Manage Stress

PSALM 37:1–8

Be still before the LORD and wait patiently for him; do not fret when people succeed in their ways, when they carry out their wicked schemes.
PSALM 37:7

Laurie Jones, writing in *The Baltimore Sun,* emphasized that it is not necessary to be victimized by stress. She pointed out that "you, not outside events, control how extensively stress affects your life."

Jones quoted stress-management consultant Donald Tubesing, who says that stress is our response to the situation, not the situation itself. He gives this example: "If you get stuck in traffic, you can work yourself up . . . and yell at anyone who beeps his horn. Or you could view the time you're sitting there as the only uninterrupted fifteen minutes you'll have all day."

John Curtis, founder of the University of Wisconsin Stress Management Institute, says, "I believe ninety percent of stress is brought on by not living in the present moment—worrying about what's already happened, what's going to happen, or what could happen."

The advice of these stress management experts can be helpful. Our best counsel, however, comes from Psalm 37. When faced with trouble, we should "be still before the LORD and wait patiently for him" (v. 7). As we ask for God's help, claim His promises, and trust Him to carry us through, we can relax and stop worrying.

That's how to manage stress.

RICHARD DEHAAN

Worry is futile but faith is fruitful.

Hurting Your Heart

PSALM 37:1–8

Refrain from anger and turn from wrath;
do not fret—it leads only to evil.

PSALM 37:8

Anger can do a lot of damage. When we allow it to control our thoughts and actions, we not only hurt other people but we also hurt ourselves.

In fact, recent medical research has found new evidence linking heart disease and anger. According to an Associated Press release, Dr. Redford B. Williams Jr. and some of his colleagues did a personality study of one hundred eighteen students in law school. They were graded on their hostility. Twenty-five years later, twenty percent of those who had scored highest as being angry persons had died, compared with only five percent of those who had registered lowest.

Dr. Williams said that people who are inclined toward anger may "get furious, for instance, in slow-moving bank lines. They complain to themselves about why other customers haven't filled out their deposit slips ahead of time and may show their unhappiness by making sour faces or even surly comments to those ahead of them."

No question about it, anger is hurtful to the heart—both physically and spiritually.

The New Testament says, "Get rid of all bitterness, rage and anger" (Ephesians 4:31), and "let the peace of Christ rule in your hearts" (Colossians 3:15).

PAUL VAN GORDER

For every minute you are angry,
you lose an opportunity for sixty seconds of happiness.

A Strategy of Patience

PSALM 37:1–11

Trust in the LORD and do good; dwell in the land and enjoy safe pasture. . . .
Be still before the LORD and wait patiently for him; do not fret when people
succeed in their ways, when they carry out their wicked schemes.

PSALM 37:3, 7

Patient perseverance should characterize the life of every believer.

While reading the book *They Call Me Coach* by John Wooden, I came across a passage that illustrates this virtue. The author, a highly successful basketball coach at UCLA for many years, said, "In game play, it has always been my philosophy that patience will win out. By that, I mean patience to follow our game plan. If we do believe in it, we will wear the opposition down and will get to them. If we break away from our style, however, and play their style, we're in trouble. And if we let our emotions command the game rather than our reason, we will not function effectively. I constantly caution our team, 'Play your game. . . . Eventually, if you play your game, stick to your style, class will tell in the end! This does not mean that we will always outscore our opponent, but it does ensure that we will not beat ourselves.'"

In Psalm 37, God is saying, in effect, "Do what's right and trust Me. Regardless of how badly you may seem to be losing, do My will and leave the outcome to Me." Such a strategy will not only keep us from beating ourselves but it will also lead to victory!

MART DEHAAN

God's clock is never slow, but sometimes ours is fast.

The Treasure Myth

PSALM 37:7–20

What good is it for someone to gain the whole world,
yet forfeit their soul?

MARK 8:36

When the great ocean liner *Titanic* sank in 1912, it was rumored to have gone down with a fortune in jewels and gold. That longstanding myth was dispelled, however, by the discovery of the ship's manifest, which showed that the ship was carrying raw feathers, linen, straw, hatter's fur, tissue, auto parts, leather, rabbit hair, elastics, hairnets, and refrigerating equipment.

There is another persistent rumor about riches. It is widely believed that a wealthy person should be honored and valued, even though he may be ungodly. On the other hand, a godly, self-disciplined person is considered by some to be of little worth if he is not wealthy.

David, the author of Psalm 37, cautioned the poor and needy not to be envious of the rich and prosperous. In time, the cargo manifest of the ungodly will be uncovered, revealing that their lives contain nothing of enduring value.

This life is only the beginning of an everlasting existence. So don't look longingly at the ungodly and their riches. They have no lasting treasures. Instead, be like those who wait with patience for their eternal God (vv. 7, 9)—no matter what their economic situation may be. They alone know where to find real treasure.

MART DEHAAN

It's better to be poor and walk by faith
than to be rich and walk by sight.

Just a Moment

PSALM 38

A good name is more desirable than great riches;
to be esteemed is better than silver or gold.

PROVERBS 22:1

I think of Proverbs 22:1 when I recall a college friend who never got in trouble or caused any difficulty. But one day, in a moment of ill-conceived mischief, he threw a match into a waste can and started a fire that left part of our dorm scorched and his reputation burned beyond recognition. Whatever else he has done since then, his name remains associated with that reckless prank.

Often we think young people should be the most careful about their reputation, and indeed they need to protect their good name. But adults too can throw away their good name through one poor choice.

Think of David, who for many years bore the stigma of his sinful, adulterous liaison with Bathsheba. Even though he was forgiven, his reputation had been stained. We can't be sure of the specific occasion for the writing of Psalm 38, but in it David describes the agony of living with the results of his sin. To avoid such pain, Scripture tells us to guard our heart (Proverbs 4:23), to walk wisely (Ephesians 5:15), and to follow in Jesus's steps (1 Peter 2:21).

It takes just a moment to destroy your good name and your testimony for God. Instead, let's use each moment to bring glory to God's name.

DAVE BRANON

If we take care of our character,
our reputation will take care of itself!

The Path of Wisdom

PSALM 38:1–15

LORD, I wait for you; you will answer, Lord my God.
PSALM 38:15

Albert Einstein was heard to say, "Only two things are infinite, the universe and human stupidity, and I'm not sure about the former." Sadly, it does seem that far too often there is no limit to the foolishness we get ourselves into—or the damage we create by our foolishness and the choices it fosters.

It was in such a season of regret that David poured out his struggle and complaint to God in Psalm 38. As he recounted his own failings, as well as the painful consequences he was enduring because of those failings, the shepherd-king made an insightful comment: "My wounds fester and are loathsome because of my sinful folly" (v. 5). Although the psalmist does not give us the details of those choices or of his worsening wounds, one thing is clear—David recognized his own foolishness as their root cause.

The answer for such destructive foolishness is to embrace the wisdom of God. Proverbs 9:10 reminds us, "The fear of the LORD is the beginning of wisdom, and knowledge of the Holy One is understanding." Only by allowing God to transform us can we overcome the foolish decisions that cause so much trouble. With His loving guidance, we can follow the pathway of godly wisdom.

BILL CROWDER

God's wisdom is given to those who humbly ask Him for it.

Running from God

PSALM 38

I confess my iniquity; I am troubled by my sin. . . .
Come quickly to help me, my Lord and my Savior.

PSALM 38:18, 22

Our dog had fleas. For a while they just about drove him crazy. When we realized what his problem was, we bathed him with flea shampoo, dusted him with flea powder, and fumigated his bedding with flea spray. Then, just when we thought we had eliminated them, they showed up again. Where were they coming from?

Well, he had recently come of age and was determined to run after new loves whenever he could find a crack in the door. We would scold and threaten him, but he was deaf to our calls. The dog was bound to run whenever he could. And he brought back problems, for him and for us.

In a much more serious sense, David faced the discomfort of problems that resulted from his waywardness. When he felt the hand of his Master pressing down on him, he knew the reason (Psalm 38:2). God was using painful consequences to rid David of his foolishness.

When we run away from God and bring trouble on ourselves, we can get help. As David did in Psalm 38, we need to recognize God's correcting hand and make a new start. Better yet, we can avoid His chastening if we go to the Lord in repentance before He must correct us.

MART DeHAAN

Running from God always brings trouble.

0 to 40

PSALM 39

*Show me, LORD, my life's end and the number of my days;
let me know how fleeting my life is.*

PSALM 39:4

The full-page newspaper advertisement for a new car was clever, and it made me think. In bold type it proclaimed that this automobile "Goes 0–40 as fast as you did!" It went on to say, "What happened? One minute you're studying for mid-terms, then you take a little nap and somehow wake up two years later with a job, a mate, and a couple of kids."

It's always a little startling to be confronted with the speed at which our years fly away. Centuries ago, the psalmist David sought God's help as he grappled with the brevity of life. He wrote, "Show me, LORD, my life's end and the number of my days; let me know how fleeting my life is. You have made my days a mere handbreadth; the span of my years is as nothing before you. Everyone is but a breath, even those who seem secure" (Psalm 39:4–5).

Rather than concluding that nothing really matters because life is so brief, the psalmist asked God for deliverance from his sins (v. 8) and for strength to live his remaining days (v. 13).

A popular slogan says, "Life Is Short—Party Hard." But God, who gives us eternal life through faith in Jesus Christ, reminds us, "Life Is Short—Live It Well!"

DAVID MCCASLAND

**It's not how long you live that counts,
but how well you live.**

Stuck in the Mud

PSALM 40:1–5

He lifted me out of the slimy pit, out of the mud and mire;
he set my feet on a rock and gave me a firm place to stand.

PSALM 40:2

We were absolutely stuck! While I was laying the wreath in place on my parents' grave, my husband eased the car off the road to allow another car to pass. It had rained for weeks and the parking area was sodden. When we were ready to leave, we discovered that the car was stuck. The wheels spun, sinking deeper and deeper into the mud.

We weren't going anywhere without a push, but my husband had a damaged shoulder, and I had just come out of the hospital. We needed help! At a distance I saw two young men, and they responded cheerfully to my frantic waves and shouts. Thankfully, their combined strength pushed the car back onto the roadway.

Psalm 40 recounts God's faithfulness when David cried for help. "I waited patiently for the LORD to help me, and he . . . heard my cry. He lifted me out of the pit of despair, out of the mud and the mire" (vv. 1–2 NLT). Whether this psalm refers to an actual pit or to challenging circumstances, David knew that he could always call on God for deliverance.

God will help us too when we call on Him. Sometimes He intervenes directly, but more often He works through other people. When we admit our need to Him—and perhaps to others—we can count on His faithfulness.

MARION STROUD

Hope comes with help from God and others.

Joy in the Morning

PSALM 40:1–5

For his anger lasts only a moment, but his favor lasts a lifetime;
weeping may stay for the night, but rejoicing comes in the morning.
PSALM 30:5

Angie could not see through the fogged-up windows in her car. Inadvertently, she pulled out in front of a truck. The accident caused such damage to her brain that she could no longer speak or take care of herself.

Over the years, I have been amazed at the resiliency of Angie's parents. Recently I asked them, "How have you managed to get through this experience?" Her father thoughtfully responded, "In all honesty, the only way we have been able to do this is by drawing close to God. He gives us the strength we need to help us through."

Angie's mother agreed and added that around the time of the accident their grieving was so deep that they wondered if they would ever have joy again. As they both leaned upon God, they experienced countless unexpected provisions for the physical and spiritual care of Angie and their entire family. Although Angie may never regain her ability to speak, she now responds to them with wide smiles and this gives them joy. Her parents' favorite verse continues to be: "Weeping may stay for the night, but rejoicing comes in the morning" (Psalm 30:5).

Have you experienced extreme sorrow? There is the promise of future joy amid your tears as you lean upon our loving Lord.

DENNIS FISHER

Leave your sorrows with Jesus, the "Man of Sorrows."

Unusual Places

PSALM 40:1–8

From inside the fish Jonah prayed to the LORD his God.
JONAH 2:1

Walking past my barn one day, I heard a frantic chirping inside. When I investigated, I found a poor blue jay beating its wings against the window. Had it not cried and chirped, I would not have heard. Its cry for help prompted me to look inside, open the door wide, and allow it to fly out to freedom.

We who are in God's family sometimes get ourselves into some unusual places and unhappy circumstances. Consider the following incidents:

- Jonah in a fish's belly, running from God (Jonah 2:1).
- David in enemy territory, acting insane (1 Samuel 21:10–15).
- Abram in Egypt, lying about his wife (Genesis 12:10–13).
- Lot in Sodom, living with the wicked (Genesis 13:12–13).
- Elijah in the desert, wallowing in self-pity (1 Kings 19:4).
- Peter in a courtyard, denying his Lord (Luke 22:55–62).

Yes, we sometimes find ourselves in the wrong place.

Are you in a place you shouldn't be today? Are you far from God, feeling defeated, trapped, and unhappy? Then cry out to the Lord, confess your sin, and be restored by His abundant mercy (1 John 1:9). He is waiting to hear your cry of repentance and open the door of freedom in Jesus.

M. R. DeHaan

No place is beyond the reach of God's grace.

What's Worth Waiting For?

PSALM 40

I waited patiently for the LORD; he turned to me and heard my cry.
PSALM 40:1

Psalm 40 is tough to take. It recalls a time when David was forced to wait. But as he looked back later with a new song in his heart, he saw that the wait was worth it. By implication, when we are in the middle of a chaotic situation, we must wait patiently for the Lord (v. 1).

That advice looks better in the Bible than it does in life. Patience is hard for those of us who get impatient with a download if it takes more than a few seconds, depend on the one-hour dry cleaners, and grab breakfast at a drive-through window.

We cook dinner in microwave ovens and gulp down remedies that offer "fast, fast relief." Overnight mail is too slow, and waiting at traffic lights drives us crazy. The people we live with, work with, play with, and worship with can absolutely unnerve us. They can be obstinate, frustrating, selfish, insulting. It's hard to be patient with them, and it's harder still to wait on the Lord.

Nineteenth-century hymnwriter Phillips Brooks ("O Little Town of Bethlehem") admitted, "The hardest task in my life is to sit down and wait for God to catch up with me." Yet patience, God's strategy for maturing us as Christians, is a lost skill we all need to cultivate.

If you have no joy because you're always in a rush, slow down. God will give you a new song—but first you must wait patiently for Him (vv. 1–3).

HADDON ROBINSON

Patience is a virtue that carries a lot of wait!

A Most Fitting Response

PSALM 40:1–5

He put a new song in my mouth, a hymn of praise to our God.
Many will see and fear the LORD and put their trust in him.

PSALM 40:3

Pastor Thomas DeWitt Talmage (1832–1902) told the story of an accident that occurred on a Great Lakes ferry. A little child standing by the rail suddenly lost her balance and fell overboard.

"Save my child!" cried the frantic mother. Lying on the deck was a great Newfoundland dog, which plunged into the water at the command of his master. Swimming to the girl, he took hold of her clothing with his teeth and brought her to the side of the boat, where both were lifted to safety. Although still frightened, the little girl threw her arms around that big shaggy dog and kissed him again and again. It seemed a most natural and appropriate thing to do.

Likewise, a response of love and gratitude should flow from every person who has been rescued by the Savior through His self-sacrificing death on the cross. He came from heaven's glory to suffer and die that we might have eternal life. The apostle Paul expressed his gratitude when he wrote, "Giving thanks to the Father who has . . . delivered us from the power of darkness and conveyed us into the kingdom of the Son of His love" (Colossians 1:12–13 NKJV).

Is your heart filled with praise and gratitude for everything God has done for you in Christ? It is a most fitting response.

PAUL VAN GORDER

Praise is the song of a soul set free.

Consider the Poor

PSALM 41:1–3

Blessed is he who considers the poor;
the LORD will deliver him in time of trouble.

PSALM 41:1 (NKJV)

You may have heard of the blessings Jesus spoke of in His Sermon on the Mount (Matthew 5:1–10). Here's a "blessing" from the Old Testament that is less well-known: "Blessed is he who considers the poor" (Psalm 41:1 NKJV).

The Hebrew word translated *considers* means "to take thought for others." The word translated *poor* means "those in need."

There are many people around us who are poor—in love, in hope, and in the knowledge of God. Even though we cannot solve all their problems, we can show them we care.

We may not have lots of money, but we can give of ourselves. We can let needy people know we're thinking of them. We can listen as they tell their stories. We can treat them with courtesy and respect. We can pray for them. We can write letters of encouragement. We can tell them about Jesus. If we can do nothing else, we can love them.

Think about those who live only for themselves, always trying to get ahead, looking for the next thing to make them happy. Compare them with people who give themselves to others. Which ones possess inner calm, strength, and joy?

The place of God's blessing is easily entered: Consider the poor.

DAVID ROPER

Giving is the true measure of love.

Really Thirsty

PSALM 42

As the deer pants for streams of water,
so my soul pants for you, my God.
PSALM 42:1

Have you ever been really thirsty? Years ago, I visited my sister Kathy in Mali, West Africa. During an afternoon of seeing the sights, the temperature had risen far above 100°F. Parched, I told her, "Hey, I need something to drink." When Kathy told me she had forgotten to bring along a supply of filtered water, I began to get a bit desperate. The longer we drove, the more I wondered what it was like to truly die of thirst.

Finally, Kathy said, "I know where we can go," as she drove up to the gate of an embassy. Inside I beheld the most beautiful sight—a water cooler! I grabbed one of the tiny paper cups and filled it again and again. My body had been deprived too long and now required lots of liquid to reverse the effects of dehydration.

The psalmist compared physical thirst with spiritual thirst: "As the deer pants for streams of water, so my soul pants for you, my God" (Psalm 42:1). His thirst was that of a desperate longing for God—the one and only living God (v. 2).

Do you long for something this world can't provide? This dissatisfaction is a thirst of the soul for God. Run to the One who alone can quench that thirst. "He satisfies the thirsty and fills the hungry with good things" (Psalm 107:9).

CINDY HESS KASPER

Only Jesus, the Living Water, can satisfy the thirsty soul.

The God Who Paints

PSALM 42

My soul thirsts for God, for the living God.
When can I go and meet with God?
PSALM 42:2

Nezahualcoyotl (1402–1472) may have had a difficult name to pronounce, but his name is full of significance. It means "Hungry Coyote," and this man's writings show a spiritual hunger. As a poet and ruler in Mexico before the arrival of the Europeans, he wrote, "Truly the gods, which I worship, are idols of stone that do not speak nor feel. . . . Some very powerful, hidden and unknown god is the creator of the entire universe. He is the only one that can console me in my affliction and help me in such anguish as my heart feels; I want him to be my helper and protection."

We cannot know if Nezahualcoyotl found the Giver of life. But during his reign he built a pyramid to the "God who paints things with beauty," and he banned human sacrifices in his city.

The writers of Psalm 42 cried out, "My soul thirsts for God, for the living God" (v. 2). Every human being desires the true God, just as "the deer pants for streams of water" (v. 1).

Today there are many Hungry Coyotes who know that the idols of fame, money, and relationships can't fill the void in their souls. The Living God has revealed himself through Jesus, the only One who gives us meaning and fulfillment. This is good news for those who are hungry for the God who paints things with beauty.

KEILA OCHOA

Beneath all of our longings is a deep desire for God.

Encourage Yourself

PSALM 42

David was greatly distressed because the men were talking of stoning him; each one was bitter in spirit because of his sons and daughters. But David found strength in the LORD his God.

1 SAMUEL 30:6

Talking to oneself is something many people ridicule in others and vow they'll never do themselves. They assume it's a sign of losing touch with reality. In light of what we read today in Psalm 42, though, let's think about it.

Before the psalmist talked to God about his depressed soul, he talked to his depressed soul about God. He said, "Why, my soul, are you downcast? Why are you so disturbed within me? Put your hope in God, for I will yet praise him" (v. 5). David was talking to himself, but he certainly was not losing his mind. His words sound like someone in touch with reality!

A few years ago, I urged a new Christian to testify to others about the change Jesus had made in his life. I knew that his own faith would be encouraged as he talked to others. He agreed with my suggestion, but he surprised me by saying, "I even testify to myself!"

When you're feeling down, remember to take advantage of the spiritual antidepressants in today's psalm. Question your soul, testify about God's goodness, admonish yourself to hope in the Lord. Minister to yourself, as David did, by personally applying the very encouragement you've given to others (1 Samuel 30:6).

JOANIE YODER

To change your outlook, remember who's looking out for you.

Night

PSALM 42

*By day the L*ORD *directs his love, at night his song is with me—
a prayer to the God of my life.*

PSALM 42:8

In his riveting and unsettling book *Night*, Elie Wiesel describes his boyhood experiences as one of the countless victims of the Holocaust. Ripped from his home and separated from everyone in his family except his father (who would die in the death camps), Wiesel suffered a dark night of the soul such as few will experience. It challenged his views and beliefs about God. His innocence and faith became sacrifices on the altar of man's evil and sin's darkness.

David experienced his own dark night of the soul, which many scholars believe motivated his writing of Psalm 42. Harried and hounded, probably as he was pursued by his rebellious son Absalom (2 Samuel 16–18), David echoed the pain and fear that can be felt in the isolation of night. It's the place where darkness grips us and forces us to consider the anguish of our heart and ask hard questions of God. The psalmist lamented God's seeming absence, yet in it all he found a night song (v. 8) that gave him peace and confidence for the difficulties ahead.

When we struggle in the night, we can be confident that God is with us in the darkness. We can say with the psalmist, "Put your hope in God, for I will yet praise him, my Savior and my God" (v. 11).

BILL CROWDER

When it is dark enough, men see the stars. —Emerson

Steady as She Goes

PSALM 43

Send me your light and your faithful care, let them lead me;
let them bring me to your holy mountain, to the place where you dwell.

PSALM 43:3

The Lord has charted a safe course for us in His Word. We run into trouble when we "change course" and decide to go our own way. The psalmist knew this, and that's why he prayed, "Send me your light and your faithful care, let them lead me." God's light and His care were the psalmist's chart and compass.

In his book *A Thirst for God*, Sherwood Wirt tells of serving briefly as the quartermaster of the *Teal*, an eighty-foot patrol boat belonging to the Alaska Game Commission. He was at the helm when Captain Cole took over briefly and changed their course north toward Juneau. He pointed to the compass reading and told Wirt, "Steady as she goes!"

As the ship cruised along, Wirt noted that they seemed to be edging toward the mainland, so he altered the course slightly and steered the *Teal* straight up the channel. In a few minutes Captain Cole came on the bridge and snapped, "You're off course! Go back to the reading I gave you." Wirt remarked in his book, "My dead reckoning had led me to believe one thing, but the chart indicated something else. Following my intuition might have led to shipwreck."

The Bible is God's chart. Life's hazards are clearly marked. So are the channels of safety. We must set our course and say, "Steady as she goes."

DAVID EGNER

To stay in the channel of blessing, follow the course of obedience.

Storytelling

PSALM 44:1–8

Blessed are those who have regard for the weak;
the LORD delivers them in times of trouble.

PSALM 41:1

As I sat at the restaurant table across from my friend, I felt caught up in his nervous energy. He was struggling with so many painful problems. That particular day had been an especially difficult one, and he was worse for the wear. He was a Christian, but he had little sense of the Lord's provision. I wanted to tell him to trust the Lord, but words of consolation stuck in my throat. I didn't know how to break through his anxiety.

I silently asked the Lord for help. A few minutes later I found myself telling the story of how the Lord had answered one of my prayers within the last couple of days. My friend listened. I explained how God met needs that I could not handle. Still my friend listened. Then he began to relax, and so did I. Together, we sensed anew God's ability to answer our prayers and work in our lives.

I left my friend that night reminded of something I had forgotten. The Scriptures encourage storytelling as a way of giving witness to God's faithfulness, and as a way of helping others.

Let's not forget those personal stories of God's working in our lives. They allow us to be firsthand witnesses to what the Lord can do. And sometimes our accounts of the Lord's ability to meet our needs will help to meet the needs of others.

MART DEHAAN

Telling what God has done for you personalizes
what God can do for others.

One Tongue Is Enough

PSALM 45

My heart is stirred by a noble theme as I recite my verses for the king;
my tongue is the pen of a skillful writer.

PSALM 45:1

All of us who want to proclaim the riches of Christ and His good news know the limitations of having only one tongue. In one of his hymns, Charles Wesley wrote, "O for a thousand tongues to sing my great Redeemer's praise!"

The fact is, though, our one tongue has much more potential than most of us will ever put to use. A tongue devoted to God can accomplish much.

For example, a man from Chicago was blind and had neither arms nor legs. But like the psalmist, his heart was overflowing with God's love, and his tongue was fully dedicated for His use. This man learned to read the braille Bible using his tongue! As a result of this painstaking accomplishment, he was able to use his tongue in a different way—to teach the Word of God and to share his radiant testimony.

Joni Eareckson Tada, another believer with physical disabilities, has spoken to millions about Christ. She often affirms, "With God, less is more."

Are you sometimes discouraged, thinking that you have little to offer God? If you have Christ's love in your heart and a willing tongue in your mouth, you can offer them boldly to God today and begin to bring praise and honor to the Lord. One tongue is enough.

JOANIE YODER

Little is much when God is in it.

Be Quiet!

PSALM 46

"Be still, and know that I am God;
I will be exalted among the nations, I will be exalted in the earth."

PSALM 46:10

Some people can't stand silence. They turn on the radio the instant they get in the car. They sit in front of a blaring TV set all evening or have music booming through the house. They've become so adjusted to our noisy age that they are uncomfortable when it's quiet. As a result, they never hear the sweet, tranquil, early morning melodies of nature. They never hear the nightingale's song in the evening. And worst of all, they miss the still, small voice of God.

The blessedness of silent interludes in a noisy world is vividly expressed in Psalm 46. The writer opens with an affirmation of confidence in the protection of God in the face of destructive forces beyond man's power—erupting volcanoes, angry tidal waves, and powerful earthquakes. Next, he portrays a softly flowing river that distributes its life-giving water throughout the land. This scene is followed by a portrait of violent, antagonistic world powers raging against the Lord but being destroyed. After reviewing God's majestic triumph, the writer then says, "Be still, and know that I am God" (v. 10). The whole psalm is an eloquent call to the kind of silence that helps us sense that the Lord is active amid the clamor and tumult of our restless world.

God's voice can be heard in the soft sounds of nature and in the comforting promises of His Word. He wants to let us know that He is present and in control. But we must be quiet.

HERB VANDER LUGT

God still speaks to those who take time to listen.

Look to the Stars

PSALM 46

No matter how many promises God has made, they are "Yes" in Christ.
And so through him the "Amen" is spoken by us to the glory of God.
2 CORINTHIANS 1:20

One afternoon a terrible storm forced two prospectors to seek shelter in a cave. When it had passed, they emerged to a disheartening sight. Trees had been uprooted; familiar landmarks were gone. All of the notations and observations they had made to guide them out of the forest were useless. One man sat down in despair. But the other said, "We are not lost. Night is soon coming, and when the stars shine again, we'll get our bearings. The stars are still up there in the sky, and we can find our way home by looking at them."

The storms of life can leave us feeling lost. Former securities vanish in a whirlwind of trouble. The death of a loved one, the trauma of divorce, the loss of position, the anguish of incurable disease, or even our own sins can tear us loose from all that once gave us purpose, meaning, and identity. The force of any one of these tragedies can so overwhelm us that we wonder if we will ever recover.

So, what is the answer? We must refocus our lives on the unchanging promises of God.

Our lives are "hidden with Christ in God" (Colossians 3:3). He loves us; He is in control; He is with us. These promises will never change. If life is in turmoil, we shouldn't fix our eyes on relationships that can be broken and securities that can vanish. Instead, we look to God's unfailing promises and begin anew. Because they are always shining like stars, life is never hopeless.

DENNIS DEHAAN

The believer's future is as bright as the promises of God.

MAY 6

A Sure Refuge

PSALM 46

God is our refuge and strength, an ever-present help in trouble. . . .
The LORD Almighty is with us; the God of Jacob is our fortress.
PSALM 46:1, 11

We can construct buildings to withstand earthquakes, hurricanes, or tornadoes. Nations can arm themselves with an arsenal of weapons to deter hostile nations or warring factions. But no building is absolutely safe in an earthquake or a major storm. And there's always the possibility that some deranged leader could call for war or large-scale terror.

The writer of Psalm 46 vividly portrayed natural destructive phenomena—the melting of the earth in volcanic eruptions, the tottering of mountains and crashing of rocks in an earthquake, and the angry roaring of waters in a tempest. He also depicted nations raging in conflict. But into this word picture he painted a river that supplies cool, clear water to Zion. That flowing stream symbolized God's presence in the midst of all the turmoil.

None of us knows what lies in store for us in our troubled world. Injury or disease may strike. Or we may enjoy good health and prosperity until God calls us home. But no matter what, we have one certainty—God is our ultimate safety in time of danger. He is with us, and He is a sure refuge.

HERB VANDER LUGT

Safety is not the absence of danger but the presence of God.

A Good God

PSALM 46

The Lord is a refuge for the oppressed, a stronghold in times of trouble.
PSALM 9:9

When my brother-in-law was a missionary in Mali, West Africa, he was involved in a traffic accident. A man had wandered into the road in front of Chuck's motorcycle. The cycle struck the man and sent Chuck and the bike sliding along the ground for more than 200 feet. Shortly after Chuck regained consciousness in the hospital, his doctor told him he had been "really lucky." Chuck smiled and replied, "God is good."

Later he thought about the day's events. The man who was struck hadn't received any permanent injuries, and Chuck would also recover from his injuries. But what if one of them had been killed? He thought, *God would be no less good.*

When we experience tragedy, we may wonder about God's goodness. Is God always good? Yes, He is. He doesn't promise that bad things will never happen to us, but He does promise to be "our refuge and strength" (Psalm 46:1). He doesn't promise that we will never walk through heart-wrenching circumstances, but He promises that we won't be alone (23:4).

God is good—no matter what suffering we are experiencing. Even when we don't understand, we can say with Habakkuk, "Yet I will rejoice in the Lord, I will be joyful in God my Savior" (3:18).

CINDY HESS KASPER

God tests our faith so that we may trust His faithfulness.

Awesome!

PSALM 47

For the LORD Most High is awesome, the great King over all the earth.
PSALM 47:2

It's an often-used word, and we hear it in the most unusual contexts. It's the word *awesome*.

My grandson Josh and I were playing with a radio-controlled racecar set on the living room floor. Several times he commented on the action of the cars by saying, "Awesome!"

On another occasion, as my wife and I were leaving a restaurant, the manager, who was standing by the door, asked, "How was everything, folks?" "Fine," I replied. "Awesome!" he said.

These two occasions set me to thinking: While it's fun to play with my grandson and to enjoy a meal at a restaurant, are these experiences really awesome? So I consulted the dictionary. The primary definition lists awesome as "deeply reverent," "dreadful," "awful." I remembered the time I stood on the south rim of the Grand Canyon. That was truly an awesome experience.

Then I thought of a more awe-inspiring reality still: Knowing the Creator and Sustainer of the entire universe. No wonder the psalmist wrote, "The LORD Most High is awesome" (Psalm 47:2).

The next time we hear the word *awesome*, may it remind us of our great God, who truly is deserving of that description!

DENNIS DEHAAN

Nothing is more awesome than to know God.

Thoughtful Praises

PSALM 47

For God is the King of all the earth;
sing to him a psalm of praise.
PSALM 47:7

I wonder what God thinks about the way we sing at church. I'm not talking about the quality of our voices, but the honesty of our words. If we're being truthful, the following rewritten hymn titles might more accurately express what's in our hearts as we sing:

"Just As I Am" is "Just As I Pretend to Be."

"O How I Love Jesus" becomes "O How I Like Jesus."

"I Surrender All" is actually "I Surrender Some."

"He's Everything to Me" means "He's Quite a Bit to Me."

Jesus said that we are to worship Him in truth (John 4:24). Singing sincerely and with understanding is a serious challenge (Psalm 47:7).

Let's take up the challenge by seeking God's help to make the original titles of these hymns true for us. In repentance and without pretense, let's turn to Him just as we are. In His forgiving presence, let's declare total love for Jesus by surrendering all to Him. As a result, Jesus truly will become everything to us. Then we will be able to sing honestly about Jesus Christ and our love for Him.

As we make melody in our hearts to the Lord (Ephesians 5:19), let's worship in spirit and in truth.

JOANIE YODER

To sing God's praise, keep your heart in tune with Him.

God Reigns

PSALM 47

God reigns over the nations; God is seated on his holy throne.
PSALM 47:8

During the days of the nuclear arms race in the early 1980s, this startling headline appeared in the *Grand Rapids Press*: "Computer Error Could Start War."

The article that followed was equally alarming. It reported: "For the second time in seven months, a computer at the nation's missile warning center erroneously put US strategic forces on alert against a Soviet missile attack on the United States."

The idea of nuclear war is horrifying enough, but to think that one could have been caused by a computer mistake is even more appalling.

We who believe in the God of the Bible, however, know that He has not abdicated His throne, and that everything is under His control. He's aware of what's going on, and nothing can happen to violate His sovereignty. The long-range good that God has in mind for all who love Him cannot be thwarted.

Clearly, this doesn't mean that there will be no more wars. But we can be sure that God rules over the nations, and He orders the affairs of this world. Everything is under His control.

Headlines about potential disasters need not cause us to panic. In God's plan there are no mistakes. The Lord God reigns!

RICHARD DEHAAN

**If you know that God's hand is in everything,
you can leave everything in God's hands.**

Take Time

PSALM 48

Within your temple, O God, we meditate on your unfailing love.
PSALM 48:9

A friend and I were on our way to the hardware store when we decided to make a quick stop for donuts in a small coffee shop. As we were talking, my friend stopped and pointed to a poster tacked on the wall behind the counter. It showed a peaceful lake scene. A father and son were visible through the early morning mist, fishing in a rowboat. All was quiet and serene. The boat was not moving on the still water, and the fishermen were watching two motionless bobbers on the placid lake. The silence and stillness left an overwhelming impression. In the corner of the poster were printed these two words: TAKE TIME.

Those two words sound like a foreign language to us. We tend to speed along in life much like we drive our cars on the freeway—going faster than we should. Our lives are a blur of frantic activity. We're in the "fast lane," traveling as quickly as our bodies and minds will allow. In so doing, we often leave God behind.

Even if the busyness of our lives is made up of worthwhile activities: kids' games and practices, church events, and the like, we may have left God back in the dust somewhere. Perhaps we should think about slowing down a bit and doing as the writer of Psalm 48 did. He meditated on God's lovingkindness. And that takes time.

We honor our Lord when we pause from the race of life and take time for Him.

DAVID EGNER

When you spend time with God, you invest in eternity.

Holy Is the Lord

PSALM 48

"Holy, holy, holy is the LORD Almighty;
the whole earth is full of his glory."
ISAIAH 6:3

There are some things God cannot do. For example, God cannot tell a lie. He can't do anything that conflicts with His holy character. What God is determines what God does. Since He is holy, all His attributes share in that perfection.

Let me explain what this means to us on a practical level. As a holy God, He is perfect in His righteousness, justice, truthfulness, and faithfulness.

His perfect righteousness assures us that we can trust His will because He'll always do what is right. "Will not the Judge of all the earth do right?" (Genesis 18:25).

His perfect justice means that God will be unquestionably fair. Christians will be rewarded for what they have done (2 Corinthians 5:10), and the wicked will be punished according to their works (Revelation 20:13).

His perfect truthfulness assures us that we can take Him at His word. Numbers 23:19 says, "God is not a man, that He should lie" (NKJV).

His perfect faithfulness tells us that He will never let us down. We read, "His compassions never fail. They are new every morning; great is your faithfulness" (Lamentations 3:22–23).

We can have absolute confidence in our righteous, just, truthful, and faithful God—because He is holy!

RICHARD DeHAAN

The holiness of God convicts the sinner and comforts the saint.

Weak Beneath the Surface

PSALM 49:6–13

Surely the lowborn are but a breath, the highborn are but a lie. If weighed on a balance, they are nothing; together they are only a breath.

PSALM 62:9

A man visited a doctor in Florence, Italy. Anxious and exhausted from lack of sleep, he couldn't eat, and he avoided his friends. The doctor found that he was in prime physical condition. Concluding that his patient needed to have a good time, the physician told him about a circus in town and its star performer, a clown named Grimaldi. Night after night he had the people rolling in the aisles. "You must go and see him," the doctor advised. "Grimaldi is the world's funniest clown. He'll make you laugh and cure your sadness." "No," replied the despairing man, "he can't help me. You see, *I am Grimaldi!*"

Many people today are like that clown—weak beneath the surface. The psalmist refers to them as having riches and honor and as giving the appearance of confidence and strength. Yet they lack spiritual understanding and will perish like the animals.

It's true. People sometimes appear to be something they aren't. In front of the cameras, behind the desk, or dressed in their finest clothes, they are pictures of strength. But let's not kid ourselves; we are all made of the same flesh, and apart from the grace and power of God we are helpless and pathetic. Only by yielding to the Holy Spirit can we find the inner resources we need.

Let's display His power by growing strong in His might.

MART DEHAAN

A sickly saint often resembles a healthy hypocrite.

The Voice of God at Sunset

PSALM 50:1-6

The Mighty One, God, the LORD, speaks and summons the earth from the rising of the sun to where it sets.

PSALM 50:1

Who has not marveled at the beauty of a sunset? We stand motionless, awestruck, hushed by the flaming sky as the sun moves over the western horizon. Seeming to hesitate a moment, the glowing orb suddenly drops out of sight, leaving the sky ablaze with brilliant shades of pink, orange, and red. Somehow the frustrations of the day are put to silence by the majestic, yet soothing voice of God as we view a glorious sunset.

Because the sun's rays are slowed down slightly and bent by the earth's atmosphere, the sun appears to be oval-shaped rather than round. That, along with the dust or smog in the air, explains the dazzling array of colors that give us so much visual pleasure at day's end. And scientists tell us that a sunset can be even more beautiful than most of us have seen. Writing in the *Encyclopedia Science Supplement*, astronomer John B. Irwin said, "When conditions are just right, the last diminishing bit of the yellow-orange sun suddenly changes into a brilliant emerald green. This green flash puts an exciting exclamation point to the end of the day."

Every sunset is an exclamation point given to us by God the Creator to end the day. It's as if the Lord were saying, "Set aside your worries. Rest from your labors. Forget about those disappointments. I am still here, taking care of My universe. Look up beyond the sun to Me and be at peace."

No wonder the psalmist spoke of the voice of God at sunset!

DAVID EGNER

In nature we can hear the voice of God.

Profitable Praying

PSALM 51

For I know my transgressions, and my sin is always before me.
PSALM 51:3

When Robert Louis Stevenson was a boy, he once remarked to his mother, "Momma, you can't be good without praying."

"How do you know, Robert?" she asked. "Because I've tried!" he answered.

This brings to mind a story about another little fellow—one who had been sent to his room because he had been bad. A short time later he came out and said to his mother, "I've been thinking about what I did and I said a prayer." "That's fine," she said, "if you ask God to make you good, He will help you." "Oh, I didn't ask Him to help me be good," replied the boy. "I asked Him to help you put up with me."

I don't think that little boy is alone in his prayers. Sometimes we ask the Lord to adjust our circumstances or to change people—instead of asking Him to deal with us. Praying about our spiritual growth becomes effective only when we first come clean with the Lord about our own sin. Look at David's prayer in Psalm 51. He acknowledged his sin (v. 3), asked for mercy (v. 1), sought a clean heart (v. 10), and requested that the joy of his salvation be restored (v. 12). David made no excuse.

Let's settle for nothing less than total honesty when we talk with the Lord. That kind of praying is not always comfortable—but it sure is profitable!

DENNIS DeHAAN

Until man has gotten into trouble with his heart, he is not likely to get out of trouble with God. —A. W. Tozer

The Old Tractor

PSALM 51

Restore to me the joy of your salvation
and grant me a willing spirit, to sustain me.
PSALM 51:12

My friend Gary restores tractors. He told me about an old John Deere that had been sitting in a farmer's field for years after serving its owner faithfully for decades.

When Gary began working on the tractor, its engine was in such bad shape that it couldn't have pulled a child's wagon, much less a plow. The belts were cracked, the wires were split, the plugs were rusted, and the carburetor was way out of adjustment.

Gary dug right in to repair the old beast. He replaced the plugs and points and adjusted the carburetor. When he put it all back together and fired it up, its engine purred like a kitten. It can now pull a plow as strongly as it ever did. Under Gary's restorative skill, it will do all it was designed to do.

In Psalm 51, David repented of his sin with Bathsheba and asked God to restore him to the place of fellowship he once enjoyed. He prayed, "Create in me a pure heart, O God. . . . Restore to me the joy of your salvation" (vv.10, 12).

Through neglect or sin, have you ended up like that old tractor—by the wayside? Turn right now to the Lord. Place yourself in His caring hands. Confess your sin, repent, and ask His forgiveness. He is waiting to restore you to himself and make you a productive Christian again.

DAVID EGNER

God specializes in restoration.

Halfhearted or Wholehearted?

PSALM 51:1–13

*If we confess our sins, he is faithful and just
and will forgive us our sins and purify us from all unrighteousness.*

1 JOHN 1:9

Did you read about the man whose guilty conscience prompted him to send a letter to the Internal Revenue Service? The note read, "I haven't been able to sleep because last year when I filled out my income tax report I deliberately misrepresented my income. I am enclosing a check for $150, and if I still can't sleep, I'll send you the rest."

Now, it's commendable that the man confessed his wrongdoing, but his halfhearted restitution showed the shallowness of his regret. His confession was prompted by his desire for personal peace, not by remorse for a moral transgression.

Because we are defiled by sin in our day-by-day walk, we need the daily cleansing of confession—even if we have been redeemed by faith in Jesus. This confession helps us maintain a strong relationship between our heavenly Father and us. But our confession must be genuine. We must come to Him with a sincere sorrow for our sins and an honest desire to forsake them.

Only when we are truly sorry that we sinned can we have the assurance that we have been restored to fellowship.

RICHARD DEHAAN

God has promised pardon to those who repent.

Praise from Pure Hearts

PSALM 51:7–17

My sacrifice, O God, is a broken spirit;
a broken and contrite heart you, God, will not despise.

PSALM 51:17

During my friend Myrna's travels to another country, she visited a church for worship. She noticed that as people entered the sanctuary they immediately knelt and prayed, facing away from the front of the church. My friend learned that people in that church confessed their sin to God before they began the worship service.

This act of humility is a picture to me of what David said in Psalm 51: "My sacrifice, O God, is a broken spirit; a broken and contrite heart you, God, will not despise" (v. 17). David was describing his own remorse and repentance for his sin of adultery with Bathsheba. Real sorrow for sin involves adopting God's view of what we've done—seeing it as clearly wrong, disliking it, and not wanting it to continue.

When we are truly broken over our sin, God lovingly puts us back together. "If we confess our sins, he is faithful and just and will forgive us our sins and purify us from all unrighteousness" (1 John 1:9). This forgiveness produces a fresh sense of openness with Him and is the ideal starting point for praise. After David repented, confessed, and was forgiven by God, he responded by saying, "Open my lips, Lord, and my mouth will declare your praise" (Psalm 51:15).

Humility is the right response to God's holiness. And praise is our heart's response to His forgiveness.

JENNIFER BENSON SCHULDT

Praise is the song of a soul set free.

Fresh

PSALM 51:8–13

Restore to me the joy of your salvation
and grant me a willing spirit, to sustain me.
PSALM 51:12

What do you think of when you hear the word *fresh*? When the weather is nice, my husband and I enjoy going to the farmers market so we can buy produce that was picked that very morning. To me, *fresh* means just-harvested fruits and vegetables—not stale or spoiled, but crisp and full of exquisite flavor.

I need that kind of freshness in my relationship with God. I can have too many stale attitudes—impatience, criticism, and selfishness—and not enough "forbearance, kindness, . . . gentleness," which are "the fruit of the Spirit" (Galatians 5:22–23).

As David repented of the sin in his life, he prayed, "Create in me a pure heart." Then he petitioned God: "Restore to me the joy of your salvation" (Psalm 51:10–12). Confession and repentance of our sin renews our fellowship with the Lord and allows us to joyously begin anew.

There's no better time than today to ask God to give you a newness of spirit, a freshness of faith, and a renewed appreciation of Him!

Lord, we want the fruit of our lives to always be "fresh and flourishing" (Psalm 92:14 NKJV). Help us to experience your love, compassion, and faithfulness that are "new every morning" (Lamentations 3:22–23). Amen.

CINDY HESS KASPER

To bear good fruit, clear out the weeds of sin.

Deleted Documents

PSALM 51

*"I, even I, am he who blots out your transgressions,
for my own sake, and remembers your sins no more."*
ISAIAH 43:25

I don't know where they go. One minute the computer screen is full of words that I typed. Then, with one stroke on my keyboard, I can eliminate them all. Suddenly they are gone. It's not like a wad of paper that I throw away—I can still keep track of that as it goes from waste can to garbage truck to landfill. Computer words, when deleted, are gone for good and can't be recalled.

Isn't that the way it is with our sins that have been forgiven by God? In Isaiah 43, the Lord says something about sin that seems like the Old Testament equivalent of deleting a document on a computer: "I, even I, am he who blots out your transgressions" (v. 25). Just as an Old Testament writer would scribe something on a papyrus scroll and then get rid of it forever by blotting it out, so God wipes our sin from His record.

Consider David's use of the words "blot out" in Psalm 51:9. He had fallen into the sins of sexual immorality and murder, yet he knew he could come to God for forgiveness. He knew that God deletes sin's penalty through forgiveness.

Sometimes we struggle regarding sins that God has forgiven. We need to remember that they are gone. If God has blotted out your sins, it's time for you to delete them too.

DAVE BRANON

When God deletes a sin, let's not save it in our memory.

Murder by Slander

PSALM 52:1–7

You who practice deceit, your tongue plots destruction;
it is like a sharpened razor.

PSALM 52:2

None of us who claim to be Christ-followers should ever engage in slander—the deliberate attempt to harm or destroy someone by spreading rumors or telling lies. Yet this often occurs because a church member who feels slighted or wronged uses his words to get revenge. James said it bluntly: "Brothers and sisters, do not slander one another" (4:11).

In his book *Did I Say That?* Leslie B. Flynn told of a bitter message that was discovered on a gravestone in Milford, New Hampshire. It charged that a certain church had "murdered" one of its members by gossip and false accusations. After her name and the date of her death in 1838 these words were inscribed: "Age 33, she was accused of lying in church meeting by the pastor and a deacon [their names are given]—was condemned by the church unheard. She was reduced to poverty." At this point the inscription stated that the church closed the matter to all discussion. The message on the marker concluded, "The intentional and malicious destruction of her character and happiness, as above described, destroyed her life. Her last words on the subject were, 'Tell the truth and this iniquity will come out.'"

The tongue has tremendous power to destroy. It has often been used in the name of religion as the source of vicious attacks on others. Let's never defame a person's reputation or character. It may feel good for the moment, but God will hold us accountable for murder by slander.

DAVID EGNER

Words break no bones, but they do break hearts.

A Fool's Argument

PSALM 53

The fool says in his heart, "There is no God." They are corrupt,
and their ways are vile; there is no one who does good.

PSALM 53:1

Some people spend a great deal of time and effort trying to disprove the existence of God. By doing so, however, they undermine their own arguments. In *Interpreting Basic Theology*, Addison Leitch wrote, "Unless [an atheist] is carrying on his fight against absolute nothingness—and this makes us wonder about his zeal—then he must be [arguing] against something he finds ingrained in himself and in others."

This inherent belief in God doesn't prove He exists, but it strongly hints in that direction. When C. S. Lewis was an atheist, he rejected the idea of a divine Being because of all the injustice in the world. But when he asked himself where he had gotten the idea of justice in the first place, he had a problem. "Man doesn't call a line crooked unless he has some idea of a straight line," wrote Lewis. "What was I comparing this universe with when I called it unjust?" Lewis realized that his case for atheism was too simple. If the idea of justice were merely a product of his own imagination, that would have destroyed his argument, which depended on real injustices. Injustice in the world, in fact, pointed to a God who himself set the standard of justice.

The fool says that there is no God (Psalm 53:1). So be wise instead and make it your primary goal to love the God who is there.

DENNIS DEHAAN

How can we know what is evil if we deny the God who is good?

Get Up!

PSALM 54

Surely God is my help; the Lord is the one who sustains me.
PSALM 54:4

I hadn't been water-skiing in fifteen years, but when friends offered to take my son-in-law Todd and me out on the lake, how could I say no? It seemed like a good idea until I watched Todd have trouble getting upright on his skis. He had done a lot of skiing, but as he tried to get up on one ski, he kept falling. So when it came to my turn, I didn't have a lot of confidence.

Fortunately, my friend, who is a competitive skier, stayed with me in the water and coached me about what to do. She said, "Let the boat pull you up," and "Be strong!" These seemingly contradictory statements made all the difference. I did both—I trusted the boat to do its job, and I hung on with all my strength. The first time the boat took off, I got up and enjoyed a great ride around the lake.

When life has you down—whether through sorrow that seems too hard to bear or circumstances that make each day a morning-to-night grind—my friend's advice can help. First, let God pull you up by His power (Psalm 54:1–4). Then, hold on to His hand. Cling to Him and "be strong in the Lord and in his mighty power" (Ephesians 6:10).

Trust His power and hold on. He will give you the strength to keep from falling (Isaiah 40:31).

DAVE BRANON

Those who wait on the LORD shall renew their strength.
—Isaiah 40:31 NKJV

The Survival Float

PSALM 55:4–23

Cast your cares on the LORD and he will sustain you;
he will never let the righteous be shaken.

PSALM 55:22

Sunlight glittered on the swimming pool in front of me. I overheard an instructor speaking to a student who had been in the water for quite a while. He said, "It looks like you're getting tired. When you're exhausted and in deep water, try the survival float."

Certain situations in life require us to spend our mental, physical, or emotional energy in a way that we can't sustain. David described a time when his enemies were threatening him, and he felt the emotional weight of their anger. He needed to escape the distress he was experiencing.

As he processed his feelings, he found a way to rest in his troubled thoughts. He said, "Cast your cares on the LORD and he will sustain you" (Psalm 55:22). He recognized that God supports us if we dare to release our problems to Him. We don't have to take charge of every situation and try to craft the outcome—that's exhausting! God is in control of every aspect of our life.

Instead of trying to do everything in our own effort, we can find rest in God. Sometimes it's as simple as asking Him to handle our problems. Then we can pause, relax, and enjoy the knowledge that He is sustaining us.

JENNIFER BENSON SCHULDT

God is a safe resting place.

Carry or Cast?

PSALM 55:16–22

Do not be anxious about anything, but in every situation,
by prayer and petition, with thanksgiving, present your requests to God.
PHILIPPIANS 4:6

Are you burdened by a load of care? Pause for a moment and remind yourself of God's faithfulness to you in times past. You will have reason to agree with Paul, who said, "do not be anxious about anything" as you give your requests to the Lord in prayer (Philippians 4:6).

British preacher Charles Spurgeon (1834–1892) loved to tell about his grandfather, a minister, who was very poor. The one cow he owned had died, and his ten children were without milk. His wife asked, "What will we do now?" "I cannot tell," he said, "but I know what God will do. We must have milk for the children, and He will provide for us."

The next morning a man brought Spurgeon's grandfather a gift of twenty pounds from the ministers' relief fund, even though help had not been requested. A few days before, the relief committee had divided the funds for distribution and an amount of five pounds was left over. One of the members said, "There is poor Mr. Spurgeon down in Essex. Suppose we send it to him." "We'd better make it ten," said the chairman, "and I'll give an extra five." That made it fifteen. Another man added five more pounds. Those men knew nothing about Spurgeon's cow, but God knew.

As His children we may choose to carry our cares or give them over to the Father. Life's journey is a lot easier if we learn to cast rather than carry.

PAUL VAN GORDER

Burdens need not overcome you,
for God's arms are underneath you.

A Bag of Potatoes

PSALM 55:16–23

"Be careful, or your hearts will be weighed down with carousing, drunkenness and the anxieties of life, and that day will close on you suddenly like a trap."

LUKE 21:34

Isaac Page tells the story of a poor man in Ireland who was plodding along toward home, carrying a huge sack of potatoes. A horse and wagon came along, and the driver stopped to offer him a ride. The man accepted and climbed up on the seat alongside the driver but kept holding the bag of potatoes in his arms. When the driver suggested that he lay the bag down on the wagon floor, he replied warmly in his Irish brogue, "I don't like to trouble you too much, sir. You're a givin' me a ride already, so I'll just carry the potatoes!"

We sometimes do the same when we try to carry life's burdens by worrying instead of turning them over to God. When we do that, we become weary, our hearts faint within us, and we lose courage. Any circumstance can become a "bag of potatoes" if we fret and worry about the outcome. Some burdens must be borne, but even those become lighter when we trust the Lord to give us the grace to bear them.

The next time you start worrying, ask yourself, "Is this a burden God wants me to bear? Or does He want me to let Him carry it?" Remember, He can handle it!

HENRY BOSCH

God tells us to burden Him with whatever burdens us.

When Fear Creeps In

PSALM 56

When I am afraid, I put my trust in you.
PSALM 56:3

When my daughter exclaimed, "Mommy, a bug!" I looked where she was pointing and saw the largest spider I have ever encountered outside of a pet shop. Both the spider and I knew that he would not be allowed to stay in our house. And yet, as I faced him, I found I could not take one step closer to end the standoff. My pulse quickened. I swallowed and gave myself a pep talk. Still, fear kept me frozen in place.

Fear is powerful; it can override logical thinking and produce irrational behavior. Thankfully, Christians don't have to let fear of anything—people, situations, or even spiders—rule our actions. We can declare, "When I am afraid, I put my trust in [God]" (Psalm 56:3).

Taking this stand against fear is consistent with the Bible's instruction to "trust in the LORD with all your heart and lean not on your own understanding" (Proverbs 3:5). Our own understanding may lead us to overestimate the object of our fear and underestimate God's power. When we are afraid, we can depend on God's understanding (Isaiah 40:28) and trust in His love for us that "drives out fear" (1 John 4:18). The next time fear creeps into your life, don't panic. God can be trusted in the darkness.

JENNIFER BENSON SCHULDT

Trusting God's faithfulness dispels our fearfulness.

A Stroll with God

PSALM 56:1–4

The eternal God is your refuge, and underneath are the everlasting arms.
DEUTERONOMY 33:27

Etty Hillesum was a young Jewish woman living in Amsterdam in 1942. During that time, the Nazis were arresting Jews and herding them off to concentration camps. As she awaited inevitable arrest, and with a fear of the unknown, she began to read the Bible—and met Jesus. She simply put her hand in God's hand and found rare courage and confidence.

Etty wrote in her diary: "From all sides our destruction creeps up on us and soon the ring will be closed and no one at all will be able to come to our aid. But I don't feel that I am in anybody's clutches. I feel safe in God's arms. And whether I am sitting at my beloved old desk in the Jewish district or in a labor camp under SS guards, I shall feel safe in God's arms. For once you have begun to walk with God, you need only keep on walking with Him, and all of life becomes one long stroll."

Etty was a living, courageous picture of the psalmist's declaration: "When I am afraid, I put my trust in you. . . . What can mere mortals do to me?" (56:3–4). What a challenge for anyone plagued by fear!

As we sense the strength of God's everlasting arms beneath us (Deuteronomy 33:27), we can stroll through life with confidence, holding the hand of our unseen Companion.

VERNON GROUNDS

**You can be confident about tomorrow
if you walk with God today.**

A Healthy Fear

PSALM 56

In God I trust and am not afraid.
PSALM 56:4

On the evening before D-Day during World War II, the captain of a Navy vessel called his men together to prepare them for crossing the English Channel. He knew they were filled with anxiety, so he tried to encourage them by saying, "When you stop to think about it, fear is a very healthy thing." A third-class yeoman spoke up, "Captain, if what you say is true, I'm the healthiest man in the entire Navy!"

Although fear is one of the most harmful emotions, it can also be one of the most helpful. The fear of getting burned causes us to handle hot objects with care. A fear of heights can caution us to keep a safe distance from the edge of a cliff. Fear of failure motivates us to redouble our efforts to succeed. But the greatest benefit of fear occurs when it directs us to the Lord for His help. David, while a captive of the Philistines, wrote that when he was fearful he would place his confidence in the Lord (Psalm 56:3).

Are you facing a seemingly insurmountable challenge? Is your heart filled with anxiety? Have you received unsettling news? Is your future uncertain? Let your fear drive you to the Lord. Commit yourself to His care and provision. Trust Him to keep His Word. Count on Him to be faithful. That's how to have a healthy fear.

RICHARD DeHAAN

When troubles call on you, call on God.

When You Are Afraid

PSALM 56

In God I trust and am not afraid.

PSALM 56:11

It was all-out war! The kids I hung around with were battling the kids who lived on the other side of Evanston Avenue. The weapons? Green apples. The stakes? Neighborhood pride and honor.

Then it happened. After an especially bitter green-apple battle, my mother sent me on an errand that would force me to ride my bike right down the street where most of the enemy lived. I was as terrified as a ten-year-old could be. My palms were sweaty. The skin on my back crawled. I was sure I would be discovered and attacked. I was petrified.

Psalm 56 describes how David felt when he was in a similar but far worse situation (see 1 Samuel 21:10–15). On the run from King Saul, he took refuge in enemy territory. He was in terrible danger and he knew it. But he also knew what to do in times of fear. He said to the Lord, "When I am afraid, I put my trust in you" (v. 3). Then he wrote, "In God I trust and am not afraid" (v. 4).

When you are feeling insecure and vulnerable to danger, remember that you are in the Lord's protective care. Do what David did. Believe that God is in control of your situation. He is more powerful than any threat to your well-being. Believe His promises. That's what to do when you're afraid.

DAVID EGNER

Running from danger? Instead, run to God.

Your Spiritual Pipeline

PSALM 57

Have mercy on me, my God, have mercy on me, for in you I take refuge.
I will take refuge in the shadow of your wings until the disaster has passed.

PSALM 57:1

The Trans-Alaska Pipeline stretches eight hundred miles through Alaska. Because it was built through an earthquake zone, engineers had to be sure the pipe could withstand earth trauma. They decided on a network of Teflon sliders designed to ease the shock when the ground moved below the pipes. Engineers were delighted when the first big test came. In 2002, an earthquake occurred, causing the ground to move eighteen feet to one side. The Teflon sliders moved gently to accommodate the movement without any damage to the pipe. The key was flexibility.

The believer's spiritual pipeline to heaven is built upon firm trust in God. But if we are inflexible in our expectations of how God should work, we can run into trouble. In a crisis, we can make the mistake of shifting our focus from God to our painful circumstances. Our prayer should be, "God, I don't understand why you have allowed this painful situation. But I am trusting in your ultimate deliverance despite all that's going on around me." The psalmist expressed this so well when he wrote: "My soul trusts in You . . . until these calamities have passed by" (Psalm 57:1 NKJV).

When the earth seems to move under us, let's be flexible in our expectations but firmly confident in God's steadfast love and care.

DENNIS FISHER

God may delay or deny our request,
but He will never disappoint our trust.

Our Source of Safety

PSALM 57

Blessed are all who take refuge in [the Lord].
PSALM 2:12

Before heading out into battle, the soldier checks and rechecks his weapon to make sure it is working smoothly.

The police officer dons his tactical vest and helmet and lifts his ballistic shield as he approaches a house on a drug raid.

The only believer on the women's basketball team knows she's going to be the object of rough treatment after she has spoken out for the Lord. She prepares for the persecution by spending time with the Lord. Why? She knows that her security is in God.

This young believer has learned what David discovered long ago. He wrote Psalm 57 while hiding in a cave from the murderous King Saul. David knew that his security was not in the cave, nor in his cunning, but in God. That's why he wrote: "I will take refuge in the shadow of your wings" (v. 1). He felt secure (v. 7), and he would sing God's praise when it was all over (v. 9).

When we are faced with opposition, we sometimes try to manipulate people or arrange circumstances to make sure we are safe. But we need to learn that our protection is not in our man-made defenses. God is our true source of safety!

DAVID EGNER

No life is more secure than one shielded by God.

God's Justice

PSALM 58

The righteous will be glad when they are avenged,
when they dip their feet in the blood of the wicked.

PSALM 58:10

Many years ago a man was executed by the state of Illinois for kidnapping, torturing, and murdering thirty-three young men. That murderer was an evil, cruel, hateful man, and I confess that when he was executed I was glad he was no longer a threat to society.

But that raises difficult questions in my mind. What should a believer's attitude be when the wicked are punished? Should we rejoice when cruel people pay for the suffering they have caused?

We get some help in Psalm 58, where David prayed that God would execute justice on the evil people who opposed him. "Break the teeth in their mouths," he entreated (v. 6). "May they be like . . . a stillborn child" (v. 8). Those are strong words!

But a key observation must be made here. David was praying that God's justice would be carried out against the incorrigibly wicked who, "like the cobra that has stopped its ears," ignored all attempts to turn them from their error (vv. 3–5).

God is a God of justice. His holiness is affirmed when child molesters, mass murderers, and the defrauders of the innocent pay for their crimes.

Let's rejoice that God cannot tolerate evil. But let's also rejoice that God is merciful. Through the sacrifice of His Son, we are forgiven and God's justice is satisfied.

DAVID EGNER

"Vengeance is Mine, I will repay," says the Lord.
—Romans 12:19 NKJV

The Power of Music

PSALM 59:6–16

I will sing of your strength, in the morning I will sing of your love.
PSALM 59:16

In the country of Wales, the music of men's chorus groups is deeply engrained in the culture. Prior to World War II, one Welsh glee club had a friendly yet competitive rivalry with a German glee club, but that bond was replaced with animosity during and after the war. The tension was gradually overcome, though, by the message on the trophy shared by the two choruses: "Speak with me, and you're my friend. Sing with me, and you're my brother."

The power of music to heal and help is a gift from God that comforts many. Perhaps that is why the Psalms speak so deeply to us. There we find lyrics that connect with our hearts, allowing us to speak to God from the depth of our spirits. "I will sing of your strength, in the morning I will sing of your love; for you are my fortress, my refuge in times of trouble" (59:16). Amazingly, David wrote this song as he was being hunted down by men seeking to kill him! Despite his circumstances, David remembered God's power and mercy, and singing of them encouraged him to go on.

May our God give us a song today that will remind us of His goodness and greatness, no matter what we may face.

BILL CROWDER

"I will make music to the LORD, the God of Israel."
—Judges 5:3 (NLT)

City of Refuge

PSALM 59:10–17

You are my strength, I sing praise to you;
you, God, are my fortress, my God on whom I can rely.

PSALM 59:17

As we entered a town in Australia, we were greeted by a sign that declared: "We welcome all who are seeking refuge and asylum." This kind of welcome seems to resonate with the Old Testament concept of the cities of refuge. In the Old Testament era, cities of refuge (see Numbers 35:6) were established to be a safe haven for people who had accidentally killed someone and needed protection. God had the people establish such cities to provide that refuge.

This concept, however, was not intended to be simply a practice for ancient Israel. More than that, cities of refuge reflected the heart of God for all people. He himself longs to be our safe haven and our city of refuge in the failures, heartaches, and losses of life. We read in Psalm 59:17, "You are my strength, I sing praise to you; you, God, are my fortress, my God on whom I can rely."

For the hurting heart of every generation, our "city of refuge" is not a place. Our city of refuge is a Person—the God who loves us with an everlasting love. May we find our refuge and rest in Him.

BILL CROWDER

Refuge can be found in the Rock of Ages.

A Place of Shelter

PSALM 61

*I long to dwell in your tent forever and take refuge
in the shelter of your wings.*

PSALM 61:4

Homeless people in Vancouver, British Columbia, have a new way to find nighttime accommodations. A local charity, RainCity Housing, has created specialized benches that convert into temporary shelters. The back of the bench pulls up to create a roof that can shield a person from wind and rain. At night, these sleeping spaces are easy to find because they feature a glow-in-the-dark message that reads: THIS IS A BEDROOM.

The need for shelter can be physical, and it can be spiritual as well. God is a refuge for our souls when we are troubled. King David wrote, "I call as my heart grows faint; lead me to the rock that is higher than I" (Psalm 61:2). When we're emotionally overloaded, we are more vulnerable to Satan's tactics—fear, guilt, and lust are a few of his favorites. We need a source of stability and safety.

If we take refuge in God, we can have victory over Satan as he tries to influence our hearts and minds. "You have been my refuge, a strong tower against the foe," David said to the Lord. "I long to . . . take refuge in the shelter of your wings" (vv. 3–4).

When we are overwhelmed, peace and protection are ours through God's Son, Jesus Christ. "In me you may have peace," Jesus said. "In this world you will have trouble. But take heart! I have overcome the world" (John 16:33).

JENNIFER BENSON SCHULDT

God is our refuge.

The Beauty of Silence

PSALM 62:1–8

Truly my soul finds rest in God; my salvation comes from him.
PSALM 62:1

Written on the wall behind the pulpit of the church we attended in my teens were these words: "The LORD is in his holy temple: let all the earth keep silence before him" (Habakkuk 2:20 KJV). And keep silence we did! All eight of us boys said nothing to one another as we sat waiting for the service to begin.

I loved this quiet time and often succeeded in pushing thoughts about girls and the Detroit Tigers out of my mind. The best I could, I tried to reflect on the wonder of God and His salvation. And in the silence I often sensed His presence.

Today we live in a noisy world. Even many church services leave little time for quiet reflection.

In ancient times the pagans cried out in a noisy frenzy to their idols (1 Kings 18:25–29). In sharp contrast, the psalmist saw the wisdom of silence, because in quiet reverence God can be heard. In the stillness of the night under a starry sky, in a hushed sanctuary, or in a quiet room at home, we can meet the living God and hear Him speak.

The psalmist's words are relevant today: "Wait silently for God alone" (Psalm 62:5 NKJV).

HERB VANDER LUGT

To hear God's voice, turn down the world's volume.

Weak and Wise

PSALM 62

*Hyraxes are creatures of little power,
yet they make their home in the crags.*

PROVERBS 30:26

In Proverbs 30:26, God is calling our attention to an unusual little creature.

The hyrax is about the size of a large guinea pig but is not closely linked to any other known animal. It looks like a rodent and has been characterized as a "rock rabbit." It is extremely vulnerable to attack from its predators. Among its enemies are snakes, eagles, buzzards, leopards, dogs, and other small beasts of prey such as the mongoose.

So how does this little fellow manage to survive? The answer is simple. It makes its home in holes or clefts of the rock, frequently along the side of a steep cliff.

In many ways we are a lot like the hyrax. We are susceptible to many dangers. Disease, depression, war, accident, and isolation threaten us constantly. If only we could find a way to survive like that little creature! Well, we can. We too have a Rock in which to hide—the Lord God himself. Trusting Him doesn't exempt us from life's troubles, but it does give protection to our soul.

It's not bad to be weak—if you are wise enough to take refuge in God.

MART DEHAAN

**If you're between a rock and a hard place,
take refuge in the Rock of Ages.**

Heart to Heart

PSALM 62

Trust in him at all times, you people;
pour out your hearts to him, for God is our refuge.
PSALM 62:8

We would expect King David to be extremely upset, because his enemies were scheming to dethrone him. Yet in Psalm 62 he testified that his soul was quietly confident before God. How was this possible in the midst of such turmoil? Verse 8 offers a clue—one I discovered for myself several years ago.

I had just returned home, battle-weary, alone, and at my wits' end. As I began pouring out my woes before God, I suddenly stopped myself and said, "Father, forgive me. I'm treating you like a counselor!" But the torrent of words flowed on, followed by the same embarrassing apology. Then God's Spirit whispered deep within, "I *am* your Great Counselor."

But of course! Hadn't He, the Creator of my physical and spiritual makeup, also created my emotions? How reasonable, then, to spread out my ragged feelings before Him. Then came His comforting, corrective counsel, ministered skillfully by the Holy Spirit through His Word. My problems didn't evaporate, but like David, I could rest in God alone. I was at peace again.

Never hesitate to pour out your heart to God. In your day of trouble, you'll find that prayer is the shortest route between your heart and God's.

JOANIE YODER

God fills our heart with peace when we pour out our heart to Him.

Preparing for Heaven

PSALM 63

You, God, are my God, earnestly I seek you;
I thirst for you, my whole being longs for you, in a dry
and parched land where there is no water.

PSALM 63:1

Some people openly declare that they don't want to go to heaven. I've had people tell me that they would rather be with their drinking buddies in hell than with the church-going crowd in heaven.

Most people, however, say they hope to go to heaven when they die, but I've often wondered what makes them think they would be happy there. These are people who ignore Jesus Christ and avoid any references to God. They have no interest in Bible reading, prayer, and worship. I wonder why they think they will suddenly enjoy fellowship with God on the other side?

Although David makes no reference in Psalm 63 to spending eternity with God, there is no doubt about his deep longing for the Lord. I believe that the godly attitudes and actions we are nurturing in our lives here and now prepare us for heaven's enjoyments throughout eternity.

That raises some heart-searching questions. How passionately do we seek fellowship with God? How much time do we spend reading His Word, praying, and worshiping? How earnestly do we want to please Him? Does our soul thirst for Him and our heart long for Him? If so, we can say with David, "My soul follows close behind You" (v. 8 NKJV).

HERB VANDER LUGT

One of life's greatest joys is the sure hope of heaven.

In the Middle of a Muddle

PSALM 63

Because your love is better than life, my lips will glorify you.
I will praise you as long as I live, and in your name I will lift up my hands.

PSALM 63:3–4

Praise doesn't come easily when we're struggling with a problem. But magnifying the Lord while we're in the middle of a muddle is an important aspect of praise.

The psalmist David clearly understood and practiced this. He composed Psalm 63 in the wilderness when he was fleeing from those who sought his life. British preacher Charles Spurgeon called it a "wilderness hymn." Its timeless words apply to any believer whose circumstances have become a wilderness.

Spurgeon described David's hymn of praise like this: The first eight verses express his longing after God and his confidence in Him; the remaining three verses prophesy the overthrow of his enemies. In verses 1 through 8, we find no less than sixteen statements of love and faith, revealing David's confidence in a personal God. He said, "You, God, are my God" (v. 1), "Your love is better than life" (v. 3), "I sing in the shadow of your wings" (v. 7), and "your right hand upholds me" (v. 8).

Are you stuck in the middle of a mess and long for God to deliver you so you can praise Him later? Like David, why not let your praises precede the victory. Praise God now!

JOANIE YODER

There's no better time to praise God than right now.

The Hand of God

PSALM 63:1–8

I cling to you; your right hand upholds me.
PSALM 63:8

When NASA began using a new kind of space telescope to capture different spectrums of light, researchers were surprised at one of the photos. It shows what looks like fingers, a thumb, and an open palm showered with spectacular colors of blue, purple, green, and gold. Some have called it "The Hand of God."

The idea of God reaching out His hand to help us in our time of need is a central theme of Scripture. In Psalm 63 we read: "Because you are my help, I sing in the shadow of your wings. I cling to you; your right hand upholds me" (vv. 7–8). The psalmist felt God's divine help like a hand of support. Some Bible teachers believe that King David wrote this psalm in the wilderness of Judah during the terrible time of his son Absalom's rebellion. Absalom had conspired to dethrone his father, and David fled to the wilderness (2 Samuel 15–16). Even during this difficult time, God was present and David trusted in Him. He said, "Because your love is better than life, my lips will glorify you" (Psalm 63:3).

Life can be painful at times, yet God offers His comforting hand in the midst of it. We are not beyond His reach.

DENNIS FISHER

**God bears the world's weight on His shoulder,
yet He holds His children in the palm of His hand.**

Squirrel Feeder

PSALM 65

You crown the year with your bounty,
and your carts overflow with abundance.
PSALM 65:11

Some years ago I placed a squirrel feeder on a fir tree a few yards from our home. It's a simple device—two boards and a nail on which to impale a corncob. Each morning a squirrel comes to enjoy that day's meal. She's a pretty thing—black with a round, gray tummy.

I sit on our back porch in the morning and watch her eat. She plucks each kernel from the cob, holds it in her paws, turns it around and eats the heart out of the kernel. At the end of the day no kernels remain, only a neat little pile of leftovers under the tree.

Despite my care for her, the creature is afraid of me. When I approach, she runs away, taking refuge in her tree and chattering at me when I get too close. She doesn't understand that I provide for her.

Some people are like that with God. They run from Him in fear. They don't realize that He loves them and richly provides them with everything for their enjoyment (Psalm 65:11).

Henry Scougal, a seventeenth-century Scottish minister, wrote, "Nothing is more powerful to engage our affection than to find that we are [loved by] One who is altogether lovely. . . . How must this astonish and delight us; how must it overcome our [fear] and melt our hearts." God's love is the perfect love that "drives out fear" (1 John 4:18).

DAVID ROPER

Your loving heavenly Father never takes His eyes off you.

The Mystery of Tragedy

PSALM 66:8–20

*Praise be to God, who has not rejected my prayer
or withheld his love from me!*
PSALM 66:20

When we suffer pain and loss, we sometimes ask the question, "If the Lord is with us, why has all this happened?" While the Bible tells us the future of human history, it supplies no specific explanation of the events that take place daily in our lives. Sometimes when tragedy strikes we understand a little, but as a rule we are unable to fathom the mystery of disease or accidents.

Even in times of perplexing trauma, we can hold fast to this faith-sustaining counsel: "Let the one who walks in the dark, who has no light, trust in the name of the LORD and rely on their God" (Isaiah 50:10).

That's what W. A. Shelton did. The former pastor of the First Methodist Church in Gadsden, Alabama, lost his dearly loved wife to death. Yet he could honestly say to his friend Denson Franklin, "I miss her greatly, but I am on God's team, and He is the quarterback. He calls the plays, and I run where He tells me. He has called the play. I do not understand it, but I shall continue to play on His team."

Are you going through circumstances you don't understand? Cry out to the Lord (Psalm 66:17, 19–20), and continue to trust in His wisdom and goodness. He understands it all and cares for you.

VERNON GROUNDS

**When all things seem to be against you,
remember that God is for you.**

The Purpose of God's Goodness

PSALM 67

*May God be gracious to us and bless us
and make his face shine on us.*

PSALM 67:1

When I was growing up, we often sang a song in Sunday school that went like this: "God is good to me! God is good to me! He holds my hand and helps me stand! God is good to me!"

I need to say right away that I believe God is good, and He takes delight in doing good things for people. He does indeed hold our hand in times of trouble and helps us stand against the onslaught of life's difficulties. But I wonder if you've ever asked yourself, "Why is He good?" It certainly is not because we deserve it or because He feels the need to buy our love and allegiance with His benefits.

The psalmist prays for God to bless him so that "[the Lord's] ways may be known on earth, your salvation among all nations" (Psalm 67:2). God's daily blessings are proof positive that He is indeed a good God who cares for His own. But how will our world know this about God if we never praise Him for His goodness to us? (v. 3).

So the next time God blesses you, be sure to look for ways to appropriately give Him the credit. Consuming His blessings without communicating His goodness shortchanges the very purpose of His gifts of grace in our lives.

JOE STOWELL

**God is good—make sure the people in your world
know what He has done in your life.**

Pigs Don't Pray

PSALM 68:4–10

Praise be to the Lord, to God our Savior,
who daily bears our burdens.

PSALM 68:19

A Christian farmer went to the city on business and stopped at a small restaurant for lunch. When his food was served, he bowed and gave God thanks, just as he did at home. A young fellow at the next table noticed that the farmer was praying. Thinking he was a little backward and not in touch with "city ways," he asked loudly to embarrass him, "Say, farmer, does everyone do that out in the country where you live?" The earnest Christian turned to him and replied kindly, "No, son, the pigs don't."

The more I observe people, the more I notice that it is the exception rather than the rule to see people bow and give thanks to God in public. We seem to have become a very self-indulgent and ungrateful society.

In Psalm 68, David reviewed the many ways God had cared for His people Israel. After surveying Jehovah's faithfulness, he exclaimed, "Praise be to the Lord, to God our Savior, who daily bears our burdens" (v. 19). From a heart overflowing with love for the Lord, David gave thanks often. Should we not respond in like manner for every blessing God has so freely given? Shouldn't we express to Him our gratitude at all times?

Let's remember to say thanks to God for our daily supply of blessings—even in a crowded restaurant. Let's not be like the pigs.

PAUL VAN GORDER

A thankful heart enjoys blessings twice—
when they're received and when they're remembered.

For the Children

PSALM 68:5; MARK 10:13–16

When Jesus saw this, he was indignant. He said to them,
"Let the little children come to me, and do not hinder them,
for the kingdom of God belongs to such as these."
MARK 10:14

As the teenagers left Robin's Nest orphanage near Montego Bay, Jamaica, many of them were in tears.

"It's just not fair," one girl said after their too-brief visit. "We have so much, and they don't have anything." In the two hours we visited, handing out stuffed animals and playing with the kids, she had been holding a sad little girl who never smiled. We learned that before she was rescued she had been abused by her parents.

Multiply this little girl's plight by the millions, and it's easy to feel overwhelmed. My teenage friends were right. It's not fair. Abuse, poverty, and neglect have turned the lives of millions of little ones into a nightmare.

How this must grieve God's heart! Jesus, who said, "Let the little children come to me" (Mark 10:14), is surely saddened by the way these children are treated.

What can we do? In Jesus's name, we can give monetary support to good orphanages. When possible, we can offer physical help. If we feel led, we can seek to provide homes for these precious children. And all of us can pray—beseeching God to help those for whom life is so unfair.

Let's show children the love of God through our hearts and our hands.

DAVE BRANON

Be Jesus to a child today.

Deep Water

PSALM 69:13–18

*Do not let the floodwaters engulf me or the depths swallow me up
or the pit close its mouth over me.*
PSALM 69:15

The builders of sport utility vehicles (SUVs) like to show us their products in mind-boggling situations. High on a mountain crag—where no truck could seemingly go. Or in a swamp so impassable you'd need a hovercraft to negotiate it. We're supposed to think SUVs are invincible.

That's why I found unintended humor in the disclaimer in an ad for a four-wheel-drive SUV. A photo showed the vehicle up to its headlights in water as it forged across a foreboding river. The ad said: "Traversing deep water can cause damage, which voids the vehicle warranty."

Deep water is a problem not only for cars but also for us. As we travel the roadways of life, we often find ourselves surrounded with oceans of grief or crashing waves of broken relationships. We need help.

The writers of the Psalms told of that needed assistance. They said God is "a stronghold in times of trouble" (9:9), and that "in the day of trouble he will . . . set me high upon a rock" (27:5). No disclaimers here. Traversing deep water won't affect our spiritual warranty. God will always be there to guarantee His support.

Are you in deep water? Reach up and grab God's hand of mercy.

DAVE BRANON

When trouble overtakes you, let God take over.

The Other Eighty Percent

PSALM 69:29–36

Let heaven and earth praise him, the seas and all that move in them.
PSALM 69:34

Recently I saw a billboard stating that eighty percent of all life on Earth is found in the seas. That staggering number is difficult to process, largely because most of that life is out of sight.

As I considered this, it reminded me of how much greater God's creation is than we typically appreciate. While we can easily have our breath taken away by a majestic mountain range or a panoramic sunset, we sometimes fail to see His extraordinary work in the details that require more careful study and examination. Not only is much of God's creation hidden by the oceans but other parts are also too small for our eyes to observe. From the microscopically small to the unsearched reaches of the universe, it is all the work of our Creator. In those magnificent structures—seen and unseen—God's creative glory is revealed (Romans 1:20).

As we grow to understand the wonder of creation, it must always point us to the Creator himself—and call us to worship Him. As the psalmist said, "Let heaven and earth praise him, the seas and all that move in them" (Psalm 69:34). If creation itself gives praise to the Creator, we can and certainly should join the chorus. What a mighty God we serve!

BILL CROWDER

**The wonder of creation causes us to say,
"What a wonderful God!"**

Time to Pray?

PSALM 70

Hasten, O God, to save me; come quickly, LORD, to help me.
PSALM 70:1

One morning, when I was a young child, I was sitting in the kitchen, watching my mother prepare breakfast. Unexpectedly, the grease in the skillet in which she was frying bacon caught fire. Flames shot into the air and my mother ran to the pantry for some baking soda to throw on the blaze.

"Help!" I shouted. And then I added, "Oh, I wish it was time to pray!" "It's time to pray" must have been a frequent household expression, and I took it quite literally to mean we could pray only at certain times.

The time to pray, of course, is any time—especially when we're in crisis. Fear, worry, anxiety, and care are the most common occasions for prayer. It is when we are desolate, forsaken, and stripped of every human resource that we naturally resort to prayer. We cry out with the words of David, "Hasten, O God, to save me" (Psalm 70:1).

John Cassian, a fifth-century Christian, wrote of this verse: "This is the terrified cry of someone who sees the snares of the enemy, the cry of someone besieged day and night and exclaiming that he cannot escape unless his Protector comes to the rescue."

May this be our simple prayer in every crisis and all day long: "Lord, help me!"

DAVID ROPER

There is no place or time we cannot pray.

Small Boats

PSALM 70

But as for me, I am poor and needy; come quickly to me, O God.
You are my help and my deliverer; LORD, do not delay.

PSALM 70:5

Fishermen living in the Brittany peninsula of France would often say this prayer as they set out to sea: "Keep us, our God; for your ocean is so wide and our boat is so small."

Commenting on this prayer, an unknown author wrote, "How very beautiful those words! Might not they be uttered by those who know the Lord as they journey on the sea of life? We are so weak, so helpless, so forgetful of God's loving-kindness. Tossed to and fro at the mercy of the world, except He hold us, we perish."

At times the challenges and difficulties of life threaten to overwhelm us. We sense our weaknesses and inability to overcome them. The problems are so great and perplexing that we feel there's no solution or end in sight. We feel like crying out to the Lord in the words of the psalmist, "I am poor and needy . . . You are my help and my deliverer" (70:5).

When God's children call on the Lord and cast themselves on Him in simple trust, they can depend on Him and His great power and wisdom to carry them through even the most severe storms of life.

Yes, in our "small boats," on a "wide ocean," we can trust our God to protect us even in the worst of storms. Let's ask Him to keep us today.

RICHARD DEHAAN

God is no security against life's storms,
but He is perfect security in life's storms.

Life's Seasons

PSALM 71:1–21

From birth I have relied on you;
you brought me forth from my mother's womb.
I will ever praise you.

PSALM 71:6

How ironic! When we are young, we can't wait to grow up! When we are old, we look back longingly to former years. God intends that we joyfully take each season of life as it comes. Whatever the age, He imparts what we need to be all we can be. He asks us to commit our way to Him and to accept what He allows of struggle and what He provides of strength.

A woman who was facing the trials of aging asked J. Robertson McQuilkin, longtime president of Columbia International University, "Why does God let us get old and weak?" McQuilkin thought a moment, then replied, "I think God has planned the strength and beauty of youth to be physical. But the strength and beauty of old age is spiritual. We gradually lose the strength and beauty that is temporary so we'll be sure to concentrate on the strength and beauty that is forever. And so we'll be eager to leave the temporary, deteriorating part of us and be truly homesick for our eternal home. If we stayed young and strong and beautiful, we might never want to leave."

Are you in life's springtime? Trust God's timing to fulfill your dreams. Are you in life's summer or autumn? Face your daily challenges head on. And if you feel winter's chill, concentrate on knowing God better. His presence will make every season of life one of strength and beauty.

DENNIS DEHAAN

Life is ten percent how we make it and
ninety percent how we take it.

A Wish for the Aged

PSALM 71:9–18

Do not cast me away when I am old;
do not forsake me when my strength is gone.
PSALM 71:9

"As a white candle in a holy place, so is the beauty of an aged face." This line from a poem by Joseph Campbell applies to people who have served the Lord all their lives and are still bearing fruit in old age.

Behind the aged face of a longtime Christian are memories of family and friends. Wrinkles stand for earnest times of prayer, loving care, and decades of useful work. The beauty is no longer the skin-deep charm of youth but the time-honored loveliness of a life well lived.

For many years, my wife ministered to beautiful aged people as a nurse in a rest home. Special people they were—like the man who gave her a weather report each night she worked, and like the woman who served God for years and continued as a prayer warrior as the sun was setting on her earthly life.

But the elderly are not always appreciated. Unscrupulous people take advantage of them. Others suggest that they are an unnecessary burden.

As Christians, we must resist and reverse this trend. Many of these precious people feel rejected and abandoned. Let's pray for the aged, care for them, and love them in Jesus's name. Perhaps we can be the answer to their prayer: "Do not cast me away when I am old."

DAVE BRANON

Kindness to the elderly helps brighten their sunset years.

Grain on the Mountaintop

PSALM 72:12–20

May grain abound throughout the land; on the tops of the hills may it sway.
May the crops flourish like Lebanon and thrive like the grass of the field.
PSALM 72:16

I've been on a number of mountaintops in the US in my time, and I can tell you that not much grows up there. The summits of mountains are bare rock and lichen. That's not where you would normally find an abundance of grain.

But Solomon, who wrote Psalm 72, petitioned God: "may grain abound . . . ; on the tops of hills may it sway," to characterize his reign as king. If grain on the mountain is so unusual, what is Solomon suggesting? That God's power can produce results in even the most unpromising soil?

Perhaps you think of yourself as an insignificant person—with very little to bring to the kingdom. Take courage: God can produce an abundant harvest through you. This is one of the ironies of faith: God uses the small to accomplish the great. Not many of us are wise or noble; most of us are anonymous and far from extraordinary. Yet all of us can be used. And contrary to what we might think, it is because of our weakness that we can be used by God (1 Corinthians 1:27–29; 2 Corinthians 12:10).

It's possible to be too big or proud for God to use, but we can never be too little. Our "weakness" can be "turned to strength" (Hebrews 11:34). By God's great power, we can do all that He has called us to do.

DAVID ROPER

To experience God's power, we must first admit that we are weak.

Got Thirst?

PSALM 73:23-28

Whom have I in heaven but you?
And earth has nothing I desire besides you.
PSALM 73:25

Health experts tell us we should drink at least sixty-four ounces of water each day. It may reduce the risk of heart attack, give our skin a healthy glow, and help us lose weight. We should drink even more water during exercise or if we live in a hot or dry climate. Even if we're not thirsty, we ought to drink water anyway.

Our thirst for God is even more beneficial. When we're spiritually dry, we long to hear from Him through His Word, and we search for even a drop of knowledge about Him. When we're exercising our faith in a new way, we want to be close to Him and receive His strength. Our thirst for God may increase when we see the sinfulness of people around us or when we gain a new awareness of our own sin and need for Him.

Spiritual thirst is a metaphor used throughout Scripture. Asaph thirsted for answers in his questioning psalm. When he saw the wicked prospering, he cried out to God to understand why (Psalm 73:16). He found the Lord to be his strength and realized that he desired nothing but Him (vv. 25–26).

If we're spiritually thirsty, we can follow Asaph's example and draw near to God (v. 28). He will satisfy us, yet give us a deeper thirst for himself. We'll learn to desire Him above all else.

ANNE CETAS

A thirst for God can be satisfied only by Christ, the Living Water.

What Are You Running To?

PSALM 73

But as for me, it is good to be near God.
I have made the Sovereign LORD my refuge;
I will tell of all your deeds.

PSALM 73:28

Author and cartoonist James Thurber made this provocative observation about life: "All persons must learn before they die what they are running from and what they are running to, and why."

Our thoughts and actions in the present are shaped by something in our past: a parent who set standards that we can never reach; sexual abuse; a great potential in high school that fizzled when we got out into life; insecurity; growing up in a remote area.

We must also find out what we're running to. Some people, competing for temporary fame and fortune, are like passengers who are fighting for the best seats on a bus headed for oblivion. Others plan for their retirement—but not for old age or beyond death.

The psalmist Asaph knew what he was running from. He had lived in doubt near the neighborhood of despair. He also knew what he was running to and why. He sang, "It is good to be near God. . . . I will tell of all your deeds" (Psalm 73:28). He also said, "You guide me with your counsel, and afterward you will take me into glory" (v. 24).

Have you figured out what you are running from? More important, do you know what you are running to?

HADDON ROBINSON

Keep your eyes on the Lord and you won't
lose sight of life's purpose.

It's Who You Know That Counts

PSALM 75

It is God who judges: He brings one down, he exalts another.
PSALM 75:7

We often hear it said, "It's who you know that counts!" Sometimes I wish that were not true. The principle seems so contrary to the laws of fair play and competition because it doesn't give people of equal abilities an equal opportunity for success. Knowing the right people often means that a job is filled on the basis of favor rather than on qualifications. It happens all the time. Someone puts in a good word for a relative, a friend, or a friend's friend. With such beginnings, work is obtained and professions are launched. Now this isn't necessarily wrong. In fact, it may be highly profitable for all involved. Yet to those who are equally qualified but don't have the right connections, it all seems quite unfair.

In Psalm 75 we read that the Lord "brings one down, he exalts another." This means that the Almighty God is behind the scenes giving His own kind of "breaks," opportunities, and promotions—all according to His mercy and grace. Therefore to know Him personally holds unlimited possibilities. What's even more exciting is that anyone, from the greatest to the least, can benefit. No other reference or relationship deserves to be compared with knowing God in Christ, and from our contact with Him we find a new source of acceptance, hope, and security. The resources of God are at our disposal, as well as His unlimited power to work for our good through all the circumstances of life. Yes, it's who you know that counts, especially when you know and trust the Lord.

MART DEHAAN

Knowing the Master is the master key to success.

God's Restraint

PSALM 76:1–12

*Surely your wrath against mankind brings you praise,
and the survivors of your wrath are restrained.*
PSALM 76:10

Augustine said that God "judged it better to bring good out of evil, than not to permit any evil to exist." Thus God takes the worst evil that men and women can do to us and turns it into good. Even the wrath of ungodly men brings praise to Him (Psalm 76:10).

God has not promised that your life will be easy—indeed it may not be. But He has promised to sustain you in your struggle and uphold you with His mighty arm. If you trust Him, He will empower you to make your way bravely through extraordinary difficulty with faith, hope, and love. The trials God permits in your life will lead to His praise and glory, if only you will abide in Him.

Furthermore, there will be a restraint and a respite. The Hebrew text is somewhat obscure in Psalm 76:10. Literally it reads, "Surely the wrath of man will praise you; the remnant of wrath [God] will bind." God will use men's wrath to bring glory and praise to himself, but when that purpose is fulfilled He will then restrain it.

God will not allow you to be pressed beyond endurance. That is His sure promise. When the lesson has been learned, when the revelation of God's glory is complete and your soul has been tried and proven—then God will raise His hand and save you. He will say, "No more."

DAVID ROPER

In every desert of trial, God has an oasis of comfort.

Days of Doubt

PSALM 77

I will remember the deeds of the LORD;
yes, I will remember your miracles of long ago.

PSALM 77:11

In 1970, Ronald Dunn began keeping a record of answered prayers and special blessings in a little book. He misplaced the book but found it again several years later at a time when his faith was floundering. He was surprised that he had forgotten most of the incidents he had written about.

As he was reading, something happened. "My memory of God's faithfulness was revived and my sagging faith began to recover," he said. "Remembering had restored my confidence in the Lord." Dunn then encouraged Christians to keep a book of remembrance, recording God's activity in their lives. "One day," he wrote, "it may mean the difference between victory and defeat."

In Psalm 77, Asaph's faith was also floundering. After listing his serious doubts, he asked, "Has God forgotten to be merciful?" (v. 9). Suddenly he stopped and said: "I will remember the deeds of the LORD; yes, I will remember your miracles of long ago" (v. 11). The act of remembering obviously revived his faith. Just read the rest of the psalm!

Why not create your own book of remembrance, recording God's wonderful deeds? Then read it often, especially on days of doubt.

JOANIE YODER

Remembering God's goodness is a good cure for doubt.

"God Hides His Face"

PSALM 77:1–15

Will the Lord reject forever? Will he never show his favor again?
PSALM 77:7

Does it ever seem as if you can't get through to God in prayer? If so, you're not alone.

David Brainerd was a godly missionary to the North American Indians in colonial days. He kept a diary in which he recorded his spiritual mountain peaks as well as his valleys. At one point he wrote, "I lodge in a bundle of straw, my labor is hard and extremely difficult, and I have little appearance of success to comfort me. . . . But what makes all my difficulties grievous to be borne is that God hides His face from me."

When it seems God isn't listening, that He's "forgotten to be gracious" (Psalm 77:9 NKJV), what should you do?

- Recognize that your experience is not unique and doesn't mean you are an outcast from God's redeemed family.
- Seek out a fellow believer with whom you can share your feelings and ask for prayer (1 Thessalonians 5:25).
- Meditate on the truths of Scripture and what God has done for you in the past (Psalm 77:11–12).
- Keep on praying in faith to your great God, no matter how silent heaven may seem (Luke 18:1).

Remember, our God is "the God who performs miracles" (Psalm 77:14).

VERNON GROUNDS

When it comes to prayer, don't hang up—hang on!

Dangerous Crossings

PSALM 77:16–20

Your path led through the sea, your way through the mighty waters,
though your footprints were not seen.

PSALM 77:19

I don't wade in swift streams anymore. The bottom's too slippery, the current's too strong, and my old legs aren't what they used to be.

So many challenges that I once took on readily are now too difficult for me. Like the psalmist, I lose sleep sometimes, wondering how I can negotiate them (Psalm 77:1–4).

Then I remember the "the deeds of the LORD" and His "miracles of long ago" (v. 11). His "path . . . through the sea," though He left no footprints behind (v. 19).

That's the way it is with God. Although you can't see Him, He is surely there. Unseen, He leads His people "like a flock" (v. 20). He does not fear the currents and storms of life, for His strength and courage are infinite.

And there's more: The Shepherd leads us through the help of other people. He led Israel "by the hand of Moses and Aaron" (v. 20). He leads us in the wise counsel of a father or mother, in the strong grip of a godly friend, in the loving encouragement of a caring husband or wife, in the gentle touch of a young child.

Good hands are reaching out to us. Our Lord is a tough and tender Shepherd who leads through perilous crossings to the other side. Have you put your hand in His?

DAVID ROPER

God tells us to burden Him with what burdens us.

A Pattern for Parents

PSALM 78:1–7

Fathers, do not exasperate your children;
instead, bring them up in the training and instruction of the Lord.
EPHESIANS 6:4

A man was having a little chat with his young son. He was trying to tell him what a Christian should be like and how he should act. When he had finished talking, his son looked at him and asked a stunning question. "Daddy," the boy wondered, "have I ever seen a Christian?" What a telling commentary on the life of that father!

How would we feel if our children were to respond to us in the same way? Psalm 78 gives us some help in making sure that doesn't happen. It sets forth a pattern for parenting—a method we can use to ensure that our children know the things of God and realize that we are people of God. According to Asaph, we can do this as we "tell the next generation the praiseworthy deeds of the LORD" (v. 4). When we "teach [our] children" (v. 5) these things, they will see by our words and our testimony that we are Christians.

Speaking of God's guidelines for living, Moses said, "Impress them on your children. Talk about them when you sit at home and when you walk along the road, when you lie down and when you get up" (Deuteronomy 6:7). By word and by personal example we must guide our children. In that way, we can both tell them and show them what it means to be a Christian.

PAUL VAN GORDER

Children may close their ears to advice
but they keep their eyes open to example.

Done?

PSALM 78:1–8

We will not hide them from their descendants;
we will tell the next generation the praiseworthy deeds of the LORD,
his power, and the wonders he has done.

PSALM 78:4

The heritage of Christian workers never ends, though their work sometimes must.

I thought of this recently after hearing of an elderly woman who no longer feels useful. Despite her years of service as a Sunday school teacher (for which she is remembered fondly), as well as the spiritual influence she has already had on her children and grandchildren, she feels as if she isn't helpful anymore. But it's not true.

The Bible reminds us that God's people are to pass along to the next generation the stories of God and His people. In Joel 1, for example, the inhabitants of Judah were told to convey a story about locusts to their children. Because the story had prophetic implications, it was an important part of the heritage of the people and thus it had to be passed on. In our reading for today, Psalm 78, the message is similar. The older Israelites were to tell the young people the story of God's work in Israel's past.

Today we have a message of salvation through Jesus and an opportunity to demonstrate a life of devotion to God. If you have passed the gospel to the next generation, your impact lingers. Even when you feel as if your work is done, it keeps going. Your influence will never die.

DAVE BRANON

Telling what Christ has done for us
leaves signposts for those who follow.

Tell the Children

PSALM 78:1–8

He commanded our ancestors to teach their children.
PSALM 78:5

Imagine an evening in ancient Israel. The day's work is done, the meal is finished, and the family is gathered around a small fire that pushes away the night chill and casts a soft glow on their faces. It's story time.

Father and grandfather take turns relating to the children the "praiseworthy deeds of the LORD" (Psalm 78:4). They tell of Abraham's journey. They speak of Isaac. Their voices come alive when they tell about old Jacob. They remember Moses and Joshua and Elijah and the great King David. They recount the history of their own family. And all the time, they focus their attention on the mighty works of God in behalf of His people.

That's the way Jewish men fulfilled their responsibility to tell the next generation about the Lord. They had been told by their parents, who had been told by their parents.

Our children need to know about God. They need to learn from us about His love, His faithfulness, and His grace. They need to hear from us about the times He stepped into our lives to protect and provide.

So gather up your sons and daughters and grandchildren. Relate to them how God has worked in your life. Fulfill your responsibility, and tell the children.

DAVID EGNER

A godly parent is a child's best guide to God.

When God Thunders

PSALM 81:6–10

In your distress you called and I rescued you,
I answered you out of a thundercloud;
I tested you at the waters of Meribah.

PSALM 81:7

Thunder rolls across the Sawtooth Mountains, crashing and echoing through the peaks and canyons, shaking the ground with celestial sonic booms. My old dog cuts and runs. I stand amazed and delighted.

The storm reminds me of the "secret place of thunder" from which God answered His people (Psalm 81:7 NKJV). Israel cried out from the straw pits and brick kilns of Egypt. In time, God's salvation rolled over the land in peals of thunder (Exodus 9:13–34).

Another psalm speaks of the storm that overshadowed Israel as they passed through the Red Sea (Psalm 77:16–20). Its thunder spelled doom for the Egyptians but deliverance to God's people. Each resounding clap was the comforting voice of a Father speaking to His children.

When Jesus foretold His death in John 12:28–29, He called on His Father to glorify His name. A voice answered from heaven saying, "I have glorified it, and will glorify it again." To the crowd, it sounded like thunder.

Are you in trouble? Cry out to God in your sorrow and distress. You may not hear the thunder roll, but it will reverberate through the heavens once again as He answers you "in the secret place of thunder." God will speak comfort to your heart and deliver you from your fears.

DAVID ROPER

Those who trust in God find comfort in His power.

Open Wide

PSALM 81

*I am the LORD your God, who brought you up out of Egypt.
Open wide your mouth and I will fill it.*

PSALM 81:10

As a boy, I was always thrilled to discover a newly constructed robin's nest. It was fascinating to watch for the eggs and then to wait for those featherless little creatures with bulging eyes and gaping mouths to break out of their shells. Standing at a distance, I could see their heads bobbing unsteadily and their mouths wide open, inviting mother robin to give them their dinner.

As I recall those childhood scenes, I think of God's promise: "I am the LORD your God . . . . Open wide your mouth and I will fill it" (Psalm 81:10). In spite of this gracious offer to Israel, the people ignored God, and He "gave them over to their stubborn hearts to follow their own devices" (v. 12). If they had accepted God's offer, they "would be fed with the finest of wheat; with honey from the rock" (v. 16).

God longs to give us spiritual food. And He will satisfy our spiritual hunger as we study His Word, worship with others, listen to faithful Bible teachers, read literature with good spiritual content, and daily depend on Him.

If we refuse God's provisions, we will suffer spiritual malnutrition and fail to grow. But if we open our mouth wide, be assured, God will fill it.

RICHARD DEHAAN

To have a fulfilled life, let God fill you.

Help the Children

PSALM 82

"Whoever welcomes one of these little children in my name welcomes me; and whoever welcomes me does not welcome me but the one who sent me."
MARK 9:37

"Eat your beans! There are children in this world who would give anything to have those!" What child hasn't heard that kind of speech coming from parents who love them enough to encourage good nutrition?

Actually, millions of children have never heard that line—children who wouldn't recognize a good meal if they saw one, who live on the streets instead of in a house, who'll never see the inside of a school.

According to one estimate, one hundred million children worldwide have no mom or dad to give them a meal nor do they have a place to call home. These kids are outcasts and treated as trash to be discarded.

This sobering fact should cause us to take a different approach. If we have the comforts that a good job and a modern society offer through God's graciousness, we should not cite examples of starving children as a way to get our kids to eat. We should try to help the starving children instead.

The hurting children of the world need two things: First, the gospel of Jesus, who told us that in helping them we would be doing His work (Mark 9:37). And second, they need the hope that comes from someone who cares enough to feed, clothe, and shelter them.

What can your family do to help the children?

DAVE BRANON

Give hope to a child—share the love of Christ.

Father to the Fatherless

PSALM 82:1–4

Defend the weak and the fatherless;
uphold the cause of the poor and the oppressed.
PSALM 82:3

It was one of the most touching displays of human compassion and love my family had ever seen. We watched with tears of joy as a network news program reported on the stunning rescue of children from an ill-equipped European orphanage.

Because the government of that beleaguered country was unable to care for these neglected children, they agreed to let American couples adopt them. Blind children. Malnourished children. Children who had been given up as worthless. Family after family—hundreds of them—put up with endless red tape, crossed the ocean, and welcomed these needy children into their hearts and homes.

That scene brought to mind the words of Psalm 68:5. David wrote, "A father to the fatherless, a defender of widows, is God in his holy dwelling." God cares for those who can't care for themselves. He helps orphaned children by means of people whose hearts are filled with compassion.

We who know Christ as our Savior know God as a loving Father. He has rescued us, so we can sympathize with the fatherless and oppressed of this world. We don't have to look far to find children who need loving care. Let's do what we can to point them to the heavenly Father.

DAVE BRANON

Because we are children of the heavenly Father,
we can show His love to the fatherless.

None So Blind

PSALM 82:3-4

"The King will reply, 'Truly I tell you, whatever you did for one of the least of these brothers and sisters of mine, you did for me.'"
MATTHEW 25:40

Singer Ray Stevens is generally given credit for writing the phrase "There is none so blind as he who will not see," a line from the song "Everything Is Beautiful." But preacher Matthew Henry used the phrase 250 years ago when commenting on the lyrics of another songwriter, Asaph.

Asaph's lyrics were not as upbeat Stevens'. His song was a rebuke to the Israelites for failing to fulfill their God-given purpose. God had chosen them to show the world how to live right and judge justly, but they were failing miserably. Instead of defending the weak and fatherless, they were defending the unjust and showing partiality to the wicked (Psalm 82:2–3).

In his commentary on Psalm 82, Henry wrote: "A gift in secret blinds their eyes. They know not because they will not understand. None so blind as those that will not see. They have baffled their own consciences, and so they walk on in darkness."

Jesus confirmed God's interest in the weak and helpless. He explained that whatever is done for the "least of these" is done for Him (see Matthew 25:34–40). And He chided His disciples for keeping children away from Him (Luke 18:16).

Those who have eyes that see what God sees find ways to help the helpless.

JULIE ACKERMAN LINK

A test of true Christian love:
Do you help those who can't help you in return?

Sunshine for Your Soul

PSALM 84

For the LORD God is a sun and shield; the LORD bestows favor and honor; no good thing does he withhold from those whose walk is blameless.

PSALM 84:11

Many people feel cheerful in fair weather, but they are depressed when skies are gray. The travel industry thrives on this fact by luring millions of people to brighter climates. There's nothing wrong with enjoying the sun and its many benefits. But if we rely on good weather to maintain our good cheer, the climate of our inner world will be as changeable as the weather.

This was my condition before I became a Christian while in my teens. Each morning I would check out the weather. If it was bright, I felt happy; if it was gloomy, so was I.

One night I realized I needed Jesus. Kneeling by my bed, I accepted His forgiveness for my sins and invited Him into my life. The next morning I forgot to check the weather! It simply didn't matter anymore. The "Sun of Righteousness" had risen in my heart (Malachi 4:2) and had replaced my fickle source of happiness with himself.

Since then, my personal world has known some dark times, but the Lord has been my constant "sun and shield" (Psalm 84:11). I still prefer sunny days, but I'm no longer a "sun-worshiper." Instead, I'm a worshiper of God's Son, who shines brightly within me—whatever the weather.

Which kind of worshiper are you?

JOANIE YODER

**Lasting happiness doesn't come from sunny days
but from the Son of God.**

More Than Results

PSALM 84

My soul yearns, even faints, for the courts of the LORD;
my heart and my flesh cry out for the living God.
PSALM 84:2

It was the eve of the US National Day of Prayer, and a Christian leader was being interviewed on national television. With a question that seemed devised to trip up his guest, the interviewer referred to the nation's worsening moral crisis and said, "Does that mean the Lord didn't listen to last year's prayer?"

"No," came the insightful reply. "God is sovereign, and you have to accept how He works and when He works." How true that is!

Many people think of prayer only in terms of asking and receiving. But it's more than results. It's about relationship. One of the most powerful reasons to pray is to maintain a strong relationship with God.

Prayer is conversation with Someone we love and with whom we want to stay close. It is communication with our heavenly Father. Notice how the writer of Psalm 84 longed to be near to God: "My heart and my flesh cry out for the living God" (v. 2). When we pray, we are enriched by the growing bond that develops between the Lord and us.

Prayer is complex. But we mustn't miss the great truth that when we as God's children draw near to Him in prayer He draws near to us (James 4:8). That's all the motivation we need to make every day a day of prayer.

DAVE BRANON

Praying is talking to our best friend.

He Can Be Trusted

PSALM 84

LORD Almighty, blessed is the one who trusts in you.
PSALM 84:12

I was sitting in my chair by the window, staring out through fir and spruce trees to the mountains beyond, lost in thought. I looked down and saw a young fox, staring up at my face. She was as still as a stone.

Days before, I had seen her at the edge of the woods, looking nervously over her shoulder at me. I went to the kitchen for an egg, and rolled it toward the place I had last seen her. Each day I put another egg on the lawn, and each day she ventured out of the trees just long enough to pick it up. Then she would dart back into the woods.

Now she had come on her own to my door to get an egg, convinced, I suppose, that I meant her no harm.

This incident reminded my wife of David's invitation: "Taste and see that the LORD is good" (Psalm 34:8). How do we start doing that? By taking in His Word. As we read and reflect on His compassion and lovingkindness, we learn that He can be trusted (84:12). We lose our dread of getting closer to Him. Our fear becomes a healthy respect and honor of Him.

You may at times distrust God, as the fox was wary of me at first. But give Him a chance to prove His love. Read about Jesus in the Gospels. Read the praises to God in the Psalms. Taste and see that He is good!

DAVID ROPER

No one is beyond the reach of God's love.

The Antidote for Pessimism

PSALM 85

The LORD will indeed give what is good,
and our land will yield its harvest.

PSALM 85:12

Just as the sun can be blotted out by an eclipse, so moods of pessimism and doubt can plunge us into spiritual darkness. At times our situation may seem so desperate that we think even God himself can't carry us through.

That was the gloomy attitude of Robert Cushman, who recorded his despair on the *Mayflower* in 1620. He wrote, "If we ever make a plantation in New England, God works a miracle! Especially considering how scant we shall be of victuals [vittles], and (worst of all) ununited amongst ourselves. If I should write you of all the things that foretell our ruin, I should overcharge my weak head and grieve your tender heart. Only this I pray you. Prepare for evil tidings of us every day. I see not in reason how we can escape. Pray for us instantly." In spite of Cushman's fears, God brought the pilgrims to their destination and enabled them to establish a home in the wilderness.

The author of Psalm 85 praised that same providence of God. He knew how the Lord had provided for Israel in the past (vv. 1–3). Now he called on God to deliver His repentant people from the present evil (vv. 4–7), and he confidently anticipated the answer to that prayer (vv. 8–13).

Let's not doubt God's all-sufficient enablement. He will carry us through life's darkest hours.

VERNON GROUNDS

When life gets you down, keep looking up!

God Is Great!

PSALM 86

For you are great and do marvelous deeds; you alone are God.
PSALM 86:10

"Only God is great." That was the solemn and unexpected declaration of Jean-Baptiste Massillon as he began his sermon at the funeral service of King Louis XIV.

The king, who liked to be referred to as Louis the Great, had ruled France from 1643 to 1715 with absolute power and incredible splendor. His funeral was held in a magnificent cathedral that was lit by a single candle alongside the ornate coffin. When it was time for Massillon to speak, he reached out and extinguished the flame. Then he broke the silence with the words, "Only God is great."

We recognize and admire some of our fellow mortals who are considered to be great thinkers, great scientists, great inventors, and great achievers in every field of endeavor. In many ways they tower above all of us ordinary people, but they still have the same needs we do. They experience aches and pains. They have troubled minds and hungry hearts. They cannot stave off death nor guarantee life beyond the grave.

Only God is truly great—great enough to meet all our needs, great enough to forgive all our sins, and great enough to carry us through the dark valley of death into eternity to be with Him forever. So we declare with the psalmist, "You are great, . . . you alone are God" (Psalm 86:10).

VERNON GROUNDS

In a world of empty superlatives, God is the greatest.

The Listening Prayer

PSALM 86:1–12

Teach me your way, LORD, that I may rely on your faithfulness;
give me an undivided heart, that I may fear your name.
PSALM 86:11

How do you feel when you talk with someone who isn't listening to you? It can happen with a friend who has his own plans for how a conversation should go. Or it can happen when the other person simply doesn't want to hear what you have to say.

Now think about this in regard to your prayer-life. Could it be that the way we talk to God is a one-sided conversation dominated by us? Notice the observation of William Barclay in *The Plain Man's Book of Prayers*: "Prayer is not a way of making use of God; prayer is a way of offering ourselves to God in order that He should be able to make use of us. It may be that one of our great faults in prayer is that we talk too much and listen too little. When prayer is at its highest, we wait in silence for God's voice to us."

We might call this "the listening prayer," and it's a practice we need to develop. We need to find a way to get alone with God in quiet, to speak to Him in earnest, taking time to listen to the urgings of the Spirit and the instruction of His Word. We must say, "Teach me your way, LORD, that I may rely on your faithfulness" (Psalm 86:11).

Are we talking so much that we don't hear what God says? If so, we need to learn the art of the listening prayer.

DAVE BRANON

God speaks through His Word—take time to listen.

Born Here!

PSALM 87:1–7

The LORD will write in the register of the peoples:
"This one was born in Zion."

PSALM 87:6

For many years, a popular bumper sticker in Colorado bore a single word—NATIVE. It proclaimed to every new arrival, "You just moved in, but I was born here. This is my state, my heritage, and I belong."

Our nationality, citizenship, and sense of belonging are usually determined by birth. This was especially true for the Israelites in Old Testament times. They were not only the people of Israel but also the people of God.

It may seem surprising, then, to read in Psalm 87 that people of rival Gentile nations will one day be treated as if they had been "born" in Zion (vv. 4–5). Herbert Lockyer says of this passage: "Whether some were born in Egypt or came from Ethiopia, all [will be] equally honored as home-born sons of the city of God. The proud from Egypt, the worldly from Babylon, the wrathful from Philistia, the covetous from Tyre [will be] brought under the regenerating, transforming power of the Spirit of God." That is, they will be spiritually reborn.

Through faith in Jesus, we too are born again (John 3:1–18). We are now citizens of "the city of the living God, the heavenly Jerusalem," and our names are "written in heaven" (Hebrews 12:22–23). Praise God! We have been born into His family with all of the accompanying privileges!

DAVID MCCASLAND

Jesus was born to die, so we could be born again.

When You Feel Like Heman

PSALM 88

If your law had not been my delight, I would have perished in my affliction.
PSALM 119:92

We can all relate to Heman. As we read Psalm 88, we quickly realize that things weren't going very well for him. Although he began by addressing the Lord as the One who could save him, he continued with seventeen verses of darkness.

Whenever we feel as Heman did, we too can be honest with God. As we do that, we need to remind ourselves of the truths of the Bible that can restore our hope. Perhaps we would benefit from a new outlook that would encourage us to:

- Turn our attention to God (Psalm 121:1–2). One of the ironies of trouble is that it can bring us closer to God—which is where we want to be anyway.
- Praise God for our salvation (Habakkuk 3:17–18; Ephesians 1:3–8). Let's remember what the Lord has done for us through Christ. His love is far greater than any difficulty we can face.
- Look for the truths that come out of affliction (James 1:2–4). A life of ease teaches less than a life of trouble and pain. We need to learn what God is trying to teach us through the struggles.
- Celebrate God's faithfulness (Psalm 119:89–92). Charles Spurgeon said, "We must be tried or we cannot magnify the faithful God, who will not leave His people."

Feeling like Heman? Talk to the Lord about it. Read and meditate on the Bible passages above and ask Him to renew your hope. Look for the ways God is faithful—even on the darkest days.

DAVE BRANON

When you feel hopeless, look to the God of hope.

On Loan from God

PSALM 89:5–12

Command those who are rich in this present world not to be arrogant nor to put their hope in wealth, which is so uncertain, but to put their hope in God, who richly provides us with everything for our enjoyment.

1 TIMOTHY 6:17

I am surrounded every day by things that don't belong to me, yet I call them mine. For instance, I refer to the computer I am using to write this article as "my Mac." I talk about "my office," "my desk," and "my phone." But none of this equipment belongs to me. It is all the property of Our Daily Bread Ministries. It's mine to use, but not mine to keep. When the ministry "gave" it to me, we both knew what that meant: It was on loan.

This kind of situation is not unique to employer-employee relationships. In reality, that's the way it is with all of us and all of the things we call our own. When we speak of our family, our house, or our car, we are speaking of people and things that God has allowed us to enjoy while here on earth, but they really belong to Him. Notice the psalmist's praise to God, "The heavens are yours, and yours also the earth" (89:11).

Understanding who really holds the title to all we possess should change our thinking. Just as I am aware that ODB Ministries lets me use its equipment to help me do my work here more efficiently and effectively, so also we should be aware that everything we have on earth is given to us to advance God's cause.

Our time, talents, and possessions are all given so that we can do God's work effectively.

DAVE BRANON

**Our worth is not determined by what we have
but by what we do with what we have.**

A Life-and-Death Issue

PSALM 90:1–10

Our days may come to seventy years, or eighty,
if our strength endures; yet the best of them are but trouble and sorrow,
for they quickly pass, and we fly away.
PSALM 90:10

By altering the gene that controls aging, scientists believe they can extend the average human lifespan to one hundred by the end of this century. This would be well beyond the proverbial seventy years mentioned in Psalm 90:10. But even if people do live longer, life's final chapter will still read, "they quickly pass" (v. 10).

Moses, who wrote Psalm 90, lived to be one hundred and twenty years old. He saw death as inevitable in a world cursed by the effects of sin. Yet he didn't become pessimistic. He asked God to teach him to number his days so he could gain "a heart of wisdom" (v. 12). He wanted to be satisfied with God's mercy so he could rejoice and be glad (v. 14). He also asked God to show His glory to the next generation (v. 16). That's how Moses faced the reality of death thousands of years ago.

Like all people since Adam and Eve, we suffer the effects of sin, and death is certain (Romans 6:23). Yet we can live with hope and joy, because God sent His Son to die for our sins. Jesus conquered death when He rose from the grave. And if we receive Him as our personal Savior and Lord, we too can experience God's forgiveness and look forward to being with Him in heaven forever. Have you faced and settled this life-and-death issue?

DENNIS DEHAAN

You're not ready to live until you're ready to die.

Time Flies

PSALM 90:10–17

Teach us to number our days, that we may gain a heart of wisdom.
PSALM 90:12

Many metaphors are used in literature to describe life's brevity. It is a dream, a swift runner, a mist, a puff of smoke, a shadow, a gesture in the air, a sentence written in the sand, a bird flying in one window of a house and out another. Another symbolic description was suggested by a friend of mine who said that the short dash between the dates of birth and death on tombstones represents the brief span of one's life.

When we were children, time loitered. But as we get closer to the end of our lives, time moves with increasing swiftness, like water swirling down a drain. In childhood we measured our age in small increments. "I'm 6 1/2," we would say, for it seemed to take so long to get older. Now we have no time for such childishness. Who claims to be 60 1/2?

It's good to ponder the brevity of life now and then. Life is too short to treat it carelessly. In Psalm 90, after describing the shortness of life, Moses prayed, "Teach us to number our days, that we may gain a heart of wisdom" (v. 12).

To make the most of our earthly existence, we must lose ourselves in the will of God (1 Peter 4:2). This we can do even when time is running out. It's never too late to give ourselves totally to God.

DAVID ROPER

Don't just count your days; make your days count.

Where Are We Going So Fast?

PSALM 90:1-12

My days are swifter than a weaver's shuttle,
and they come to an end without hope.

JOB 7:6

Scientific measurements indicate that we are moving even when we are standing still. Continental landmasses sit on enormous slabs of rock that slide very slowly at the rate of one to eight inches per year. America is gradually moving westward, away from Europe, at the rate of three inches per year.

If that doesn't blow your hair back, consider this. Our Milky Way galaxy is hurtling through space at 375 miles per second or 1.3 million miles per hour. But that's not all. Within our own galaxy the sun and its solar system are zooming along at 12.4 miles per second (43,000 mph) in the direction of the star Vega in the constellation Lyra.

A man lying on his back in a quiet park on a cloudless day may feel as though all time and movement have stopped under the hot rays of a noonday sun. But the scientist and the godly person know otherwise. Just as we are hurtling through the heavens at unimaginable speeds, so too we are moving from here to eternity. Our days and opportunities to live for the Lord pass so rapidly that we cannot afford to waste time.

Teach us to number our days, Lord. Help us to live without desperation or futility as we travel so quickly from our home to yours.

MART DEHAAN

How you spend time determines how you spend eternity.

The Right Focus

PSALM 90

*Satisfy us . . . with your unfailing love,
that we may sing for joy and be glad all our days.*
PSALM 90:14

We call life's older years the "sunset years." But are they really that rosy? For some, they are. But for many others, even Christians, the sunset years may become clouded with bitterness or despair.

To minimize this, we must make it our goal early in life to get the right focus. Robert Kastenbaum understood this. He wrote, "I do feel an increased sense of responsibility to this future self and to all those who cross my path. What kind of old man will I be, given the chance? The answer to that question depends largely on the kind of person I am right now."

As I have observed contented older people, I've learned that it is our focus more than our feelings that determines the sort of people we are. I once visited a godly woman in her nineties who was feeling her age in every joint and organ. "Old age ain't for sissies!" she groaned honestly. Then, as always, her groans gave way to praise for God's goodness. A focus of gratitude, begun early in life, parted the clouds and let the sun shine through.

What is your focus today, regardless of your feelings? Is it one of gratitude for Jesus and His gift of eternal life? If so, you'll grow sweeter as you grow older.

JOANIE YODER

**What you will be tomorrow depends on
the choices you make today.**

Holding on for Life

PSALM 91

*I will say of the LORD, "He is my refuge
and my fortress, my God, in whom I trust."*
PSALM 91:2

Try to remember a time when you were in a frightening situation. It could have been a near-miss in your automobile or footsteps behind you as you walked down a dangerous street. Possibly you had to face an angry employer. What about the time you were asked to give an oral report before an audience? In all those situations, did you long to have someone close by to give you support and encouragement?

I remember taking my family to the beach on a summer's day when the waves were quite big. My little daughter Katie wanted to go swimming, but she was afraid of those huge breakers. Only after she realized that they didn't move me and that she was secure as long as she held onto me tightly, could she enjoy the water and the splashing of those waves. She had someone she could depend on for support.

Psalm 91 describes many frightening situations in which we need the assistance of someone stronger than we are. The psalmist told us that when troubles assailed him from all angles, he went to One who was as strong and unmovable as a fortress. He clung to God for his very survival, for he had learned that when troubles created waves in his life, he could find security and help in Him.

Are you encountering frightening and unnerving situations? Cling to your refuge and fortress, the Almighty God. He's the only one to hold onto—for life.

KURT DEHAAN

When troubles call on you, call on God.

Dial 91:1

PSALM 91

Whoever dwells in the shelter of the Most High
will rest in the shadow of the Almighty.
PSALM 91:1

Most people know that dialing the numbers 9-1-1 in the United States will get them in touch with emergency help. It's so simple that even preschoolers have saved the lives of family members by using it. Three numbers do it all.

In one case, a woman's car had been hijacked with her and her infant son inside. She dialed 9-1-1 on her cellular phone, but the hijacker was totally unaware of what she had done. With the police dispatcher listening, the young mother cleverly included clues about her location as she talked to the hijacker. Police were able to locate her and her baby and arrest the criminal.

In an emergency, help is as close as three pushes on the phone keypad. Often, though, the situations we face cannot be remedied by human rescuers. Many times our crisis requires divine assistance. When that happens, we can call a different kind of 9-1-1—Psalm 91:1. There we find the help and protection of our Almighty God. This verse reminds us that God is our "shelter" and that we can rest in His shadow.

When we face the crises of life, we often try to survive on our own. We forget that what we need most, God's protection and the comfort of His presence, are available for the asking. The next time spiritual danger strikes, dial Psalm 91:1.

DAVE BRANON

We need not fear life's dark shadows when we
abide under the shadow of God's wings.

Secret Security

PSALM 91

*For he will command his angels concerning you
to guard you in all your ways.*

PSALM 91:11

Feeling secure is a high priority in this unsafe, volatile world. A private investigation agency in Florida promises to "work diligently to restore the sense of security and safety that you and your family deserve."

The psalmist found a "secret place," where he felt safe (Psalm 91:1). And we can rest secure in that same place. He described it with these phrases:

"In the shadow of the Almighty" (v. 1). Shadows provide protection from the direct heat of the sun. If the heat is severe, the shade reduces what we actually feel. When we're under God's shadow, we do not face the full heat of our difficulties.

"My refuge and my fortress" (v. 2). God is the strongest protector we could ever have, and we can run to Him for help. Nothing can penetrate Him to get to us unless it's part of His loving plan for our ultimate good.

"Under his wings" (v. 4). God is soft and tender like a caring mother bird. When troubles rage, He draws us close. We don't need to fear that He will cast us out—we are His.

"Your dwelling" (v. 9). Our Father will be our home, our abiding place—now and forever.

True security can be found only in our Lord, who promises to save us and be near us (vv. 15–16).

ANNE CETAS

No one is more secure than those who are in God's hands.

Give Thanks

PSALM 92

It is good to praise the LORD
and make music to your name, O Most High.

PSALM 92:1

A minister wrote that the author of Psalm 92 was a selfish person because he thanked God for judging his enemies. This same preacher also said that people who gather in their comfortable homes and thank God for their abundance while so many people are homeless and hungry are "selfish hypocrites."

But is this true? As we read Psalm 92, we discover that the psalmist was thanking God for being the kind of God He is—One who deals justly with the wicked (vv. 7–11) and who abundantly blesses the righteous (vv. 12–15). He was not praying selfishly, as that minister charged.

We need not feel guilty for enjoying the blessings of health, freedom, food, shelter, and salvation. We should be thankful. But we should also be concerned about those who are less fortunate—the ill, the oppressed, the hungry, the homeless, and the unsaved. We should desire good things for them. We should pray regularly for them and give our time and money to help them.

If we are truly thankful for what God has given us, we will be more generous with others. Gratitude, contrary to that minister's criticism, actually leads to unselfishness.

Yes, it is good to give thanks to the Lord.

HERB VANDER LUGT

Gratitude to God generates generosity.

Keep Going for God!

PSALM 92

They will still bear fruit in old age, they will stay fresh and green.
PSALM 92:14

A familiar saying goes something like this: "Old age is a matter of mind over matter. If you don't mind, it doesn't matter!"

That must have been John Kelley's attitude. Kelley, who died in 2004 at the age of ninety-six, ran in fifty-eight Boston Marathons (that's 26.2 miles each time)—including his last one in 1992 when he was eighty-four years old.

Kelley's remarkable feat is a reminder to each of us that we must stay active as long as we can. Far too many folks hit middle age and put the body in neutral. And Christians too often put their service for Jesus Christ in the same inactive mode.

Each of us has a responsibility to God, as long as He gives us physical and mental strength, to work heartily "as working for the Lord" (Colossians 3:23). We are never called to retire from life and coast home to heaven.

The psalmist said that the righteous "will still bear fruit in old age" (Psalm 92:14). For those who are physically able, that means continuing in active service. For those who can no longer move about, that means being active in prayer and in quiet service.

Let's make sure old age doesn't stop us from bearing fruit. We need to keep going for God.

DAVE BRANON

To stay youthful, stay useful.

Divine Mystery

PSALM 93

*The LORD reigns, he is robed in majesty; the LORD is robed in majesty
and armed with strength; indeed, the world is established, firm and secure.
Your throne was established long ago; you are from all eternity.*

PSALM 93:1–2

At one point along the Saguenay River in southeastern Canada, the water flows through a chasm between two rugged rock formations. Their pinnacles tower over 1,600 feet into the sky. Early pioneers were so awestruck by these majestic crags that they named them Trinity and Eternity.

The two great truths expressed by these words create a sense of awe in the heart of every Christian. The Bible tells us of God's eternity—His timeless existence (Psalm 93:2), and His triune nature—the threefold expression of himself as God the Father, God the Son, and God the Holy Spirit (Matthew 28:19).

Both of these affirmations baffle our minds. If we try to comprehend either of them, the question asked by Job's friend comes to mind: "Can you probe the limits of the Almighty?" (Job 11:7). The answer is obvious. When we try to behold the triune God, we feel like someone who gazes up into the midday sun to study it.

At the heart of the Christian faith is mystery, because at the heart of our faith is the eternal, triune God. We have the Father who loves us, the Savior who died for us, and the Spirit who helps us to be holy. This divine mystery gives us reason to bow down and worship our eternal God.

HADDON ROBINSON

**To understand God is impossible;
to worship Him is imperative.**

Angry Floods

PSALM 93

*The seas have lifted up, LORD, the seas have lifted up their voice;
the seas have lifted up their pounding waves.*

PSALM 93:3

Trouble comes our way, according to Psalm 93, in relentless waves that surge and pound against our souls and break upon them with furious force. "The seas have lifted up, LORD, the seas have lifted up their voice," and they are deafening (v. 3).

Yet above the tempest we hear the psalmist's refrain: "Mightier than the thunder of the great waters, mightier than the breakers of the sea—the LORD on high is mighty" (v. 4).

Indeed, "the LORD reigns" (v. 1). He is clothed with majesty and strength. He sits as King, exalted higher than the waves that rise above us, deeper than their immeasurable depths, greater than their strongest surge. The storm is in His all-powerful hands: "The world is established, firm and secure," for His rule over it was established long ago (v. 1). He rules the raging of the sea; the "wind and the waves obey Him" (Mark 4:37–41). He speaks and they are still.

The storm will not last forever. Yet, while it rages, you can cling to the Lord's promises of love and faithfulness, for His "statutes . . . stand firm" (Psalm 93:5). Waves of trouble and grief may sweep over you, but you will not be swept away. He "is able to keep you from stumbling" (Jude 24). Our Father in heaven is holding your hand.

DAVID ROPER

**When adversity is ready to strike us,
then God is most ready to strengthen us.**

What Do You Think?

PSALM 94:1–11

But the things that come out of a person's mouth
come from the heart, and these defile them.

MATTHEW 15:18

How would you like to have your every thought for the past six months flashed on a screen for all your acquaintances, neighbors, and church friends to see? You would probably want to leave town! It is sobering to realize that even though we can hide our thoughts from others, God knows what we're thinking (Psalm 94:11).

We need to give careful attention to our thoughts not only because God knows them but also because our thoughts determine our character. Jesus said that our words and actions spring from our heart (Matthew 15:18–19).

While visiting Mammoth Cave in Kentucky, one can see enormous pillars that have been formed by the steady dropping of water. A single drop finds its way from the surface down through the ceiling of the cavern to deposit its minute sediment on the floor of the cave. Another drop follows it, and still another, until the "icicle of stone" forms a pillar of rock.

A similar process is going on in each of our hearts. Every thought that sinks into the soul makes its contribution, producing the pillars in our character. The ideas you hold in your mind help to form the facets of your personality that make up the real "you."

So, how is your thought-life?

HENRY BOSCH

Pure thinking builds godly character.

The True Owner

PSALM 95:1–7

All things have been created through him and for him.
COLOSSIANS 1:16

Did you hear about the church that didn't have enough room for parking? Fortunately, it was located right next to a store that was closed on Sundays, so a church member asked the store owner if they could overflow into his parking lot. "No problem," he said. "You can use it fifty-one weeks out of the year. On the fifty-second week, though, it will be chained off." The man was grateful, but asked curiously, "What happens that week?" The store owner smiled, "Nothing. I just want you to remember that it's not your parking lot."

It's easy to take for granted all the material and spiritual blessings that God has given us. That's why we need to stop and remember that Scripture says the true owner of all we possess is God: "Everything in heaven and earth is yours. Yours, LORD, is the kingdom; you are exalted as head over all" (1 Chronicles 29:11). Even our bodies do not belong to us: "Do you not know that your bodies are temples of the Holy Spirit . . . ? You are not your own; you were bought at a price" (1 Corinthians 6:19–20).

In 1 Timothy 6:17, Paul reminds us: "God . . . richly provides us with everything for our enjoyment." We are so abundantly blessed with good things! Let's never take our heavenly Father for granted, but use wisely and gratefully all that He has given us.

CINDY HESS KASPER

God gives blessing to us so we can give glory to Him.

Daytona Rogue

PSALM 95

Come, let us bow down in worship,
let us kneel before the LORD our Maker.
PSALM 95:6

People who lived in Daytona Beach, Florida, on July 3, 1992, saw an amazing phenomenon on their Atlantic Ocean shoreline. On that day a rogue wave twenty-seven miles long, eighteen feet high, and two hundred fifty feet wide suddenly rose out of a calm sea and crashed ashore. Apparently triggered by an undersea landslide, the huge wave piled sailboats on top of vehicles along a popular road along the Florida beach.

This bizarre Daytona moment is a snapshot of life. There is no escape from the unexpected. There is no way to foresee the unpredictable. Everywhere we turn there are potential calamities. Yet worrying about such things won't give us a shred of security.

The psalmist found the answer to living joyfully in an uncertain world. Because he understood the heart of a shepherd, he found security in remembering that God's people are the sheep of His pasture (Psalm 95:7). The mountains, valleys, seas, and dry ground are in His hand (vv. 4–5). Every hill and wave come under His careful attention.

Unpredictability seems like a reason for anxiety. But the psalmist didn't have time to worry about what might happen. Instead, he made the choice to praise his Maker, who never loses control. We can make the same choice.

MART DEHAAN

Even though you can't control your circumstances,
you can control your attitude.

Knowing God

PSALM 96

Let the one who boasts boast about this: that they have the understanding to know me, that I am the LORD, who exercises kindness, justice and righteousness on earth, for in these I delight," declares the LORD.

JEREMIAH 9:24

It is one thing to know about God, but it is quite another to know Him by personal experience. We can repeat a formal statement about Him without sensing His nearness in our everyday round of activities. Let's see how this distinction applies when considering some of God's attributes.

- The thought that God is present everywhere is staggering. But to be actually aware of His presence brings comfort and hope in times of need.
- The thought that God knows everything is mind-boggling. But to trust Him completely, having the confidence that no detail of our situation escapes His attention, is to enjoy a peace that endures through every trial.
- The thought that God is all-powerful makes us marvel at His greatness. But to have Him, who "is able to do immeasurably more than all we ask or imagine" (Ephesians 3:20) actually work in, through, and for us encourages us to relax in His mighty arms.
- The thought that God is love is most wonderful to contemplate. But to know Him as a loving Redeemer through the provision of His own love-gift, Jesus Christ, brings the joy of sins forgiven and the sure hope of spending eternity in heaven.

The writer of Psalm 96 knew God. And for us, it all begins by receiving Christ, whom to know is life eternal.

RICHARD DEHAAN

Life's greatest tragedy is to lose the sense of God's presence and not miss it.

How to Pray

PSALM 96:1–9

In the same way, the Spirit helps us in our weakness.
We do not know what we ought to pray for, but the Spirit himself
intercedes for us through wordless groans.

ROMANS 8:26

Prayer is one of the most important spiritual exercises for a believer. Jesus, the Son of God and Lord of all things, spent whole nights in prayer while He lived on earth.

In those night-long encounters, Jesus communed with His Father. His prayers were not just petitions to get something. Too often we think of prayer as a way to get God to do things for us or for others, but the highest purpose of prayer is to deepen our relationship with Him.

Prayer does involve petition and intercession, but it also includes communion. In petition God does something *for* us, in intercession He does something *through* us, and in communion He does something *in* us.

When we pray, how much of our time is spent communing with the Lord? Our prayers will become less self-centered and more God-centered as we draw closer to Him, seek His glory, and subordinate our petitions to His will. Communion is the line that connects our soul with the battery of God's power. When this line is down, our petitions are but idle chatter. God's power must flow into our lives as we bow before Him and recognize Him as Lord of all. Communion with God is a great privilege and the most important element of prayer.

M. R. DeHaan

Adoration of God should come before asking of God.

God in the Thunderstorm

PSALM 97:1–6

Clouds and thick darkness surround him;
righteousness and justice are the foundation of his throne. . . .
His lightning lights up the world; the earth sees and trembles.

PSALM 97:2, 4

It had been a long Michigan winter and my three-year-old granddaughter had forgotten all about thunderstorms. So she was frightened one spring afternoon when the sky grew dark, lightning flashed, thunder began to roll, and rain came pouring down. She climbed onto her dad's lap. He reassured her that God knows all about thunderstorms, and then he used the occasion to tell her about God's awesome power.

Psalm 97:1–6 also uses the imagery of a thunderstorm to illustrate the mighty works of the Lord. The writer paints a scene of rolling clouds, jagged forks of lightning, and rumbling thunder to describe God's power. The thick, dark clouds that hide the sun remind me that man cannot stand the full view of God's glory (v. 2). In the lightning I see a picture of God's fiery wrath on His foes (vv. 3–4). In all of these forces of nature I see the glory of God (v. 6).

We've all witnessed the power of a thunderstorm. And sometimes we are afraid. But each storm that rolls across the sky can bring to mind great truths: God is awesome in power, He judges His foes, and His glory fills the earth.

So, when the next storm comes, join the psalmist in praising God for His wondrous power and majesty. See God in the thunderstorm.

DAVID EGNER

When we trust God, His power is not a danger but a comfort.

For Him

PSALM 98

I will sacrifice a thank offering to you and call on the name of the LORD.
PSALM 116:17

A seventeen-year-old girl and her male co-worker at a department store were meeting for lunch. He had some questions about life, and she was glad to talk to him about her faith. As they sat down with their tacos, the girl bowed her head to thank the Lord for her food. When she looked up, her co-worker said, "I didn't pray. Will God kill me for that?"

His response reveals much about how people view God. Many think our Godward actions—prayer, singing, worship, reading Scripture—are done as safety devices to prevent the Lord from zapping us. When we think of Him that way, we will have wrong motives for any God-directed action. That kind of thinking leads us to pray and worship God for personal gain or approval.

Our worship of the Lord is not done so we can somehow benefit. Instead, every heavenward thought or action should be done out of honor for Him and His greatness. Our hearts and voices should be filled with the kind of praise expressed in Psalm 98. Our expressions of thanksgiving are a sacrifice to Him (Psalm 116:17).

Sure, we benefit when we turn our attention to God, but that should not be our motivation. It's not for us that we worship God. It should always be for Him.

DAVE BRANON

**We don't worship God to gain His benefits—
we already have them.**

Worship Worthy

PSALM 99

Exalt the LORD our God and worship at his footstool; he is holy.
PSALM 99:5

In Exodus we read that as Moses was tending his father-in-law's sheep in the desert, his attention was drawn to a strange sight. A bush burned without being consumed. When Moses turned to look more closely at this phenomenon, God said to him, "Take off your sandals, for the place you are standing is holy ground" (Exodus 3:5). Joshua had a similar experience when he approached the captain of the host of the Lord. As Joshua drew nearer, he was given this command: "Take off your sandals, for the place where you are standing is holy" (Joshua 5:15).

The experiences of Moses and Joshua vividly teach us that a holy God demands our reverence and respect. True, we are encouraged to "approach God's throne of grace with confidence" (Hebrews 4:16), and we can enter the presence of God with boldness because Christ has opened the way for us through His substitutionary death on the cross. But never are we to approach God with disrespect. Never are we to profane His name. Our heavenly Father is not "the man upstairs." He is God, the One who is high and lifted up. And because of His majesty and holiness, we are to exalt and worship Him. As the one true God, He is worthy of our adoration. He deserves our highest praise.

Let us therefore enter His presence with reverence.

Let us worship Him with gratitude and exaltation. God not only desires our devotion but He also deserves it. He is worthy of our heartfelt worship.

RICHARD DeHAAN

True worship acknowledges the true worthship of God.

Make a Joyful Shout

PSALM 100

Shout for joy to the LORD, all the earth.

PSALM 100:1

Duke University's basketball fans are known as "Cameron Crazies." When Duke plays archrival North Carolina, the Crazies are given these instructions: "This is the game you've been waiting for. No excuses. Give everything you've got. Cameron [Indoor Stadium] should never be less than painfully loud tonight." Clearly, Duke fans take allegiance seriously.

The songwriter of Psalm 100 took his allegiance to the Lord seriously and wanted others to do the same. "Shout for joy to the LORD!" he exclaimed (v. 1). His people were to freely express their praise to Him because He was the covenant God of Israel—the God over all other so-called gods. They were called to focus all their energies on Him and His goodness.

God's goodness and grace should motivate us to freely express our love and allegiance to Him with shouts of joy. This may mean that those who are more reserved must push back the boundaries of restraint and learn what it means to be expressive in their praise to God. Those who are so expressive that they miss the beauty of silence may need to learn from those whose style is more reflective.

Worship is a time to focus on our Creator, Redeemer, and Shepherd, and celebrate what He has done.

MARVIN WILLIAMS

Our thoughts about God should lead us to joyful praise.

Serve Joyfully

PSALM 100

Worship the LORD with gladness; come before him with joyful songs.
PSALM 100:2

When I walked into the gift shop, I was greeted with a cheery "Good afternoon!" The young salesperson chattered brightly as she pointed out the shop's unique products, shared my observations about the weather, helped me choose a gift, and neatly wrapped my purchase.

"You must really enjoy what you're doing," I said. "Actually, I hate it," she replied. "I'm only doing this because I have to. I can't wait till six o'clock comes so I can join my friends on the beach!"

As I walked away, I reflected on this young woman's behavior. She had given me the impression that she enjoyed her work. In reality, however, she was merely putting in time.

I began to ask myself if I live like that. Do I greet people with a bright smile and pretend that I am serving God enthusiastically, even though there is no joy in my heart? Some of us are masters at wearing a mask of joy when we are actually serving the Lord grudgingly out of a sense of duty.

The Bible tells us to do everything "with all your heart, as working for the Lord" (Colossians 3:23), and to serve Him "with gladness" (Psalm 100:2). If there is no joy in our lives, let's ask Him to search our hearts, to forgive our sin, and to restore our joy (51:12).

DAVID EGNER

Duty can be drudgery, but duty with love for God is delight.

Gates of Worship

PSALM 100

Enter his gates with thanksgiving and his courts with praise;
give thanks to him and praise his name.

PSALM 100:4

When you visit some of the greatest cities in the world, you can encounter famous gates such as the Brandenburg Gate (Berlin), the Jaffa Gate (Jerusalem), and the gates at Downing Street (London). Whether the gates were built for defensive or ceremonial purposes, they all represent the difference between being outside or inside certain areas of the city. Some are open; some are closed to all but a few.

The gates into the presence of God are always open. The familiar song of Psalm 100 is an invitation for the Israelites to enter into the presence of God through the temple gates. They were told to "shout for joy" and "come before him with joyful songs" (vv. 1–2). Shouting for joy was an appropriate expression when greeting a monarch in the ancient world. All the earth was to sing joyfully about God! The reason for this joyful noise was that God had given them their identity (v. 3). They entered the gates with praise and thanksgiving because of God's goodness and His steadfast and enduring love, which continues through all generations (vv. 4–5). Even when they forgot their identity and wandered away from Him, God remained faithful and still invited them to enter His presence.

The gates into God's presence are still open, inviting us to come and worship.

MARVIN WILLIAMS

The gates into the presence of God are always open.

The Gallery of God

PSALM 100

The LORD is good and his love endures forever.
PSALM 100:5

Psalm 100 is like a work of art that helps us celebrate our unseen God. While the focus of our worship is beyond view, His people make Him known.

Imagine the artist with brush and palette working the colorful words of this psalm onto a canvas. What emerges before our eyes is a world—"all the earth"—shouting for joy to the Lord (v. 1). Joy—because it is the delight of our God to redeem us from death. "For the joy that was set before Him," Jesus endured the cross (Hebrews 12:2 NKJV).

As our eyes move across the canvas we see an all-world choir of countless members singing "with gladness" and "joyful songs" (Psalm 100:2). Our heavenly Father's heart is pleased when His people worship Him for who He is and what He has done.

Then we see images of ourselves, fashioned from dust in the hands of our Creator and led like sheep into green pasture (v. 3). We, His people, have a loving Shepherd.

Finally, we see God's great and glorious dwelling place—and the gates through which His rescued people enter His unseen presence while giving Him thanks and praise (v. 4).

What a picture, inspired by our God. Our good, loving, and faithful God. No wonder it will take forever to enjoy His greatness!

DAVE BRANON

Nothing is more awesome than to know God.

Just Because He's Good

PSALM 100

Give thanks to the LORD, for he is good!
PSALM 136:1

Joel and Lauren decided to move from Washington State back home to Michigan. Wanting to make one last special memory, they bought coffee from their favorite cafe and then stopped at their favorite bookstore. There they picked up two bumper stickers with a favorite motto of the town they were saying goodbye to: "It's an Edmonds kind of day."

After two weeks and a three thousand mile drive, they entered Michigan. Hungry and wanting to celebrate their arrival, they stopped and asked about where to find a restaurant. Although they had to backtrack a few miles, they found a quaint little cafe. Emma, their waitress, excited to learn they were from her home state of Washington, asked, "What city?" "Edmonds," they replied. "That's where I'm from!" she said. Wanting to share the joy, Joel got their extra bumper sticker from the car and handed it to her. Amazingly, the sticker was from her mother's store! It had gone from her mom's hands to theirs, across 3,000 miles, to her hands.

Mere coincidence? Or were these experiences good gifts orchestrated by a good God who loves to encourage His children? Proverbs tells us, "A person's steps are directed by the LORD" (20:24). In response, let's "praise his name. For the LORD is good" (Psalm 100:4–5).

ANNE CETAS

Every good gift comes from the Father.

What Do You Hate?

PSALM 101

Let those who love the LORD hate evil, for he guards the lives of his faithful ones and delivers them from the hand of the wicked.

PSALM 97:10

Nineteenth-century pastor Henry Ward Beecher told of a mother in the wild frontier country who was washing clothes beside a stream. Her only child was playing nearby. Suddenly she realized he was gone. She called his name, but there was no answer. Alarmed, the mother ran to the house, but her son was not there.

Frantically, the woman dashed out to the forest. There she found the child, but it was too late. The youngster had been killed by a wolf. Heartbroken, she picked up his lifeless body, drew him close to her heart, and tenderly carried him home. Beecher concluded, "Oh, how that mother hated wolves!"

Every Christian should have a similar hatred for evil (Psalm 101:3–8). Yet many mothers and fathers who are so careful to guard their youngsters from physical harm don't notice the evil forces that threaten their spiritual welfare. As a result, they leave them unprotected. They show little concern for the kinds of friends their children make, the computer activities they are a part of, or the entertainment media they watch. But whenever these influences are bad, they should be seen as a deadly threat, and we should protect our children from them.

It's not wrong to hate when we hate what is wrong.

RICHARD DeHAAN

If we do not hate evil, we cannot love good.

Integrity 101

PSALM 101

I will be careful to lead a blameless life—when will you come to me?
I will conduct the affairs of my house with a blameless heart.

PSALM 101:2

A few years ago, officials in Philadelphia were astonished to receive a letter and payment from a motorist who had been given a speeding ticket in 1954. John Gedge, an English tourist, had been visiting the City of Brotherly Love in the mid-1950s when he was cited for speeding. The penalty was $15, but Gedge forgot about the ticket for more than fifty years—until he discovered it in an old coat. "I thought, I've got to pay it," said the eighty-four-year-old Brit, who lived in a nursing home in East Sussex. "Englishmen pay their debts. My conscience is clear."

This story reminded me of the psalmist David's commitment to integrity. Although he made some terrible choices in his life, Psalm 101 declares his resolve to live blamelessly. His integrity would begin in the privacy of his own house (v. 2) and extend to his choice of colleagues and friends (vv. 6–7). In sharp contrast to the corrupt lives of most kings of the ancient Near East, David's integrity led him to respect the life of his sworn enemy, King Saul (1 Samuel 24:4–6; 26:8–9).

As followers of Jesus, we are called to walk in integrity and to maintain a clear conscience. When we honor our commitments to God and to others, we will walk in fellowship with God. Our integrity will guide us (Proverbs 11:3) and help us walk securely (10:9).

MARVIN WILLIAMS

There is no better test of a person's integrity
than his behavior when he is wrong.

Five-Minute Rule

PSALM 102:1–17

He will respond to the prayer of the destitute;
he will not despise their plea.

PSALM 102:17

I read about a five-minute rule a mother had for her children. They had to be ready for school and gather together five minutes before it was time to leave each day.

They would gather around Mom, and she would pray for each one by name, asking for the Lord's blessing on their day. Then she'd give them a kiss, and off they'd go. Even neighborhood kids would be included in the prayer circle if they happened to stop by. One of the children said many years later that she learned from this experience how crucial prayer is to her day.

The writer of Psalm 102 knew the importance of prayer. This psalm is labeled, "A prayer of an afflicted person who has grown weak and pours out a lament before the LORD." The psalmist cried out, "Hear my prayer, LORD . . . ; when I call, answer me quickly" (vv. 1–2). God looks down "from his sanctuary on high, from heaven [he views] the earth" (v. 19).

God cares for you and wants to hear from you. Whether you follow the five-minute rule asking for blessings on the day or you need to spend more time crying out to Him in deep distress, talk to the Lord each day. Your example may have a big impact on your family or someone close to you.

ANNE CETAS

Prayer is an acknowledgment of our need for God.

Temporary or Eternal?

PSALM 102:24–27

So we fix our eyes not on what is seen, but on what is unseen,
since what is seen is temporary, but what is unseen is eternal.
2 CORINTHIANS 4:18

The Seven Wonders of the Ancient World were wonderful indeed! These impressive creations of human genius include the Tomb of Mausolos, built in 350 BC; the Temple of Artemis at Ephesus; the Hanging Gardens of Babylon; King Ptolemy's lighthouse near Alexandria; the one-hundred-foot statue of Apollo called the Colossus of Rhodes; the forty-foot statue of Zeus in the city of Olympia; and the great pyramids of Egypt.

Six of these remarkable achievements have been destroyed—Ptolemy's lighthouse by an earthquake, and the other five demolished by plunderers. Only the pyramids remain to fill us with awe.

We may marvel over these Seven Wonders, but we must never forget that everything in our world is temporary. I remember looking at the skyline of New York City from the stern of a ferryboat and recalling the lines of a hymn: "These all shall perish, stone on stone; but not Thy kingdom nor Thy throne."

The writer of Hebrews said, "Since we are receiving a kingdom that cannot be shaken, let us . . . worship God acceptably with reverence and awe" (12:28). These words and the words of Psalm 102 help us to keep the temporary and the eternal in perspective.

VERNON GROUNDS

Hold tightly to what is eternal and loosely to what is temporal.

Whoppers or Adventures?

PSALM 102:18–28

But you remain the same, and your years will never end.
PSALM 102:27

My grandfather loved to tell stories, and I loved to listen. Papaw had two kinds of tales. "Whoppers" were stories with a whiff of truth, but they changed with each new telling. "Adventures" were stories that really happened, and the facts never changed when retold. One day my grandfather told a story that just seemed too far-fetched to be true. "Whopper," I declared, but my grandfather insisted it was true. Although his telling never varied, I simply couldn't believe it; it was that unusual.

Then one day, while I was listening to a radio program, I heard the announcer tell a story that confirmed the truth of my grandfather's tale. My grandfather's "whopper" suddenly became an "adventure." It was a moving moment of remembrance that made him even more trustworthy in my eyes.

When the psalmist wrote about the unchanging nature of God (102:27), he was offering this same comfort—the trustworthiness of God—to us. The idea is repeated in Hebrews 13:8 with these words, "Jesus Christ is the same yesterday and today and forever." This can lift our hearts above our daily trials to remind us that an unchanging, trustworthy God rules over even the chaos of a changing world.

RANDY KILGORE

Let the sameness of God waft over your heart
with His peace in your storms.

Gratitude Is Contagious

PSALM 103

Praise the LORD, my soul; all my inmost being, praise his holy name.
PSALM 103:1

Although forgetfulness sometimes increases with age, it's really common to us all. Even children have lapses of memory and excuse themselves by saying, "I forgot!" But there's one kind of forgetfulness that is inexcusable at any age—forgetting to be grateful to God. The psalmist David was determined not to fail the Lord in this way, so he exhorted his own soul: "Forget not all his benefits" (Psalm 103:2).

David didn't keep his thanksgiving to God a secret. In Psalm 34:2 he wrote, "Let the afflicted hear and rejoice." And who were the "afflicted"? They were those who, like David, were going through tough times. Why would they be glad to hear his praises? Because their own faith was strengthened when he testified about God's help to him in times of fear (v. 4), trouble (v. 6), need (v. 10), sorrow (v. 18), or affliction (v. 19).

When was the last time you openly and unashamedly praised God for helping you in your difficulties? Someone has said, "If Christians praised God more, the world would doubt Him less." Not only is it appropriate, therefore, to express your gratitude for all His benefits, but your example may also encourage others to move from doubt to faith as you praise Him.

JOANIE YODER

An attitude of gratitude can make your life a beatitude.

Stop and Look Back

PSALM 103:1–5

Praise the LORD, my soul, and forget not all his benefits.
PSALM 103:2

Have you ever driven up the side of a mountain and then stopped to look back? I remember a winding road that zigzagged up one peak in the Great Smoky Mountains. At times, the fog was thick and the driving was treacherous. When we reached the top, we looked down over the side. There, winding below us, was the wearisome stretch over which we had come. Everything was clearly discernible, even the fog bank through which we had inched our way. What a sight!

Sometimes we as Christians need to stop along life's road and look back. Although the way might have been winding and steep, we can see how God directed us by His faithfulness. Here's how Bible scholar F. E. Marsh (1858–1919) described what the Christian can see when he looks back:

The deliverances the Lord has wrought (Deuteronomy 5:15)
The way He has led (Deuteronomy 8:2)
The blessings He has bestowed (Deuteronomy 32:7–12)
The victories He has won (Deuteronomy 11:2–7)
The encouragements He has given (Joshua 23:14).

When we face difficulties, we sometimes forget God's past faithfulness. We see only the detours and the dangerous path. But look back and you will also see the joy of victory, the challenge of the climb, and the presence of your traveling Companion, who has promised never to leave you nor forsake you.

Take courage. The One who brought you this far will continue to direct you.

PAUL VAN GORDER

**Never be afraid to trust an unknown future
to an all-knowing God.**

My Little Girl

PSALM 103:1–8

The LORD is compassionate and gracious,
slow to anger, abounding in love.
PSALM 103:8

Several years ago I read about a girl named Mary who had been born with a cleft palate. When she started school, her classmates teased and taunted her because of her imperfect appearance. Mary soon became convinced that no one could love her.

There was a second grade teacher, however, who was liked by all the children. Mrs. Leonard was a cheerful woman, full of good humor and affection. Each year she checked the children's hearing with a simple test. The students would stand across the room from her as she whispered a question such as: "What color are your shoes?" or "Do you have a new dress?" and the child would answer. When the time came for Mary's turn, she listened closely for the teacher to whisper. Then she heard these words: "I wish you were my little girl."

Those words changed Mary's life forever. She realized she was loved, despite her flawed features, by someone who mattered.

Though you may feel unworthy and unwanted, God wants you to know that He is merciful, forgiving, and full of love for you (Psalm 103:1–8). Do you know that God loves you like that?

DAVID ROPER

If God had a refrigerator, your picture would be on it.

More Than Enough

PSALM 103:1–11

The LORD . . . crowns you with love and compassion.
PSALM 103:2–4

When I entertained a large group in my home, I feared that the menu I planned wouldn't be enough to serve all the guests. I shouldn't have worried though. Several friends unexpectedly brought additional items, and all of us were able to enjoy the surprise surplus. We had more than enough and were able to share out of the abundance.

We serve a God of abundance who is consistently "more than enough." We can see God's generous nature in the way He loves His children.

In Psalm 103, David lists the many benefits our Father bestows on us. Verse 4 says that He redeems our life from destruction and crowns us with love and compassion.

The apostle Paul reminds us that God "has blessed us . . . with every spiritual blessing" and "is able to do immeasurably more than we ask or imagine" (Ephesians 1:3; 3:20).

Because of His great love, we are called children of God (1 John 3:1), and His grace gives us "sufficiency in all things" that we "may have an abundance for every good work" (2 Corinthians 9:8 NKJV).

God's love and grace, spilled over into our lives, enable us to share them with others. The God of power and provision is always the God of "more than enough"!

CINDY HESS KASPER

We always have enough when God is our supply.

Forgiven!

PSALM 103:1–12

Blessed is the one whose transgressions are forgiven,
whose sins are covered.

PSALM 32:1

A little boy named Bobby had just been tucked into bed by his mother, who was waiting to hear his prayers. But he had been naughty that day and now it was bothering him. So he said, "Mama, I wish you'd go now and leave me alone. I want to pray by myself."

Sensing that something was wrong, she asked, "Bobby, is there anything you ought to tell me?" "No, Mommy," he replied. "You would just scold me, but God will forgive me and forget about it." That little boy understood one of the greatest salvation benefits of all—the reality of sins forgiven. The Bible indicates that in Christ "we have redemption through His blood, the forgiveness of sins" (Colossians 1:14 NKJV). We who have received the Lord Jesus as Savior enjoy freedom from sin's eternal condemnation (Romans 8:1), and we can also have daily forgiveness and cleansing (1 John 1:9).

The apostle Paul said that salvation provides these added benefits: we are justified (Romans 3:24), and we are at peace with God (5:1).

We should never get the idea that our sins are taken lightly by the Lord. But when we acknowledge our guilt with true repentance, God stands ready to forgive because of what Jesus did on the cross. It's up to us to accept it.

RICHARD DEHAAN

When God forgives, He also forgets.

What's Love?

PSALM 103:1–14

This is love: not that we loved God, but that he
loved us and sent His Son as an atoning sacrifice for our sins.

1 JOHN 4:10

When asked, "What's love?" children have some great answers. Noelle, age 7, said, "Love is when you tell a guy you like his shirt, then he wears it every day." Rebecca, who is 8, answered, "Since my grandmother got arthritis, she can't bend over and polish her toenails anymore. So my grandfather does it for her all the time, even after his hands got arthritis too. That's love." Jessica, also 8, concluded, "You really shouldn't say 'I love you' unless you mean it. But if you mean it, you should say it a lot. People forget."

Sometimes we need to be reminded that God loves us. We focus on the difficulties of life and wonder, *Where's the love?* But if we pause and consider everything God has done for us, we remember how much we are loved by God, who is love (1 John 4:8–10).

Psalm 103 lists the "benefits" God showers on us in love: He forgives our sin (v. 3), satisfies us with good things (v. 5), and works righteousness and justice (v. 6). He is slow to anger and abounds in love (v. 8). He doesn't deal with us as our sins deserve (v. 10), and He has removed our sin as far as the east is from the west (v. 12). He has not forgotten us!

What is love? God is love, and He's pouring out that love on you and me.

ANNE CETAS

The death of Christ is the measure of God's love for you.

A Loving Father

PSALM 103:7–13

As a father has compassion on his children,
so the LORD has compassion on those who fear him.
PSALM 103:13

The parents were obviously weary from dragging their two energetic pre-schoolers through airports and airplanes, and now their final flight was delayed. As I watched the two boys running around the crowded gate area, I wondered how Mom and Dad were going to keep the little guys settled down for our half-hour flight into Grand Rapids. When we finally boarded, I noticed that the father and one of the sons were in the seats behind me. Then I heard the weary father say to his son, "Why don't you let me read one of your storybooks to you." And during the entire flight, this loving father softly and patiently read to his son, keeping him calm and focused.

In one of his psalms David declares, "As a father has compassion on his children, so the LORD has compassion on those who fear him" (Psalm 103:13). The tender word *compassion* gives us a picture of how deeply our heavenly Father loves His children, and it reminds us what a great gift it is to be able to look to God and cry, "Abba, Father" (Romans 8:15).

God longs for you to listen again to the story of His love for you when you are restless on your own journey through life. Your heavenly Father is always near—ready to encourage you with His Word.

BILL CROWDER

God's great love for His child is one of His greatest gifts.

He Never Changes

PSALM 103:11–22

You, LORD, sit enthroned forever;
your renown endures through all generations.

PSALM 102:12

Photographer David Crocket of Seattle's KOMO-TV knows that solid mountains can move. On May 18, 1980, he was at the foot of towering Mount St. Helens when it erupted. For ten hours he was nearly buried by the falling debris. As the atmosphere cleared, a helicopter pilot spotted him. He was dramatically rescued and flown to a hospital.

Writing about his horrendous experience, he said, "During those ten hours I saw a mountain fall apart. I saw a forest disappear. . . . I saw that God is the only one who is immovable. . . . I feel somehow that I'm being allowed to start over—whatever is in His master plan for me."

Nothing in our world, not even a mountain, is absolutely indestructible. God alone is absolutely unchangeable—He endures "forever" (Psalm 102:12). He "has established his throne in heaven, and his kingdom rules over all" (103:19).

When we trust ourselves to God's keeping, we are forever secure. He removes our sins from us "as far as the east is from the west" (103:12). And His love for us is "from everlasting to everlasting" (v. 17). He holds us in His almighty hands, and nothing can pry us loose from that omnipotent grip (John 10:28–29).

VERNON GROUNDS

Our world may crumble around us, but God never changes.

God's Helpers

PSALM 103:19–22

Praise the Lord, you his angels.
PSALM 103:20

I was having a conversation with some children about God and superheroes when Tobias asked a question. An imaginative, curious five-year-old, he asked anyone listening: "Does God have a sidekick like Hercules does?" His wiser, older brother, age seven, quickly responded: "Yes, He has thousands of them—they're His angels."

Angels are a popular topic of discussion, and people believe a number of myths about them. For instance, some people pray to angels, thinking they are on the same level as God himself. And some believe that people become angels when they die. But here's what the Bible, our authority, teaches:

- God created angels (Colossians 1:15–17).
- Angels worship God (Nehemiah 9:6) and are known by these terms: archangels (Jude 1:9), cherubim (2 Kings 19:15), and seraphim (Isaiah 6:1–3).
- They minister to God's people (Hebrews 1:13–14) by guarding and protecting them (Psalm 91:9–12).
- They are given special assignments by God (Matthew 1:20; Luke 1:26).
- God's angels rejoice when we repent of sin and turn to Christ for salvation (Luke 15:7, 10).

Only God deserves our worship. So let's join the angels in singing His praises!

ANNE CETAS

Angels are God's special helpers.

Mozart's Pet Bird

PSALM 104:1–13

The birds of the sky nest by the waters; they sing among the branches.
PSALM 104:12

Mozart (1756–1791) is revered as a genius of musical composition. In one instance, he was even inspired by the melody of a bird. Mozart had a pet starling whose song so fascinated him that some say he wrote a piece of music based on the melody he heard in the bird's chirps.

Birds were also an inspiration to the psalmist. In Psalm 104, he praises God for caring for the living creatures He put on the earth. Included in his observations are birds who fly in the heavens above, perch in the branches of trees, and sing songs of heartfelt joy: "The birds of the sky nest by the waters; they sing among the branches" (v. 12). Nature filled the psalmist's heart with praise to God, and I think that must have included the musical sounds of the birds.

Often the marvels we see in creation prompt us to worship. This theme is repeated throughout Scripture: "The heavens declare the glory of God; the skies proclaim the work of his hands" (Psalm 19:1). Creation's stimulus to praise need not be limited to the visual. It can also be widened to include hearing nature's songs. As we go about our daily routine, we can tune our hearts to the melodies God has placed in His creatures and let them serve as an added springboard of praise to the Creator.

DENNIS FISHER

All of nature is a grand symphony conducted by the Creator.

The Witness of Insects

PSALM 104:16–28

How many are your works, LORD! In wisdom you made them all;
the earth is full of your creatures.
PSALM 104:24

The more than one and a half million kinds of insects on this planet display a diversity that points to the wisdom of an infinite Creator. The common honeybee, for instance, organizes a little city inside its hive. It builds 10,000 cells for honey, 12,000 for the larvae, and a special chamber for the queen.

When temperatures inside the hive become so warm that the honey is in danger of being lost through the softened wax, squads of sentinels automatically take their places at the hive's entrance. Their fast-beating wings create a cooling system that rivals the electric fan.

French scientist René Antoine Ferchault de Réaumur examined a wasp's nest in 1719 and noted that it seemed to be made of a type of crude pasteboard. After further investigation, he discovered that most of the material was obtained from tree fibers. As a result of this study, the first successful production of paper from wood pulp was achieved. Yet God had instilled this ability in the wasp at the dawn of history.

There are millions of similar wonders in our world, more than enough to convince us that a great, all-wise Creator brought them into being. It's just another reason He deserves our heartfelt worship.

HENRY BOSCH

The natural world bears the signature of a supernatural Creator.

Fast Food

PSALM 104:23-35

When you give it to them, they gather it up;
when you open your hand, they are satisfied with good things.
PSALM 104:28

An item in the *National Geographic* magazine carried this caption: "New Spin on Fast Food." The article was about the phalarope, "a wading shore-bird that has a unique way of dining on creatures too deep for it to reach." Spinning in the water at breakneck speed—a full spin per second—it creates a vortex that "pumps up" shrimp from a depth of three feet.

According to UCLA biologist William M. Hamner, the bird is also a speedy eater. His research team has learned that "phalaropes detect prey, thrust, seize, transport, and swallow in less than half a second, at a rate of 180 pecks per minute."

The author of Psalm 104 probably never saw a phalarope, but he had observed enough of God's creative genius in nature to fill his heart with praise. He wrote, "The earth is full of your creatures. . . . living things both large and small. . . . All creatures look to you to give them their food at the proper time. When you give it to them, they gather it up" (vv. 24–28).

Do we think of our life-support systems—the food we eat, the air we breathe, the strength we receive—as coming from the hand of God? Most of us take these provisions for granted. With your Bible open to Psalm 104, look again at the marvels of God's world.

DENNIS DEHAAN

The design of creation points us to the Master Designer.

26,000 Gifts a Day

PSALM 104:24–35

Let everything that has breath praise the LORD. Praise the LORD.
PSALM 150:6

What do you do eighteen times a minute, 1,080 times an hour, 26,000 times a day, yet rarely notice? The answer: You breathe. If you are forty years old, you have already taken more than 378,000,000 breaths. And each of those breaths was a measured gift from the hand of God!

Your lungs are among the most important parts of your body. They furnish your blood with oxygen and get rid of carbon dioxide and water. A few minutes without breathing and you would lose consciousness. You could not survive much longer without oxygen.

The Bible tells us that the Lord holds in His hand "the life of every creature and the breath of all mankind" (Job 12:10). He gives us those 26,000 gifts each day so we might honor Him with the life they sustain.

A minister was at the bedside of an elderly Christian who was near death. When he asked her what Scripture she wanted him to read, she said, "Make your own selection, pastor, but let it be one of praise." Although she was breathing her last, she wanted her parting testimony to echo the psalmist: "Let everything that has breath praise the LORD" (Psalm 150:6).

Have you thanked God today for His 26,000 gifts?

HENRY BOSCH

**When it's time to breathe a prayer of thanks,
don't hold your breath.**

Oceans of Praise

PSALM 104:24–30

May the glory of the LORD endure forever;
may the LORD rejoice in his works.

PSALM 104:31

Whenever I see the ocean (which is not often enough), I am awed by its sheer volume and beauty and power. Great ships loaded with oil or food or merchandise make long journeys across its vast surface. Fishing vessels, working near the shore or hundreds of miles out at sea, harvest its rich provisions: lobster and crab, tuna and swordfish. Beneath its churning surface is a storehouse of wealth of all kinds, some still undiscovered.

The author of Psalm 104, recounting the works of God in a lofty hymn of praise, used the "vast and spacious" sea as an example of God's creative power and wisdom (vv. 24–25). The Lord rules over all this massive area of water, which is "teeming with creatures beyond number—living things both large and small" (v. 25). The psalmist referred in poetic terms to the ocean as the playground of Leviathan, a giant sea monster that God "formed to frolic there" (v. 26).

The surging ocean, both life-sustaining and dangerous, points us to the greatness of our God. He is awesome in His works, unlimited in His provision, and generous in His bestowal of all kinds of life.

Lord, truly your works are magnificent! As I think of them, I join the psalmist in praising you.

DAVID EGNER

All creation sings God's praise.

Sent by God

PSALM 105:7–22

He sent a man before them—Joseph, sold as a slave.
PSALM 105:17

If God sent you to do something significant for Him, how would you expect to be treated? Like a dignitary in a motorcade? How would you expect to feel? Important and confident? Secure in knowing exactly where you were headed and what you were to do?

Our first steps along the pathway of serving God may feel like the end of our hopes and dreams. God's beginnings for His servants often bear little resemblance to the endings He has in mind.

The story of Joseph (Genesis 37–47) is a great encouragement when God's dealings with us seem impossible to understand. Psalm 105 tells us that God "sent a man before them— Joseph, sold as a slave. They bruised his feet with shackles, his neck was put in irons, till what he foretold came to pass, till the word of the LORD proved him true" (vv. 17–19).

Being sent by God may begin with losing a job instead of landing one. It could involve the injustice of being penalized when you played fair and refused to compromise. It may hurt as much as Joseph's shackles in prison.

If God has given you a difficult beginning, ask Him for the strength to see it through. The God who sends will also sustain until you reach the end He has in mind.

DAVID McCASLAND

The God who sends you will also sustain you.

Beware of Quick Fixes

PSALM 106:1–15

*But they soon forgot what he had done
and did not wait for his plan to unfold.*

PSALM 106:13

Some people pray only in a crisis. They have a "quick fix" mentality that sees God mainly as a problem solver. When merciful solutions come, He is courteously thanked, then more or less forgotten until the next crisis.

The story is told of a young rich girl, accustomed to servants, who was afraid to climb a dark stairway alone. Her mother suggested that she overcome her fear by asking Jesus to go with her up the stairs. When the child reached the top, she was overheard saying, "Thank you, Jesus. You may go now."

We may smile at that story, but Psalm 106 contains a serious warning against dismissing God from our lives—as if that were possible. Israel took the Lord's mercies for granted, and God called that rebellion (v. 7). They developed malnourished souls because they chose to ignore Him (vv. 13–15). What a lesson for us!

Anticipate great things from God, but don't expect Him to come at your beck and call. Instead, be at His beck and call, eager to fulfill His will.

Like the little rich girl, ask God to accompany you through life's dark passageways. But instead of dismissing Him when your special needs are met, cling to Him as if your life depended on it. It does!

JOANIE YODER

God is not a vending machine.

Too Blessed

PSALM 107:1–8

*Let them give thanks to the LORD for his unfailing love
and his wonderful deeds for mankind.*

PSALM 107:8

On my daily commute to and from the office, I have plenty of time for reading—bumper stickers on cars, that is. Some are surly, others clever, and still others downright distasteful. One bumper sticker I saw recently, however, gently challenged my heart about the way I often engage life. The sticker simply said, "Too blessed to complain."

I must confess that I felt convicted as I pondered those words. Too often I find myself lamenting moments in life that don't go my way, rather than focusing on the wonderful gifts my heavenly Father has given me. Reading that simple message that day brought me a renewed commitment to be more actively and intentionally grateful because my God has been good to me in more ways than I could ever count.

Psalm 107 is a song that seeks to rectify thankless thinking. The psalmist (who many think was King David) makes a plea to hearts grown cold with ingratitude. Even in the worst of times, we have much to be thankful for. May we learn to thank God for His goodness to us!

BILL CROWDER

**We don't need more to be thankful for,
we just need to be more thankful.**

Reasons to Say Thanks

PSALM 107:1–15

Proclaiming aloud your praise and telling of all your wonderful deeds.
PSALM 26:7

Did you ever find yourself staring at the words "Thanksgiving Day" on the calendar and wondering what in the world you had to be thankful for?

It could happen if a job loss makes you wonder how you'll ever get enough money to survive. Or if you have recently heard nothing but bad news from the doctor. Or if someone you had entrusted with your heart has broken it and run away.

The reasons we may find it hard to give thanks are as many as the troubles that strike us each day. Difficulties don't pause for a Thanksgiving break.

There is a way, however, to find reasons to be thankful during even the darkest episodes of life. When the curtain of struggles seems to block out all joy, we can choose to be thankful.

One way is to look into Scripture to see all the things we have to be thankful for—things that have nothing to do with circumstances. Despite our trials, we can give thanks for God's unfailing goodness (Psalm 106:1); for God's holy name (Psalm 30:4); for deliverance from sin (Romans 7:24–25); for victory over death (1 Corinthians 15:56–57); for God's nearness (Hebrews 13:5).

When all joy seems gone, we can still find reasons to thank God—even if it means thanking Him that our difficulties will one day be replaced by the joys of heaven.

DAVE BRANON

If you pause to think, you'll have cause to thank.

He Changed My Life

PSALM 107:1–16

Let the redeemed of the LORD tell their story—
those he redeemed from the hand of the foe.

PSALM 107:2

Following the death of computer pioneer Steve Jobs in 2011, more than one million people from around the world posted tributes to him online. The common theme was how Jobs had changed their lives. They said they lived differently because of his creative innovations, and they wanted to express their appreciation and their sorrow. The screen of one tablet computer said in large letters: iSad.

Gratitude fuels expression, which is exactly what Psalm 107 describes: "Let the redeemed of the LORD tell their story—those he has redeemed from the hand of the foe" (v. 2). The theme of this psalm is "people in great trouble who were delivered by the Lord." Some were homeless and in need (vv. 4–5); some had rebelled against God's Word (vv. 10–11); others were at their wits' end when they cried out to God (vv. 26–27). All were rescued by God. "Let them give thanks to the LORD for his unfailing love and his wonderful deeds for mankind" (vv. 8, 15, 21, 31).

When we consider the greatness of God's love, His grace in sending Jesus Christ to die for us and rise again, and what He has delivered us from, we cannot keep from praising Him and wanting to tell others how He changed our lives!

DAVID MCCASLAND

Our gratitude to God for salvation fuels our witness to others.

Outside the Boat

PSALM 107:23–32

They mounted up to the heavens and went down to the depths.
PSALM 107:26

Katsushika Hokusai was one of the most prolific and celebrated artists in Japanese history. Between 1826 and 1833, when he was in his mid-sixties and early seventies, he created his greatest work—a series of color wood-block prints titled "Thirty-Six Views of Mt. Fuji." Among those paintings was his masterpiece: *The Great Wave Off Kanagawa*. This painting, created during a time of financial and emotional struggles for Hokusai, shows a towering wall of water edged with clawlike foam about to crash down on three slim boats full of rowers.

Psalm 107 also tells a story of people in peril at sea. Afloat on the waves, "they mounted up to the heavens and went down to the depths." And as a result, "their courage melted away" (v. 26). Eventually, the sailors sent an S.O.S. to God, and He responded by smoothing out the sea and guiding them to their destination (vv. 28–30).

When we face desperate circumstances, we tend to look to other people for guidance and comfort. They are in the same boat, however—lost in an ocean of life's ups and downs. Only God is outside the boat, sovereign, stable, and strong enough to calm the storms (vv. 24–25, 29). Facing trouble? Call on Him!

JENNIFER BENSON SCHULDT

We worship a God who is greater than our greatest problem.

Two Great Fears

PSALM 107:23–32

*They were glad when it grew calm,
and he guided them to their desired haven.*

PSALM 107:30

Psalm 107 tells of "those who go down to the sea in ships" (v. 23 NKJV). Along their journey at sea, they see God as the One behind the tempestuous storm and the One who calms it. In the world of sailing vessels there were two great fears. One fear was of a terrible gale, and the other was of having no wind at all.

In "The Rime of the Ancient Mariner," English poet Samuel Taylor Coleridge (1772–1834) describes tempests and doldrums at sea. Two lines have become household words:

Water, water everywhere,
    Nor any drop to drink.

In doldrum latitudes (near the equator), the wind dies down and a sailing ship remains stationary. Captain and crew are "stuck," with no relief in sight. Eventually, with no wind, their water supply runs out.

Sometimes life demands that we weather a storm. At other times it puts us to the test of tedium. We may feel stuck. What we want most is just out of reach. But whether we find ourselves in a crisis of circumstance or in a place where the spiritual wind has been taken out of our sails, we need to trust God for guidance. The Lord, who is sovereign over changing circumstances, will eventually guide us to our desired haven (v. 30).

DENNIS FISHER

God orders our stops as well as our steps.

Unexpressed Gratitude

PSALM 107:31–43

Give thanks to the LORD, for he is good;
. . . Let the redeemed of the LORD tell their story.

PSALM 107:1–2

The whole reason for saying thanks is to let the giver of a gift know how much you appreciate something. Author G. B. Stern once said, "Silent gratitude isn't much use to anyone."

When our son was young, he sometimes needed to be reminded that avoiding eye contact, looking down at his feet, and mumbling some unintelligible words was not an acceptable "thank you." And after many years of marriage, my husband and I are still learning that it's important for us to continually express our gratitude to each other. When one of us feels appreciative, we try to verbalize it—even if we've said it many times before about the same thing. William Arthur Ward said, "Feeling gratitude and not expressing it is like wrapping a present and not giving it."

Showing our gratitude is obviously important in human relationships, but it's even more essential in our relationship with God. As we think about the many blessings we have received, do we express our thanks to Him throughout the day? And when we think of the amazing gift of His death and resurrection for forgiveness of our sins, do our hearts bubble over with awe and thanksgiving? (Romans 6:23; 2 Corinthians 9:15).

Take the reminder in Psalm 107:1 to heart each day: "Give thanks to the LORD, for He is good!"

CINDY HESS KASPER

God's highest Gift should awaken our deepest gratitude.

"Now's Your Chance, Lord"

PSALM 108

Give us aid against the enemy, for human help is worthless.
PSALM 108:12

John and Betty Stam, missionaries to China who were martyred for the cause of Christ in the 1930s, had led a young girl to the Lord and later hired her to do their housework. Although converted, she had some serious problems for which there seemed to be no solution.

One day, in deep distress, she went to her bedroom and cried out to the Savior for help. John and Betty overheard her and were deeply moved. They were especially touched when she said with the utmost reverence and faith, "Now's your chance, Lord! Now's your chance!" Her earnest prayers were rewarded, for God soon helped her solve her problems.

Someone has said, "There are two ways of getting help in time of need. One is to go around to all your friends and be disappointed, and then as a last resort turn to the Lord. The other is to take a shortcut and go to Him first. Don't make a move until you have first expressed your need to Him!"

Do you feel that there is no solution to your problems in sight? Pour out your heart to the Lord. Tell Him you are unable to cope with your desperate situation. Then wait patiently for His help. He will provide the answer at just the right moment.

HENRY BOSCH

**The quickest way to get back on your feet
is to get down on your knees.**

How to Answer Accusers

PSALM 109:1-5, 26-31

In return for my friendship they accuse me, but I am a man of prayer.
PSALM 109:4

While I was a student at college, my roommate accused me of stealing $100 from him. He didn't confront me directly, but he spread his lie among his friends and reported it to the dean's office. The incident was thoroughly investigated, as it should have been.

It was the most helpless experience I have ever faced. All I could do was say, "I didn't do it." But those words seemed hollow against the accusation and rumor.

I didn't know what to do. Part of me wanted to knock the truth out of my roommate. Another part wanted to contact everyone who heard about it and tell them I was innocent. Only later did my accuser admit that he had faked the theft to get money out of his parents for a stereo.

King David had a similar experience. Someone was making terrible accusations against him, undermining his position and causing him much grief (Psalm 109:2–4).

So what did David do? Did he use his authority to have his accuser killed? No, he prayed and asked the Lord to intercede, punish the slanderer, and make it right (vv. 4–29).

When someone spreads false rumors about us, we may want to retaliate. How much better it is to answer our accusers with the power of prayer!

DAVID EGNER

To stop a rumor, start praying.

Shoot Our Wounded?

PSALM 109:21–31

*For he never thought of doing a kindness, but hounded to death the poor
and the needy and the brokenhearted.*

PSALM 109:16

A major city's newspaper reported that a patient in a local hospital was shot
and killed as he lay in his bed recovering from a previous gunshot wound.
The victim had been listed in fair condition prior to the shooting and was
looking forward to going home. Hospital patients and employees were
stunned. A spokesperson said that nothing like this had happened in the
fifty years of the hospital's existence.

Wouldn't it be wonderful if we could say the same for our churches?
Wouldn't it be encouraging if we were able to say that in fifty years of meeting together for worship, fellowship, and spiritual healing, we had not had a
single instance of a "wounded" member being cut down by the unkindness
of a fellow Christian?

Many among us have experienced the pain that David expressed in
Psalm 109. When he was hurt and vulnerable, insensitive people took
advantage of him. Certainly, if he had sinned, he needed their loving correction. What he didn't need was their scorn, gossip, and selfish neglect.

Who shoots his foot after stubbing his toe? No one in his right mind.
Neither should anyone with the mind of Christ act unmercifully toward
a wounded brother or sister in the body of Christ. Rather, we must "show
mercy" (v. 16 NKJV).

MART DEHAAN

**A hurting person needs a helping hand,
not an accusing finger.**

Active Worship

PSALM 110

Enter his gates with thanksgiving and his courts with praise;
give thanks to him and praise his name.
PSALM 100:4

Ray Stedman, for many years pastor of Peninsula Bible Church in Palo Alto, California, wanted to put you in his place. In his book *Folk Psalms of Faith*, Stedman said he wished all churchgoers could stand in the pulpit and watch the faces in the congregation during a sermon. He said that while most people in the audience seem to be giving the minister their attention, a large number of them may have their minds elsewhere.

Stedman wrote, "It would be fascinating at the end of a service to know where everybody had been!"

To gain the greatest benefit from our church attendance, we should be active participants. First, before we leave home, we must prepare our hearts. Then, at church we should become wholeheartedly involved in every part of the service—singing the songs, silently praying as the pastor leads, and rejoicing in the warm fellowship we can have with other believers. Finally, we have to discipline ourselves to listen; that is, we must intently, carefully, and openly receive the teaching of God's Word. We should have a hunger for truth that quiets our spirits, inspires worship, evokes praise to God, and moves us to action.

It's easy to blame the pastor if we leave church feeling empty and discouraged. But our minister can't do all the work. We must do our share. Those who get the most out of the service are the ones who put the most into it.

RICHARD DEHAAN

Active worship requires active involvement.

A Difficult Hill

PSALM 110

He will drink from a brook along the way,
and so he will lift his head high.

PSALM 110:7

High in a fold of Jughandle Peak in the mountains north of our home in Idaho lies a glacial lake. The route to the lake goes up a steep, exposed ridge through boulders and loose stones. It's a strenuous ascent.

At the beginning of the climb, however, there is a brook—a spring that seeps out of soft, mossy earth and flows through a lush meadow. It's a quiet place to drink deeply and prepare for the hard climb ahead.

In John Bunyan's classic allegory of the Christian life, *The Pilgrim's Progress*, Christian arrives at the foot of a steep ascent called the Hill Difficulty, "at the bottom of which was a spring . . . Christian now went to the spring and drank to refresh himself, and then began to go up the hill."

Perhaps the difficult mountain you face is a rebellious child or a serious medical diagnosis. The challenge seems more than you can endure.

Before you face your next major task, visit the spring of refreshment that is God himself. Come to Him with all your weakness, weariness, helplessness, fear, and doubt. Then drink deeply of His power, strength, and wisdom. God knows all your circumstances and will supply a store of comfort, of spiritual strengthening and consolation. He will lift up your head and give you strength to climb that difficult hill.

DAVID ROPER

"He who overrules all things . . . enabled Christian to . . . continue on his way." —John Bunyan, *The Pilgrim's Progress*

Rearview Mirror Reflections

PSALM 111

For you make me glad by your deeds, LORD;
I sing for joy at what your hands have done.
PSALM 92:4

I've always thought you can see the hand of God best in the rearview mirror. Looking back, it's easier to understand why He placed us in the home that He did; why He brought certain people and circumstances into and out of our lives; why He permitted difficulties and pain; why He took us to different places and put us in various jobs and careers.

In my own life, I get a lot of clarity (though not perfect clarity—that's heaven's joy!) about the wise and loving ways of God as I reflect on the ways He has managed my journey by "what [God's] hands have done" (Psalm 92:4). With the psalmist, it makes me glad and strikes a note of joy in my heart to see how often God has assisted, directed, and managed the outcomes so faithfully (Psalm 111).

Looking ahead, though, is not always so clear. Have you ever had that lost feeling when the road ahead seems twisted, foggy, and scary? Before you move into next year, stop and look in the rearview mirror of the year gone by, and joyfully realize that God meant it when He said, "'Never will I leave you; never will I forsake you.' So we way with confidence, 'The Lord is my helper; I will not be afraid'" (Hebrews 13:5–6).

With the promise of God's presence and help in mind, you can move ahead with utmost confidence.

JOE STOWELL

God's guidance in the past gives courage for the future.

A Good Person

PSALM 112

Praise the LORD. Blessed are those who fear the LORD,
who find great delight in his commands.

PSALM 112:1

A good person is hard to find these days. At least that's the impression you might get from a society that is having a tough time finding heroes.

Too often, though, we look in the wrong places when we're searching for role models. We look for someone who is a good athlete or who makes a lot of money or who commands respect because of leadership skills.

When we look only in these situations for good people, we fail to see that most of the godly men and women are not in the spotlight. They are just quietly and faithfully serving their families, their friends, and God.

In Psalm 112 we see a clear set of guidelines for what makes a person good. According to the psalmist, a good person fears the Lord (v. 1), delights in God's commands (v. 1), and is gracious, compassionate, and righteous (v. 4). He or she is generous and exercises discretion (v. 5). He or she is unshakable in his faith, and he or she has no fear because that person's trust is in God (vv. 6–8).

Looking for a good person? In a society where so many are anything but godly, how can we set the right example? Look at Psalm 112. It's a pattern all Christian men and women need to follow if they want to make a difference in their world.

DAVE BRANON

To make a difference in the world,
let Jesus make a difference in you.

He Lights the Way

PSALM 112

Even in darkness light dawns for the upright,
for those who are gracious and compassionate and righteous.

PSALM 112:4

A missionary in Peru went to visit a group of believers one evening. She knew that the house where they were meeting was located on a cliff and the path would be treacherous. She took a taxi as far as it could go, and then she began the hazardous ascent to the house on foot. The night was dark and the way was very difficult. As she rounded a bend, she suddenly came upon several believers carrying bright lanterns. They had come out to light the way. Her fears were relieved, and she ascended the path easily.

In a similar way, God lights our path. When we trust Jesus as our Savior, He who is the Light of the world enters our lives and removes the darkness of our sin and despair. This light continues to comfort us through times of sorrow. In the midst of sadness, trouble, illness, or disappointment, the Lord brightens the way and encourages His children by giving hope.

This may come through a word of exhortation from a fellow believer. It may be the illumination of God's Word by the ministry of the Holy Spirit. It may be calm reassurance in response to heartfelt prayer. Or it may be the miraculous supply of a specific need. Whatever the case, God sends light when we are engulfed in darkness.

Jesus gives light in the darkest night!

DAVID EGNER

God sometimes puts us in the dark
to show us that Jesus is the light.

The Work of Our Hands

PSALM 112

The righteous will never be shaken; they will be remembered forever.
PSALM 112:6

One reason we're left here on earth and not taken to heaven immediately after trusting in Christ for salvation is that God has work for us to do. "Man is immortal," Augustine said, "until his work is done."

The time of our death is not determined by anyone or anything here on earth. That decision is made in the councils of heaven. When we have done all that God has in mind for us to do, then and only then will He take us home—and not one second before. As Paul put it, "When David had served God's purpose in his own generation, he fell asleep" (Acts 13:36).

In the meantime, until God takes us home, there's plenty to do. "As long as it is day, we must do the works of him who sent me," Jesus said. "Night is coming, when no one can work" (John 9:4). Night is coming when we will once for all close our eyes on this world, or our Lord will return to take us to be with Him. Each day brings that time a little closer.

As long as we have the light of day, we must work—not to conquer, acquire, accumulate, and retire, but to make visible the invisible Christ by touching people with His love. We can then be confident that our "labor in the Lord is not in vain" (1 Corinthians 15:58).

DAVID ROPER

In God's eyes, true greatness is serving others.

Righteousness Endures Forever

PSALM 112:4–9

His righteousness endures forever.
PSALM 112:9 (NKJV)

A good deal of our unhappiness as we grow older is caused by our pining for the "good old days"—those times when we enjoyed health, wealth, position, or power. But the things of this world don't last. They are vacillating, changeable, capricious. In time, they may be taken away from us and replaced with poverty, isolation, weakness, and pain.

When we realize that this world and everything in it is unstable and unpredictable, we are left longing for something that lasts. What is left?

The psalmist wrote, "[God's] righteousness endures forever" (112:9 NKJV). It is untouched and unharmed by time and circumstances. Nothing that happens in this world can take it away. It endures when life has stripped us of every other possession.

This righteousness is ours as we draw near to God through faith in Jesus Christ (see Romans 1:17; 3:21–26). He is our rock and our salvation and the only source of true and lasting happiness. Psalm 112:1 says, "Blessed [happy] are those who fear the LORD, who find great delight in his commands."

Delight in the Lord and in His Word, and you'll find true happiness. He alone offers a righteousness that endures for all eternity.

DAVID ROPER

Happiness is ours when we delight in the Lord.

No Dumping Allowed

PSALM 113

He raises the poor from the dust and lifts the needy from the ash heap.
PSALM 113:7

For several years I've worked in a ministry to drug addicts, and I've seen Christ transform many who had lost hope. Yet in response to a newspaper article about our work, I received a letter from someone who said, "You are wasting your time working with worthless drug addicts. They should be given a lethal injection and tossed on the city dump."

How heartless! People who say such things need a massive dose of good news. They (and also that letter writer) need to hear that God doesn't cast us sinners off on some trash heap. On the contrary, He loved this world so much that He sent His only Son to die for their sins. And whoever puts his faith in Him will not perish but will be given eternal life (John 3:16).

Some people visit dumps, searching for objects to redeem and restore. According to Psalm 113, God looks compassionately on human castaways. He seeks ways to lift them out of the ash heaps of sin and death and to give them a place of honor and dignity (vv. 7–8).

If that is God's response to this world's castaways, we should make it ours. We too were lost in the depths of sin but were raised to newness of life. God says of sinners, "No dumping allowed!"

JOANIE YODER

**Christ was lifted up on the cross
that we might be lifted out of our sin.**

The Awesome Power of God

PSALM 114

Tremble, earth, at the presence of the Lord,
at the presence of the God of Jacob.
PSALM 114:7

Back and forth, back and forth go the pounding waves of the sea. From ages past, the continents have been separated by the mighty oceans. Man has learned to travel over them, to descend to the bottom of them, and to travel through them—but their immensity and the relentless force of their waves remain untamable. Rocks are crushed, shorelines are changed, and even experienced sailors can be driven aground or sent to the bottom of the sea. The combined genius of man and the most powerful equipment can do little to conquer the oceans.

They are no problem for God, however. The One who created the mighty oceans does with them what He wishes. Psalm 114 refers to the exodus of the Israelites from Egypt and the parting of the Red Sea (Exodus14:13–31) to describe God's great power. The psalmist wrote, "The sea looked and fled" (Psalm 114:3). Then he asked, "What was it, sea, that you fled?" (v. 5). The answer is implied: The seas were obeying the command of God.

When the turbulent seas of adversity are threatening, we need to remember the awesome power of God. As the seas fled before Him, so too can the obstacles that seem so overwhelming to us. They have no more resistance to God's power than water in a teacup!

DAVID EGNER

**The power of God within you is greater than
the pressure of troubles around you.**

Ice Fishing

PSALM 115:1–11

You shall have no other gods before me.

EXODUS 20:3

Two Texans went to Minnesota one winter to do some ice fishing. After setting up their tent, they pulled the cord on their chain saw to cut a hole in the ice. Then they heard a mysterious voice from above saying, "There are no fish under the ice."

"Is that you, God?" they asked in awe.

"No," came the reply, "but I know that there are no fish under the ice. I'm the owner of this ice-skating rink."

People who worship gods other than the one true God resemble fishermen ice fishing in a skating rink. The idolaters of Isaiah's day worked hard at practicing their religion. They spent exorbitant sums of money overlaying their professionally carved idols with gold and crafting silver chains for them (Isaiah 40:19–20). They bowed down and worshiped what they had constructed with their own hands (Psalm 115:4–7). Yet, there was nothing there. They appeared to be worshiping God, but their worship was as futile as fishing in an ice-skating rink.

Our great God can never be reduced to an image of man's own making. "The LORD is the everlasting God, the Creator of the ends of the earth" (Isaiah 40:28). And He wants us to worship Him in spirit and in truth (John 4:24).

HADDON ROBINSON

How foolish to worship the creature rather than the Creator!

Sight Unseen

PSALM 115

Why do the nations say, "Where is their God?"
Our God is in heaven; he does whatever pleases him.

PSALM 115:2–3

As my plane rose over Grand Rapids, I realized that the flight path would take us right over my house. I also knew that my daughter Julie would figure out that this was my plane, and she would be out in the front yard, waving. I strained my eyes, but I couldn't see Julie nor my house.

When I arrived at my destination, I called home. Julie told me that she had indeed spotted my plane and stood waving and shouting. She couldn't see me, but she knew I was there.

Julie's wave-at-the-plane routine illustrates, in a small way, our perspective of God. She knew I was there because she pieced together certain facts—like when my plane was supposed to take off and what direction it would be flying. Likewise, we have enough information to come to the conclusion that God is there, even though we cannot see Him.

Some of those indicators include the heavens (Psalms 19:1), the created world (Romans 1:18–20), the constellations (Amos 5:8), and mankind itself (Exodus 4:11). Despite the best efforts of those who wish to exclude God from this world, His handiwork gives us enough evidence to assure us that He is there.

What a comfort it is to us to know that "our God is in heaven"! (Psalm 115:3).

DAVE BRANON

All creation points to the almighty Creator.

Misplaced Love

PSALM 115

Their idols are silver and gold, made by human hands.
PSALM 115:4

Martin Lindstrom, an author and speaker, thinks that cellphones have become akin to a best friend for many owners. Lindstrom's experiment using an MRI helped him discover why. When the subjects saw or heard their phone ringing, their brains fired off neurons in the area associated with feelings of love and compassion. Lindstrom said, "It was as if they were in the presence of a girlfriend, boyfriend, or family member."

Many things vie for our affection and time and attention, and it seems we continually need to evaluate where we're focusing our lives. Joshua told the people of Israel that they were to give their affection and worship to God alone (Joshua 24:14). This was significant in contrast to the idols worshiped by the nations around them. These idols were made of metal and were only the work of men's hands (Psalm 115:4). They were totally powerless compared to the Lord. Therefore, God's people were exhorted to find their security in Him and not in other gods (Judges 10:13–16). Jesus reiterated this in His discussion of the commandments: "Love the Lord your God with all your heart and with all your soul and with all your mind" (Matthew 22:37).

The Lord alone is our "help and shield" (Psalm 115:9). May we reserve our worship for Him.

MARVIN WILLIAMS

God is most worthy of our affections.

On Creaky Knees

PSALM 116

Because he turned his ear to me, I will call on him as long as I live.
PSALM 116:2

Meet Margaret the battler. More than ninety years of memories and faith were her legacy, but she was not ready to surrender. Her life was full of the physical pain that often accompanies old age, and even though she was too weak to walk anymore, Margaret was not done with her ministry.

Despite her increasing feebleness, and despite her near deafness and inability to move around, Margaret had a ministry that reached far beyond the walls of the nursing home where she lived. Every day—often for hours at a time—she would sit in her chair with a stack of prayer cards and pray diligently for missionaries. And sometimes, when she could push her frail body to do so, she would kneel beside her bed on creaky knees to talk with God.

Margaret didn't have much more than prayer to offer her Lord. She was the essence of the answer to the question in Psalm 116:12, "What shall I return to the LORD for all his goodness toward me?" Verse 13 answers, "I will . . . call on the name of the LORD."

A lifetime of being sustained by God's love, grace, and mercy was just about over for Margaret. In the face of mounting physical weakness, she stayed spiritually strong to the end. O to have her courage and dedication—at any age!

DAVE BRANON

Christ's soldiers fight best on their knees.

The Cynical Psalmist

PSALM 116

The LORD is gracious and righteous; our God is full of compassion.
PSALM 116:5

Theodore Roosevelt understood the dangers of cynicism when he observed, "The poorest way to face life is to face it with a sneer."

The psalmist nearly succumbed to this danger. He evidently had enemies who were out to get him with vicious lies and rumors. The attacks were so unjustified and his desperation so deep that he thought he would die. In his loneliness and agony he concluded that there was no one he could trust. He confessed, "I said in my haste, 'All men are liars'" (Psalm 116:11 NKJV).

Cynicism is a virus that attacks the spirit and breaks down our relationship both to others and to God. The cynic suspects the worst even in the best of people. He can see more evil through a keyhole than others see through an open door.

The psalmist's enemies nearly defeated him, not with knives but through verbal attacks. And the greatest danger came not from the lies told about him but from their effect on his soul and his walk with the Lord.

Beware of cynicism. Avoid making snap judgments about others while under stress. The psalmist did that but eventually realized that his attitude was wrong. God delivered him and replaced his cynicism with vibrant praise. The Lord can do that for you too.

HADDON ROBINSON

Cynicism sees only evil at work; faith sees God at work.

A Real Relationship

PSALM 116:1-7

Peace I leave with you; my peace I give you.
JOHN 14:27

Phillips Brooks, former minister of Boston's Trinity Episcopal Church, is perhaps best known as the author of "O Little Town of Bethlehem." He was a very busy pastor, yet he always seemed relaxed and unburdened, willing to take time for anyone in need.

Shortly before Brooks died, a young friend wrote to him and asked the secret of his strength and serenity. In a heartfelt response, Brooks credited his still-growing relationship with Christ.

He wrote, "The more I have thought it over, the more sure it has seemed to me that these last years have had a peace and fullness which there did not used to be. It is a deeper knowledge and truer love of Christ. . . . I cannot tell you how personal this grows to me. He is here. He knows me and I know Him. It is the most real thing in the world. And every day makes it more real. And one wonders with delight what it will grow to as the years go on."

What a testimony to the strength and serenity our Savior can provide! What a motivator for all of us who know Him as Savior to cultivate daily a closer, deeper fellowship with Jesus! Only that relationship can bring abiding peace and delight.

VERNON GROUNDS

Peace floods the soul when Christ rules the heart.

Quiet Conversations

PSALM 116:5–9

Praise the LORD, my soul, and forget not all his benefits.
PSALM 103:2

Do you ever talk to yourself? Sometimes when I'm working on a project—usually under the hood of a car—I find it helpful to think aloud, working through my options on the best way to make the repair. If someone catches me in my "conversation" it can be a little embarrassing—even though talking to ourselves is something most of us do every day.

The psalmists often talked to themselves in the Psalms. The author of Psalm 116 is no exception. In verse 7 he writes, "Return to your rest, my soul, for the LORD has been good to you." Reminding himself of God's kindness and faithfulness in the past is a practical comfort and help to him in the present. We see "conversations" like this frequently in the Psalms. In Psalm 103:1 David tells himself, "Praise the LORD, my soul; all my inmost being, praise his holy name." And in Psalm 62:5 he affirms, "Yes, my soul, find rest in God; my hope comes from him."

It's good to remind ourselves of God's faithfulness and the hope we have in Him. We can follow the example of the psalmist and spend some time naming the many ways God has been good to us. As we do, we'll be encouraged. The same God who has been faithful in the past will continue His love for us in the future.

JAMES BANKS

**Reminding ourselves about God's goodness
can keep us filled with His peace.**

God Weeps with Us

PSALM 116

Precious in the sight of the LORD is the death of his faithful servants.
PSALM 116:15

What is the meaning of Psalm 116:15, "Precious in the sight of the LORD is the death of His faithful servants"? God certainly doesn't value or find enjoyment in the death of His children! If He did, why would the psalmist praise God for delivering him from death? And why did Jesus groan and weep as He saw the grief at Lazarus's tomb? (John 11:33–35). I agree with scholars who render Psalm 116:15, "Costly in the sight of the Lord is the death of His saints."

In this world, unless you are a celebrity, your passing will soon be forgotten by all but a small circle of relatives and friends. But Jesus showed us that God shares the sorrow and pain of the bereaved and that the death of the humblest believer causes His heart great pain.

This thought came to me as I attended the funeral of my brother Tunis. His family and his pastor extolled his compassion, kindness, and generosity. Afterward, people who knew him as a businessman spoke well of him. Though his name was just one of many in the newspaper obituaries, his death was a matter of great loss to us who knew and loved him. And it is comforting to know that God did not take his passing without feeling our pain. In fact, I believe He wept with us.

HERB VANDER LUGT

God shares in our sorrow.

In Brief

PSALM 117

*For great is his love toward us, and the faithfulness
of the LORD endures forever. Praise the LORD.*
PSALM 117:2

I counted once and discovered that Abraham Lincoln's Gettysburg Address contains fewer than three hundred words. This means, among other things, that words don't have to be many to be memorable.

That's one reason I like Psalm 117. Brevity is its hallmark. The psalmist said all he had to say in twenty-nine words (actually, it is fewer words than that in the Hebrew text).

"Praise the LORD, all you nations; extol him, all you peoples. For great is his love toward us, and the faithfulness of the LORD endures forever. Praise the LORD!"

Ah, that's the good news! Contained in this hallelujah psalm is a message to all nations of the world that God's love toward us is great (v. 2).

Think about what God's love means. God loved us before we were born; He will love us after we die. Not one thing can separate us from the love of God that is in Jesus our Lord (Romans 8:39). His heart is an inexhaustible and irrepressible fountain of love!

As I read this brief psalm of praise to God, I can think of no greater encouragement for our journey than its reminder of God's merciful kindness. Praise the Lord!

DAVID ROPER

**What we know about God should lead us
to give joyful praise to Him.**

No Peas

PSALM 118:1–14

*In every situation, by prayer and petition, with thanksgiving,
present your requests to God.*

PHILIPPIANS 4:6

When our kids were young, one of them bluntly said "no" when we passed him some peas for dinner. To which we replied, "No what?" We hoped he would say, "No, thank you." Instead he said, "No peas!" That led to a discussion about the importance of good manners. In fact, we had similar discussions on numerous occasions.

Beyond good manners—which are external—our Lord reminds us that we are to have a heart of gratitude. Scripture contains dozens of reminders that expressing gratitude is of primary importance in our relationship with God. Psalm 118 begins and ends with the exhortation to "give thanks to the LORD" (vv. 1, 29). We are to give thanks when we come into His presence (100:4). And the requests we bring to Him are to be wrapped in a spirit of thanksgiving (Philippians 4:6). Such an attitude of gratitude will help us remember our abundant blessings. Even in the midst of trouble and despair, God's presence and love are our constant companions.

It's no wonder, then, that the psalmist reminds us to "give thanks to the LORD, for he is good; his love endures forever" (Psalm 118:1).

JOE STOWELL

**It is only with gratitude that life becomes rich.
—Dietrich Bonhoeffer**

The Robin Response

PSALM 118:1–18

Endure hardship as discipline; God is treating you as his children.
For what children are not disciplined by their father?

HEBREWS 12:7

Our response to God's loving correction determines whether we will benefit from it. We can respond to God's chastening in one of three ways. (1) We can just resign ourselves to it without gaining instruction from it. (2) We can "buckle under" and become so depressed that we doubt God's love for us. (3) We can gratefully accept it and thank God for loving us enough to correct us. The third response is the right one, for it always benefits us and brings glory to God.

These three responses remind me of the way certain birds react in a rainstorm. The duck is indifferent to the rain—oblivious to its effect. The chicken becomes a most miserable, helpless creature in the downpour. But the robin sings in the rain, seemingly thankful for the refreshing showers.

What is our response when God lovingly chastens us? If we react like the robin, we become more than conquerors through Him who loved us. Of course, no chastening is pleasant at the time (Hebrews 12:11). However, God's Word promises that it will yield the fruit of righteousness if we let it work in us.

Have you been complaining because of God's discipline? Remember, He is working to make you more like His Son. Try praising Him! That's the right response.

PAUL VAN GORDER

What happens to us is not nearly so important
as what happens in us.

When You Are Hated

PSALM 118:1–21

The LORD is with me; I will not be afraid.
What can mere mortals do to me?

PSALM 118:6

As I was reading about Romanian believers who stood for Christ in the face of imprisonment, torture, and death, I thought of our Lord's exhortation, "Do not be afraid of those who kill the body but cannot kill the soul" (Matthew 10:28). All through church history, imprisoned and suffering Christians have found comfort in the assurance that God would deliver them—either back to their loved ones on earth or through death to the company of the saints already in heaven.

Although severe opposition to Christianity still exists in parts of the world, most of us don't face life-threatening persecution. But all Christians experience faith-testing trials.

One former professional football player who made an amazing recovery from a paralyzing injury spoke of his faith in Christ while appearing on a secular talk show. During the program, a caller vehemently denounced him for an earlier appearance on a Christian television program. The caller's hatred of Jesus Christ came through loud and clear.

Like believers down through the centuries, we can expect that we will be hated and attacked (John 15:18–19). But we need not be afraid. God is in control. He will defeat the forces of evil and honor His people. We too can say, "The LORD is with me; I will not be afraid" (Psalm 118:6).

HERB VANDER LUGT

To be right with God may cause us to be in trouble with others.

This Is the Day

PSALM 118:19–29

This is the day the LORD has made; we will rejoice and be glad in it.
PSALM 118:24 (NKJV)

In 1940, Dr. Virginia Connally, age twenty-seven, braved opposition and criticism to become the first female physician in Abilene, Texas. A few months before Dr. Connally's one-hundredth birthday in 2012, the Texas Medical Association presented her with its Distinguished Service Award, Texas's highest physician honor. Between those two landmark events, Dr. Connally enthusiastically embraced a passion for spreading the gospel around the world through her many medical mission trips while living a life of service to God and to others—one day at a time.

Dr. Connally's pastor, Phil Christopher, said, "Every day for her is a gift." He recalled a letter in which she wrote, "Every tour, trip, effort, I wonder if this will be my last and ultimate? Only God knows. And this is enough." The psalmist wrote, "This is the day the LORD has made; we will rejoice and be glad in it" (Psalm 118:24 NKJV). So often we focus on the disappointments of yesterday or the uncertainties of tomorrow and miss God's matchless gift to us: Today!

Dr. Connally said of her journey with Christ, "As you live a life of faith, you're not looking for the results. I was just doing the things that God planted in my life and heart."

God made today. Let's celebrate it and make the most of every opportunity to serve others in His name.

DAVID MCCASLAND

Welcome each day as a gift from God.

Making It Stick

PSALM 119:9–16

I have hidden your word in my heart that I might not sin against you.
PSALM 119:11

One day a young Christian came into a mission station in Korea to visit the man who had been instrumental in his conversion to Christ. After the customary greetings, the missionary asked the reason for his coming. "I have been memorizing some verses in the Bible," he said, "and I want to quote them to you." He had walked hundreds of miles just to recite some Scripture verses to his father in the faith.

The missionary listened as he recited without error the entire Sermon on the Mount. He commended the young man for his remarkable feat of memory then cautioned that he must not only "say" the Scriptures but also practice them. With glowing face, the new Christian responded, "Oh, that is the way I learned them. I tried to memorize them but they wouldn't stick, so I hit on this plan. First, I would learn a verse. Then I would practice what the verse said on a neighbor who was not a Christian. After that I found I could remember it."

Could this be the secret of retaining the Word of God? James gives this succinct command, "But be doers of the word, and not hearers only" (James 1:22 NKJV).

Try that Korean Christian's method of memorizing Scripture. Perhaps that will help make it stick.

PAUL VAN GORDER

To get ahold of Scripture, let Scripture get ahold of you.

"I'd Sit Down and Cry"

PSALM 119:9–16

I meditate on your precepts and consider your ways.
PSALM 119:15

Reading the Bible is vital for every Christian. How can we learn about God or grow spiritually if we do not spend time studying the Book in which He has made himself known to us? Taking a few minutes each day to read a chapter is a good way to start. But we should also block out extended periods of time for exploring God's Word and reflecting on what He is saying to us.

The importance of spending much time with something of great value and beauty is illustrated by a quote from *National Geographic* magazine about Carl Sharsmith, an eighty-one-year-old guide in Yosemite National Park. "Carl was back at his tent quarters after a long afternoon with tourists. His nose was flaked white and red with sunburn; his eyes were watery, partly from age but also from hearing again an old question after a half-century of summers in California's Yosemite National Park. A lady tourist had hit him with a question where it hurt: 'I've only got an hour to spend at Yosemite,' she declared. 'What should I do? Where should I go?' The old naturalist-interpreter-ranger finally found voice to reply. 'Ah, lady, only an hour.' He repeated it slowly. 'I suppose that if I had only an hour to spend at Yosemite, I'd just walk over there by the river and sit down and cry.'"

A whole lifetime is not long enough to appreciate fully the beauty and learning and value of the Bible. That's why we must take time to study its truths and make them real in our lives.

DAVID EGNER

**The deep truths of the Word are best mined
with the spade of meditation.**

The Bible and Changed Lives

PSALM 119:1–16

I delight in your decrees; I will not neglect your word.
PSALM 119:16

William Wilberforce (1759–1833) was a clever debater, a shrewd politician, and a popular socialite. At age twenty-one, he became a member of Parliament in England during a time of terrible moral and spiritual decline. The rich were making a mockery of marriage, the poor were downtrodden, and the slave trade was booming.

For a time, Wilberforce went along with these evils, thinking only of his personal ambitions. But when he was twenty-five, he traveled to France with one of his former teachers, Isaac Milner. During this trip, Wilberforce read and studied the Bible with Milner. Before long he surrendered his life to Christ and was transformed. The parties he once enjoyed now seemed indecent. The plight of the poor now troubled him. And he soon became the leader in the battle against slavery, which was abolished in England in 1833, primarily due to his efforts.

Wilberforce was transformed because he read and then obeyed the Bible. Do you want to know God and do His will? Read the Bible regularly and take its message seriously. Obeying God's Word will bring radiance and victory into your life.

HERB VANDER LUGT

**The Spirit of God uses the Word of God
to change the people of God.**

The Frog's Blackboard

PSALM 119:33–40

Turn my eyes away from worthless things;
preserve my life according to your word.
PSALM 119:37

As a young boy, one of my favorite pastimes was hunting frogs along the banks of a pond near our home. I was unaware of their unique visual powers that enabled them to elude me so easily. Later I learned that the frog's optical field is like a blackboard wiped clean, and that the only images it receives are objects that directly concern him. These little amphibians are never distracted by unimportant things, but are aware only of essentials and whatever may be dangerous to them.

In the Christian life we frequently become preoccupied with the vain things of the world. We allow our lives to become so cluttered with materialistic and insignificant concerns that we lose perspective of the things that endure. In our text the psalmist asked God for help in fixing his attention on what is good and lasting (Psalm 119:37).

The Lord's words should not depart from our eyes, but must be kept in our heart (Proverbs 4:21). Then our field of vision will be wiped clean of unnecessary things, and we will see clearly what God wants us to do.

Have you become distracted by sin so that you can no longer discern what is really important? Then take a lesson from the frog's "blackboard" and center your gaze on Christ and His will for your life.

MART DEHAAN

The more attracted we are to Christ,
the less we'll be distracted by the world.

Lasting Nourishment

PSALM 119:33-40

Teach me, LORD, the way of your decrees, ...
Preserve my life according to your word.

PSALM 119:33-37

Do you remember what your pastor spoke about eight weeks ago? Probably not. After all, it's been a while. But does that mean it wasn't a valuable message or that it was a waste of your time to hear God's Word being preached?

Absolutely not—especially if we see God's Word and its teaching as a source of keeping us alive spiritually. Former major league baseball player Shawn Boskie learned this truth while talking with fellow pro baseball veteran and Christian Mark Dewey. "Mark asked me if I remembered what I had for lunch the thirteenth of last month, and I told him I couldn't remember. He said, 'But did it nourish you?' I said, 'Yes, I guess it did.'"

Boskie got Dewey's point. "I think that's the way God's Word is," Shawn concluded. "It nourishes us even though we may not be able to remember exactly what it was we read."

The Word of God is indeed nourishment, and it comes to us from various sources: preaching, music that glorifies and praises God, and Bible-based literature, to list a few. We need to continually feed our souls—not so we can remember facts, but so we can grow stronger.

You may not recall all the details of each spiritual meal, but one thing is sure: It's lasting nourishment.

DAVE BRANON

One mark of a well-fed soul is a well-read Bible.

Use as Directed

PSALM 119:33–48

When your words came, I ate them;
they were my joy and my heart's delight,
for I bear your name, LORD God Almighty.

JEREMIAH 15:16

Dr. Smiley Blanton was a busy New York City psychiatrist who kept a Bible on his desk. Somewhat surprised to see this, a client asked, "Do you, a psychiatrist, read the Bible?"

"I not only read it, I study it," said Dr. Blanton, a devout Christian. Then he added, "If people would absorb its message, a lot of psychiatrists would go out of business."

To clarify his point, Dr. Blanton said that if clients who are plagued by guilt would read the parable of the prodigal son and his forgiving father (Luke 15:11–32), they could find the key to healing.

Do we look for healing in God's powerful Word? We may read the Bible, but do we really believe it, study it, and put its teachings into practice? The saving truth of Scripture is God's potent medicine for delivering us from the disease of sin.

The prophet Jeremiah, despite difficulties and hardships, found joy in the words of the Lord (Jeremiah 15:16). And the psalmist loved the commandments of God (Psalm 119:48) and said to Him, "I delight in your commands . . . . I may meditate on your decrees" (vv. 47–48).

Like medicine, God's Word must be taken as directed. Are you internalizing its truth?

VERNON GROUNDS

The Bible contains all the nutrition a healthy soul needs.

"I Dare You"

PSALM 119:41–48

Never take your word of truth from my mouth, for I have put my hope in your laws. I will always obey your law, for ever and ever.

PSALM 119:43, 44

I heard a story of a little church that was having a reunion. A former member who attended the celebration had worked hard and had become a millionaire. When he testified about how he had grown in the faith, he related an incident from his childhood.

He said that when he earned his first dollar as a boy, he decided to keep it for the rest of his life. But then a guest missionary preached about the urgent need on the mission fields. He struggled about giving his dollar. "However, the Lord won," the man said proudly, "and I put my treasured dollar in the offering basket. And I am convinced that the reason God has blessed me so much is that when I was a little boy I gave Him everything I possessed." The congregation was awestruck by the testimony — until a little old lady in front piped up, "I dare you to do it again!"

There's a vital truth behind that story. We must not let past attainments stop our spiritual growth. The psalmist said, "I will always obey your law" (119:44). He knew he needed to keep his commitment fresh every day.

As Christians, we cannot rest on past attainments. We must give the Lord our full devotion now. Then no one will be able to say to us, "I dare you to do it again!"

DAVID EGNER

Use the past as a springboard, not as a sofa.

The Borrowed Bible

PSALM 119:49–56

My comfort in my suffering is this: Your promise preserves my life.
PSALM 119:50

Syeed was a Bengali guard hired by missionary Tom McDonald to protect the property of a Christian hospital under construction in Bangladesh. As Jay Walsh tells the story in his book *Ripe Mangoes*, Syeed noticed another worker, Monindra, reading an unfamiliar book.

One day Syeed visited Monindra to ask what he was reading. "That's a Christian Bible," he replied. The Bible was so precious to Monindra that when Syeed asked to see it, he refused. But Syeed would not be denied. For nearly a week he would sneak into Monindra's quarters, take the Bible to a secluded place to read, and then return it unnoticed.

Then one day Syeed could not be found. After a short search, he was discovered kneeling before that Bible, calling out, "Lord Jesus, save me!" As the months and years passed, Syeed suffered severe persecution for his beliefs, yet he never backed down from the decision he made that day while reading a "borrowed" Bible.

The Word of God is indeed powerful. It did for Syeed what it did for the author of Psalm 119. It gave him life, comfort, and courage (vv. 50–53).

Has the power of God's Word revolutionized your life?

DAVE BRANON

Many books can inform, but only the Bible can transform.

Rock Bottom

PSALM 119:65–72

It was good for me to be afflicted so that I might learn your decrees.
PSALM 119:71

I was in my early thirties, a dedicated wife and mother, a Christian worker at my husband's side. Yet inwardly I found myself on a trip nobody wants to take, the trip downward. I was heading for that certain sort of breakdown that most of us resist, the breakdown of my stubborn self-sufficiency.

Finally I experienced the odd relief of hitting rock bottom, where I made an unexpected discovery: The rock on which I had been thrown was none other than Christ himself. Cast on Him alone, I was in a position to rebuild the rest of my life, this time as a God-dependent person rather than the self-dependent person I had been. My rock-bottom experience became a turning point and one of the most vital spiritual developments of my life.

Most people feel anything but spiritual when they hit bottom. Their misery is often reinforced by Christians who take a very shortsighted view of what the sufferer is going through and why. But our heavenly Father is pleased with what He intends to bring out of such a painful process. A person who knows the secret of the God-dependent life can say, "It was good for me to be afflicted so that I might learn your decrees" (Psalm 119:71).

JOANIE YODER

When a Christian hits rock bottom,
he finds that Christ is a firm foundation.

The Word Stands Firm

PSALM 119:89–96

Your word, LORD, is eternal; it stands firm in the heavens.
PSALM 119:89

When the US Congress convenes each year, senators and representatives reopen debate on how to deal with the nation's social and political problems. Throughout the year, more and more laws are passed.

I often marvel at the growing mountain of laws. It's sometimes hard to understand why we need to add and change laws so often.

Our government's law-system contrasts greatly with God's system of moral standards. Although the Bible records many regulations that no longer apply to us, it also sets forth universal truths that never change. As David said in Psalm 119:89, "Your word, LORD, is eternal; it stands firm in the heavens."

Everything God wants us to know and how He wants us to conduct ourselves has been clearly spelled out for us. And God's truth must not be amended, voted on, or vetoed.

The Bible not only provides principles that stand forever but it also gives delight (v. 92), life (v. 93), and protection (vv. 94–95) to those who read and obey it.

Our lawmakers may be doing admirable work, but they can never give us anything as valuable as the Lord's permanent statutes. And we can do no better than to live by the Word of God, which "stands firm."

DAVE BRANON

In a changing world you can trust God's unchanging Word.

One Verse

PSALM 119:89–96

For the word of God is alive and active. Sharper than any double-edged sword, it penetrates even to dividing soul and spirit, joints and marrow; it judges the thoughts and attitudes of the heart.

HEBREWS 4:12

Which of the 31,173 verses in the Bible is your favorite? And do you think that verse can make a difference in someone's life?

God has used certain verses to make a remarkable impact on the world. For example, the author of *The Pilgrim's Progress,* John Bunyan, touched the lives of thousands by preaching from John 6:37, "All those the Father gives me will come to me, and whoever comes to me I will never drive away."

Noted reformer Martin Luther greatly influenced the course of church history because of his understanding of Romans 1:17, "The righteous will live by faith." And missionary pioneer William Carey introduced the gospel to India after being touched by the words of Isaiah 54:2, "Enlarge the place of your tent."

As a young person about to embark on my first overseas missionary venture, I was moved, challenged, and comforted by Jeremiah 33:3. God used this verse to remind me to call on Him because He had "great and mighty things" (KJV) in store for me.

Maybe a specific verse from Scripture has touched your heart in a special way. Share that truth with others—because God's Word will always have an impact.

DAVE BRANON

One truth from the Bible is worth more than all the wisdom of humankind.

"That's Not Jade"

PSALM 119:97–104

Watch your life and doctrine closely. Persevere in them, because if you do, you will save both yourself and your hearers.

1 TIMOTHY 4:16

The devoted Christian who wants to stay true to the faith may wonder how he or she can detect wrong teaching. The solution is simple. Learn the truth so well you'll be able to spot false doctrine the moment you see it.

The following story from Haddon Robinson's book *Biblical Preaching* helps to illustrate the point: "A Chinese boy who wanted to learn about jade went to study with a talented old teacher. This gentleman put a piece of the precious stone into his hand and told him to hold it tight. Then he began to talk of philosophy, men, women, the sun and almost everything under it. After an hour he took back the stone and sent the boy home. The procedure was repeated for several weeks. The boy became frustrated. When would he be told about the jade? He was too polite, however, to question the wisdom of his venerable teacher. Then one day, when the old man put a stone into his hands, the boy cried out instinctively, 'That's not jade!'" He had become so familiar with the genuine that he could immediately detect a counterfeit.

Similarly, we must become so well acquainted with God's truth that we recognize any departure from it. We can say, in effect, "That's not jade."

DAVID EGNER

The best way to detect a counterfeit is to know the real thing.

Guidance and Feelings

PSALM 119:105–112

Your word is a lamp for my feet, a light on my path.
PSALM 119:105

Many Christians equate God's leading with an overriding "feeling" or an inner impression. These strong inclinations, however, are not necessarily signs that God is directing.

John Hibben, former president of Princeton University, once invited a Mr. Buchman to dinner. The guest, an eccentric believer in divine guidance, arrived late and brought along three uninvited guests. When Buchman shook hands with Mrs. Hibben, he said, "The Lord told me to bring these three other men to dinner too." Mrs. Hibben, not expecting added company, replied, "Oh, I don't think the Lord had anything to do with it." "Why not?" retorted Buchman. "Because," responded Mrs. Hibben, "God is a gentleman."

This exchange raises an important question: What is our primary source for divine guidance? We recognize that strong impressions may come to us, but we must always test them to be sure they are in line with God's revealed will.

In his book *Knowing God* J. I. Packer cautions, "Feelings with an ego-boosting, or escapist, or self-indulging, or self-aggrandizing base must be detected and discredited, not mistaken for guidance."

That's good counsel—especially since we have a lamp for our feet and a light for our path!

DENNIS DEHAAN

Feelings must be considered in light of facts and faith.

Majority Rule?

PSALM 119:137–144

Your righteousness is everlasting and your law is true.
PSALM 119:142

Majority rule is right and fair for electing mayors, representatives, and presidents. Although it sometimes allows less-than-honorable people to get into office, it is a good system.

But people go too far when they want to apply the principle of majority rule to moral standards. They say that if the majority favors certain cultural practices, then it is acceptable.

Some things, however, are not up for a vote. If we had a referendum tomorrow and one hundred percent of the voters decided to repeal the law of gravity, it wouldn't change anything. You still couldn't jump off a building without being a smash hit.

Just as God has established physical laws that cannot be broken, so too He has set up moral standards. And if we break them, we are ultimately broken by them. Even if a governing body votes to change the standard, God's law remains the only correct guideline.

We must look to the Scriptures to discover what God's moral laws say. Then we must obey them. They are never up for a vote.

DAVE BRANON

God—not the majority—is our authority.

Treasuring God's Word

PSALM 119:161–168

I have not departed from the commands of his lips;
I have treasured the words of his mouth more than my daily bread.

JOB 23:12

What would you think of a person who possessed a priceless treasure but treated it as something of little value? Well, we could be guilty of that if we were to neglect the Bible.

In his book *The Wonder of the Word of God*, evangelist Robert L. Sumner tells about a person who treasured the Bible in an unusual way. A man suffered through an explosion, and his face was badly disfigured. He lost his eyesight as well as both hands. He was just a new Christian, and one of his greatest disappointments was that he could no longer read the Bible.

Then he heard about a lady in England who read braille with her lips. Hoping to do the same, he sent for some books of the Bible in braille. Much to his dismay, however, he discovered that the nerve endings in his lips had been destroyed by the explosion. One day, as he brought one of the braille pages to his lips, his tongue happened to touch a few of the raised characters and he could feel them. Like a flash he thought, I can read the Bible using my tongue. At the time Sumner wrote his book, the man had "read" through the entire Bible four times.

O Lord, help us treasure your Word like that!

RICHARD DEHAAN

The Bible is the best gift God ever gave to man.
—Abraham Lincoln

Look Up!

PSALM 121:1–8

My help comes from the LORD, the Maker of heaven and earth.
PSALM 121:2

In a park near our home there's a trail I enjoy walking on. Along one section there's a panoramic view of red sandstone rocks in the Garden of the Gods with the majestic 14,115-foot Pikes Peak behind them. From time to time, though, I find myself walking that section occupied with some problem and looking down at the wide, smooth trail. If no one is around, I may stop and say aloud, "David, look up!"

The psalms known as "Songs of Ascents" (Psalms 120–134) were sung by the people of Israel as they walked the road up to Jerusalem to attend the three annual pilgrim festivals. Psalm 121 begins, "I will lift up my eyes to the mountains—where does my help come from?" (v. 1). The answer follows, "My help comes from the LORD, the Maker of heaven and earth" (v. 2). The Creator is not an aloof being, but a companion who is always with us, always awake to our circumstances (vv. 3–7), guiding and guarding our journey through life "both now and forevermore" (v. 8).

Along life's path, how we need to keep our eyes fixed on God, our source of help. When we're feeling overwhelmed and discouraged, it's all right to say aloud, "Look up!"

DAVID MCCASLAND

Keep your eyes on God—your source of help.

His Mind Never Wanders

PSALM 121:1–4

He will not let your foot slip—
he who watches over you will not slumber.

PSALM 121:3

Has this ever happened to you? I was driving down the road on a pleasant evening after a full day. I was paying attention to traffic and driving defensively. The next thing I knew, I heard the crunch of tires on gravel. They were mine! I snapped to attention.

My mind had wandered, and I had strayed to the edge of the road. Either I was daydreaming or I was enjoying the beauty of the evening and forgot what I was doing.

What would happen if God's mind wandered? Consider Colossians 1:17, which says that in Christ "all things hold together." This means that in His providence, the Son of God keeps our world in motion. So if His mind wandered, trees would crash to the ground. Water would pour out of the oceans. The planets would go spinning off through space. Prayers would be unheard and unanswered. And those He protects would be left vulnerable to the attack of the enemy.

But that could never happen. Why? Because the God who never sleeps is watching over our world—and us—all the time (Psalm 121:3–4). We are ever at the center of His attention and His care. We are secure because we love and serve a God whose mind never wanders.

DAVID EGNER

Because God's mind is on us, we can put our mind at ease.

He's Up Anyway

PSALM 121:3–4

Indeed, he who watches over Israel will neither slumber nor sleep.
PSALM 121:4

Linus Mandy wrote, "A friend was telling me she helped out at a kid's summer camp a few years ago. After rounding up the troops for the night, she told them, 'Let's go to sleep and put our cares in God's hands.' 'Yeah,' said one of the kids, 'He's up all night anyway!'"

We all battle with the problem of worry. Fears about the future gradually creep in. Then they get stronger and stronger, and can eventually become overwhelming. This happens when we begin to replace our faith with anxiety, shifting the burden from God's strong shoulders to our frail ones. We fret. We're afraid. We can't sleep.

At times like this we need to remind ourselves that God is always on the alert. He never sleeps (Psalm 121:4). He knows everything, including what we fear (44:21). He is everywhere (139:7–10). He is in charge of our world (Ephesians 1:11). Therefore, we do not need to be afraid.

Do you really believe that God sees all, knows all, is all-powerful, and is in control? Then put your cares in His hands. Entrust Him with whatever it is that's keeping you awake at night. He'll take care of it. He's the One who never slumbers nor sleeps.

DAVID EGNER

Worry is a burden God never meant for us to bear.

Relief from the Scorching Sun

PSALM 121

The LORD watches over you—
the LORD is your shade at your right hand.
PSALM 121:5

Living in Britain, I don't usually worry about sunburn. After all, the sun is often blocked by a thick cover of clouds. But recently I spent some time in Spain, and I quickly realized that with my pale skin, I could only be out in the sunshine for ten minutes before I needed to scurry back under the umbrella.

As I considered the scorching nature of the Mediterranean sun, I began to understand more deeply the meaning of the image of the Lord God as His people's shade at their right hand. Residents of the Middle East knew unrelenting heat, and they needed to find shelter from the sun's burning rays.

The psalmist uses this picture of the Lord as shade in Psalm 121, which can be understood as a conversation on a heart level—a dialogue with oneself about the Lord's goodness and faithfulness. When we use this psalm in prayer, we reassure ourselves that the Lord will never leave us, for He forms a protective covering over us. And just as we take shelter from the sun underneath umbrellas, so too can we find a safe place in the Lord.

We lift our eyes to the "Maker of heaven and earth" (vv. 1–2) because whether we are in times of sunshine or times of rain, we receive His gifts of protection, relief, and refreshment.

AMY BOUCHER PYE

We find refuge in the Lord.

Help Is Standing By

PSALM 121:5-8

*The LORD will watch over your coming
and going both now and forevermore.*

PSALM 121:8

The child of God is never outside the watchful care of the heavenly Father. When we feel surrounded by forces that are too much for us, we do not need to fear because "God is our refuge and strength" (Psalm 46:1).

In his book *Where in the World Is God?* Richard Harding tells of a British oceanliner headed to America during the dangerous days of World War II. The captain had orders that stated, "Keep straight on this course. Do not turn aside for any reason. If you need help, radio a message in code."

A few days out at sea, the lookout spotted an enemy ship. The captain dispatched a coded message: "Enemy sighted! What shall I do?" Back came the reply, "Keep straight ahead. Help is standing by." The captain obeyed orders and kept on course.

Soon after they had arrived safely, the passengers and crew were surprised to see a great British escort ship steam into the harbor. That battleship, though out of sight, had followed them from England to America, prepared to help if necessary.

We cannot see God. At times we do not even feel His presence. But in the daily uncertainties of life, amid the dangers around us, in our most pressing hour, God is standing by to help. He will see us safely to the other shore.

PAUL VAN GORDER

God is present, even when we feel He is absent.

The Eye That Never Sleeps

PSALM 121

I call on the LORD in my distress, and he answers me.

PSALM 120:1

Detective Allan Pinkerton became famous in the mid-1800s by solving a series of train robberies and foiling a plot to assassinate Abraham Lincoln as he traveled to his first inauguration. As one of the first agencies of its kind in the US, the Pinkerton National Detective Agency gained even more prominence because of its logo of a wide-open eye with the caption, "We Never Sleep."

There is no better feeling than knowing you are protected and secure. You feel peaceful when the doors are locked and all is quiet as you drift off to sleep at night. You feel safe. But many lie awake in their beds with fearful thoughts of the present or dread of the future. Some are afraid of commotion outside or of a spouse who has been violent. Some cannot rest because of worry over a rebellious child. Others are anxiously listening to make sure a seriously ill child is still breathing.

These are the times when our loving God encourages us to cry out to Him, to the One who will neither "slumber nor sleep" (Psalm 121:4). Psalm 34:15 reminds us that "the eyes of the LORD are on the righteous, and his ears are attentive to their cry."

Pinkerton may have been the original "private eye," but the One who really has the eye that never sleeps is listening to the cries of "the righteous" (Psalm 34:17).

CINDY HESS KASPER

We can sleep in peace when we remember that God is awake.

Trust Me

PSALM 121

*When you pass through the waters, I will be with you;
and when you pass through the rivers, they will not sweep over you.*
ISAIAH 43:2

When I was a little girl, my aunt and uncle took me to Lake Michigan. While some of my cousins ventured far out into the waves, I played close to shore. Then my Uncle Norm asked me, "Can you swim?" "No," I admitted. "Don't worry," he said. "I'll take you out there." "But it's too deep," I protested. "Just hang on to me," he assured me. "Do you trust me?" Then I took his hand and we began to walk farther out into the lake.

When my feet couldn't touch the bottom anymore, Uncle Norm held me up and reassured me, "I've got you. I've got you." Then finally he said, "Okay, let your feet down. You can stand here." I was afraid because I thought we were still in deep water, but I trusted him and happily discovered that I was standing on a sandbar.

Have you ever been in so much despair that you felt as if you were sinking in deep water? The difficulties of life can be oppressive. God doesn't promise that we will escape the turbulent seas of life, but He does promise, "Never will I leave you; never will I forsake you" (Hebrews 13:5).

We can trust our faithful God to be there in all of our struggles. "When you pass through the waters, I will be with you; when you pass through the rivers, they will not sweep over you" (Isaiah 43:2).

CINDY HESS KASPER

**Before your burden overcomes you,
trust God to put His arms underneath you.**

Glad to Go to Church

PSALM 122

I rejoiced with those who said to me,
"Let us go to the house of the LORD."

PSALM 122:1

Some people enjoy going to church. They sing joyfully, listen intently, and feel enriched as they leave. But others seem bored. I remember a man who always slept through my sermons during my days as a pastor. I blamed myself. But one Sunday I noticed that he was sleeping before I started preaching. He may not have received much spiritual uplift from the services, but I'm guessing he always left refreshed!

Why do some people, like the writer of Psalm 122, look forward to a worship experience, while others say, "What a burden"? (Malachi 1:13). It may be the way the service is conducted, but that isn't usually the problem. Some people get bored with a service that is conducted the same way every Sunday, yet others take a real interest and find enjoyment in it. Some people are uncomfortable in a service that is unstructured and highly emotional while others thoroughly enjoy that kind of meeting. These different responses stem from different attitudes. Some people just go to church because it is the thing to do. Others prepare themselves for worship and go expecting a spiritual blessing.

Preparations for Sunday worship should take place Monday through Saturday. If we are regularly reading God's Word, praying, and serving Christ, we will be glad when it's time to go to church.

HERB VANDER LUGT

Come to church for a faith lift.

Join the Cry

PSALM 122:6–9

I urge . . . that petitions, prayers, intercession
and thanksgiving be made for all people.
1 TIMOTHY 2:1

A women's prayer group in my country holds regular monthly prayer sessions for Ghana and other African countries. When asked why they pray so incessantly for the nations, their leader, Gifty Dadzie, remarked, "Look around, listen to and watch the news. Our nations are hurting: war, disaster, diseases, and violence threaten to overshadow God's love for humanity and His blessing upon us. We believe God intervenes in the affairs of nations, so we praise Him for His blessings and cry for His intervention."

The Bible reveals that God indeed intervenes in the affairs of nations (2 Chronicles 7:14). And when God intervenes, He uses ordinary people. We may not be assigned huge tasks, but we can play our part to help bring about peace and the righteousness that exalts a nation (Proverbs 14:34). We can do that through prayer. The apostle Paul wrote, "I urge, then, first of all, that petitions, prayers, intercession and thanksgiving be made for all people—for kings and all those in authority, that we may live peaceful and quiet lives in all godliness and holiness" (1 Timothy 2:1–2).

As the psalmist exhorted the ancient Israelites to "pray for the peace of Jerusalem" (Psalm 122:6), so may we pray for the peace and healing of our nations. When we pray in humility, turn from wickedness, and seek God, He hears us.

LAWRENCE DARMANI

Prayer for those in authority is both a privilege and a duty.

Let God Take Care of It!

PSALM 123

As the eyes of slaves look to the hand of their master,
as the eyes of a female slave look to the hand of her mistress,
so our eyes look to the LORD our God,
till he shows us his mercy.

PSALM 123:2

During the Great Depression, my father moved to a farm as a tenant. He signed a contract stating that he and the owner would share equally in the proceeds from milk and crops. In the fall, however, the landlord wouldn't give us our share of the money from the wheat crop. Dad's appeals to him accomplished nothing, so he consulted a Christian lawyer.

Reading the fine print in the contract, the lawyer advised my father that he could take no legal action. The landowner was unethical, but he had been clever enough to keep out of trouble. Rather humorously the lawyer said, "Mr. Vander Lugt, you have three choices. You can kill the crook and get yourself into deep trouble. You can cheat him and become like him. Or you can take the wrong and let God take care of you and him."

As Dad told us about this, he said he knew he had only one real option—put the matter in God's hands. He never got his money, but as a family we never went hungry. And we learned a valuable lesson.

The writer of Psalm 123 was distressed because enemies were treating him with ridicule and contempt (v. 4). However, he calmed his spirit by looking to the Lord as does a servant who trusts his master. Are you willing to do the same?

HERB VANDER LUGT

He who abandons himself to God will
never be abandoned by God.

Sticks and Stones

PSALM 123

We have endured no end of ridicule from the arrogant,
of contempt from the proud.
PSALM 123:4

The psalmist was fed up with the "contempt of the proud" (Psalm 123:4). Perhaps you are too. People in your neighborhood, office, or classroom may be scornful of your faith and determination to follow Jesus. Sticks and stones do break our bones, but words can wound more deeply. In his commentary on this psalm, Derek Kidner refers to contempt as "cold steel."

We can fend off the jeers of the proud by becoming like them, or we can view their attempt to humiliate us as a badge of honor. We can rejoice that we've been "counted worthy to suffer disgrace for [Jesus's] Name" (Acts 5:41). Better to bear shame for a short time than to endure "everlasting contempt" (Daniel 12:2).

We must not become like the mockers by mocking them in turn, but we should bless those who persecute us. "Bless and do not curse," Paul reminds us (Romans 12:14). Then God may draw them to faith and repentance, and turn our moments of shame into eternal glory.

Finally, as the psalmist counsels us, we must "look to the LORD our God" (123:2). He understands as no other, for He too has endured reproach. He will show compassion to us according to His infinite mercy.

DAVID ROPER

When others' treatment of you gets you down, look up to Jesus.

Looking Back

PSALM 124

If the LORD had not been on our side when people attacked us, . . . the flood would have engulfed us, the torrent would have swept over us.

PSALM 124:2, 4

Psalm 124 is a look back at the goodness of the Lord in delivering and protecting His people. Angry pagan leaders were ready to swallow Israel alive, but the Lord intervened to rescue His chosen ones. Twice the grateful psalmist proclaimed, "If the LORD had not been on our side . . ." (vv. 1–2).

When we who believe in Jesus look back, we can say the same thing. Once I was a passenger in a car as it skidded across a glare-ice expressway toward a massive pile-up. The Lord saw fit to keep us from plowing into that tangled wreckage.

There have been times when I faced strong temptations. If it had not been for the Lord, I would not have had the strength to say no.

And a few years ago I labored through a prolonged period of emptiness, painful memories, suicidal guilt, and hopelessness. If it had not been for the help of God, I would not have made it through that dark valley.

"If the LORD had not been on our side . . . ." I've said it many times. I'm quite sure you have too. When new afflictions, hardships, doubts, or temptations arise, let's remember the Lord's grace in the past and say with the psalmist, "Our help is in the name of the LORD" (v. 8).

DAVID EGNER

God gives enough grace for whatever we face.

Looking Ahead

PSALM 125

*As the mountains surround Jerusalem,
so the LORD surrounds his people both now and forevermore.*
PSALM 125:2

One day I was talking with a man who expressed his apprehension about the future. He was certain the stock market would crash. He said he thought our country would soon be taken over by evil forces, and the church would be overrun with worldliness. And even though he professes faith in Jesus Christ, he is afraid that by some quirk or oversight he will end up in hell.

Psalm 125 reminds us that we do not need to face the future with such pessimism. The psalmist praises God because He has promised to protect and preserve His people. As the mountains around Jerusalem will not be moved, the psalmist sang, so the Lord surrounds His people forever (vv. 1–2).

God promises to provide us with His grace. We are safe for all eternity because He said so. Jesus said that not one of His own will be snatched from His Father's hand (John 10:28). And Paul wrote that nothing can separate us from the love of God (Romans 8:38–39).

This does not mean we are free to go out and sin. Paul wrote emphatically about the inconsistency of practicing a sinful lifestyle when we have "died to sin" (Romans 6:1–4).

We who know the Lord and walk in His ways have every assurance that our future is as secure as the unchanging character of God.

DAVID EGNER

**You need not fear where you're going when you
know God is going with you.**

What's in Your Mouth?

PSALM 126

Our mouths were filled with laughter, our tongues with songs of joy.
Then it was said among the nations, "The LORD has done great things for them."
PSALM 126:2

Communications experts tell us that the average person speaks enough to fill twenty single-spaced, typewritten pages every day. This means our mouths crank out enough words to fill two books of three hundred pages each month, twenty-four books each year, and twelve hundred books in fifty years of speaking. Thanks to phones, voicemail, and face-to-face conversations, words comprise a large part of our lives. So the kinds of words we use are important.

The psalmist's mouth was filled with praise when he wrote Psalm 126. The Lord had done great things for him and his people. Even the nations around them noticed. Remembering God's blessings, he said, "Our mouths were filled with laughter, our tongues with songs of joy" (v. 2).

What words would you have used in verse three had you been writing this psalm? So often, our attitude may seem to be: "The Lord has done great things for me, and I—

. . . can't recall any of them right now."
. . . am wondering what He'll do for me next."
. . . need much more."

Or can you finish it by saying, "And I am praising and thanking Him for His goodness"? As you recall God's blessings today, express your words of praise to Him.

ANNE CETAS

Let no thought linger in your mind that you would
be ashamed to let out of your mouth.

The Joy of the Harvest

PSALM 126

Let us not become weary in doing good,
for at the proper time we will reap a harvest if we do not give up.

GALATIANS 6:9

It is one of those rare, beautiful autumn days as I am writing this article. I am sitting on a cement block in my shirtsleeves, admiring the labor of my hands. I have just picked ten bushels of Red Delicious apples from my two small trees.

I think ahead to the winter evening when I will sit before the fireplace with a tray of these delicious fruits at my elbow. But then my mind recalls all the past hard work it took to produce these apples.

I recall how I climbed my ladder with pruning tools to trim those trees in freezing weather. I remember spraying those trees to ward off insects and disease. I murmured to myself, "Is it really worth all this work?" Today I have the answer in ten bushels of almost perfect fruit. Yes, it was worth it all.

For the Christian, today is the sowing, growing, and pruning time. We find ourselves wondering about the difficulties we must face as we serve the Lord. But the prospect of the future urges us on. It is the promise of harvest that brightens the way and makes the burdens lighter.

Are you bowed down and discouraged? Then look ahead. Keep your eye on the future and the joy of the harvest (Galatians 6:9).

M. R. DeHaan

A fruitful harvest requires faithful service.

Fun in God's Service

PSALM 126

Our mouths were filled with laughter, our tongues with songs of joy.
Then it was said among the nations, "The LORD has done great things for them."
The LORD has done great things for us, and we are filled with joy.

PSALM 126:2–3

My grandnephew, his wife, and their daughter are serving as missionaries in New Guinea. He closes his newsletters with these words: "Having fun serving Him."

With the word *fun*, he means pleasure, not a sense of amusement. How pleasurable it is to be an instrument in God's hand—leading people to the Savior, comforting the sick and sorrowing, bringing transformation to troubled marriages, and doing good in the name of Jesus.

I'm quite sure the writer of Psalm 126 would agree. The six verses radiate with a spirit of joy and gladness from beginning to end. The psalm opens with a reminder of a time when God "restored the fortunes of Zion" (v. 1). God had miraculously delivered His people from a grave situation (exactly what it was we don't know). It was like a dream come true—and His people were filled with joy as they responded with refreshing laughter and hearty singing. It was a revival!

After a prayer for another such revival, the psalmist made a promise to all who serve God: "Those who sow with tears will reap with songs of joy" (v. 5). An abundant spiritual harvest can lead to laughter and singing. Yes, serving Him is fun!

HERB VANDER LUGT

Joy is a fruit of the Spirit that's always in season.

Sermon in a Strawberry Patch

PSALM 126

This is to my Father's glory, that you bear much fruit,
showing yourselves to be my disciples.

JOHN 15:8

Strawberries are my favorite fruit. I even love strawberry plants, for once they preached a powerful, unforgettable sermon to me.

I was on my hands and knees in my garden pulling weeds when suddenly I noticed something I had seen hundreds of times before but never caught the lesson. It was the "runners" on the berry plants. From the main vine, a number of slender shoots extended like arms in all directions. They were thin, green stems creeping along the ground, being pushed out by that mysterious power in the mother plant. After reaching out about six inches, the end penetrated the ground and developed roots. Then the leaves of a new baby plant shot upward. All the while, before the infant plant was able to sustain itself, it received nourishment from the parent through the "runner."

When the new growth was fixed in the ground, the "runner" resumed its journey and reached out another six inches, still nourished by the original clump of berries. Then the process was repeated. As I noticed this, I forgot all about the weeds and saw only the mother plant sending out its runners. "O Lord, make me like those strawberries," I prayed, "reaching out to multiply and bring forth fruit."

We must bear spiritual fruit, or the process will soon end. This was the sermon I listened to on my knees in my strawberry patch.

M. R. DeHaan

Christians must produce fruit—if they don't witness, they wilt.

Keep Laughing

PSALM 126

A cheerful heart is good medicine, but a crushed spirit dries up the bones.
PROVERBS 17:22

A judge ordered a German man to stop bursting into laughter in the woods. Joachim Bahrenfeld, an accountant, was taken to court by one of several joggers who say their runs have been disturbed by Bahrenfeld's deafening squeals of joy. He faced up to six months in jail if he was caught again. Bahrenfeld, 54, said he went to the woods to laugh nearly every day to relieve stress. "It is part of living for me," he said, "like eating, drinking, and breathing." He felt that a cheerful heart, expressed through hearty laughter, was important to his health and survival.

A cheerful heart is vital in life. Proverbs 17:22 says, "A cheerful heart is good medicine." A happy heart affects our spirit and our physical health.

But there is a deeper, abiding joy for those who trust the Lord that is based on much more than frivolity and circumstances. It is a joy based on God's salvation. He has provided forgiveness of sin and a restored relationship with himself through His Son Jesus. That gives us a deep joy that circumstances cannot shake (Psalm 126:2–3; Habakkuk 3:17–18; Philippians 4:7).

May you experience the joy of knowing Jesus Christ today!

MARVIN WILLIAMS

**Joy comes from the Lord who lives in us,
not from what's happening around us.**

While We Sleep

PSALM 127

In vain you rise early and stay up late, toiling for food to eat—
for he grants sleep to those he loves.

PSALM 127:2

One translation of Psalm 127:2 reads, "He gives to His beloved even in his sleep" (NASB). I believe there's something wonderfully significant in this verse—something easily missed unless we understand that Israel's day began in the evening, not in the morning as it does for us.

Our days often begin with a great deal of hustle. We roll out of bed, grab a quick breakfast, and rush out the door. After all, we have so much to do!

On the other hand, Israel's day began in the evening. They rested and slept, then got up in the morning to join God in a work in progress, for "he who watches over Israel will neither slumber nor sleep" (121:4).

Israel's sequence of evening and morning is significant, I believe, because it pictures the attitude we should embrace in all our efforts. Our days should begin by resting in God's infinite ability. When we begin our work, we join God in what He is already doing.

It's useless to drive ourselves in anxious frenzy, to "rise early and stay up late" (127:2), as if success depended solely on our efforts. We must work hard and be faithful in all we do, but we must also realize that everything depends on God. He never stops working on our behalf. Before we begin our day's work, we must first find our rest in Him.

DAVID ROPER

Do thy duty, that is best; leave unto the Lord the rest.
—Henry Wadsworth Longfellow

Fine Crystal

PSALM 127

Children are a heritage from the LORD,
offspring a reward from him.
PSALM 127:3

I have a friend—call her "Ann"—who tells me that her fondest memory is of the morning she broke her mother's "priceless" crystal.

Ann's mother was having a party. She had taken her fine crystal from the cupboard and carefully washed it and placed it on the table. The crystal represented the only valuable material possession her mother owned, and it was used only on special occasions.

In her rush to get things ready for her guests, Ann's mother said to her young daughter, "Would you please find some place to play where I won't trip over you?" So Ann crawled underneath the table to play. Unfortunately, she kicked the leg of the table, and the crystal crashed to the floor. "Crystal exploded like shrapnel," she recalls. She had destroyed the most elegant thing her mother possessed.

"I'm so sorry," the little girl sobbed. Her mother gathered her in her arms and whispered, "Don't cry, honey. You are far more valuable to me than mere crystal."

Children are indeed our most valuable possession, more precious than anything we could ever buy or earn. They are "a heritage from the LORD" and "a reward" (Psalm 127:3).

Do your children know how precious they are to you? Why not tell them today.

DAVID ROPER

Little children are of great value to God.

Reasons to Be Admired

PSALM 127–128

Unless the LORD builds the house, the builders labor in vain.
PSALM 127:1

In a survey by national magazine, American teenagers revealed some surprising news about themselves. When asked whom they admire most, more than seven out of ten teens chose their parents over media stars, political leaders, and athletes.

Encouraging as these figures are, they should also challenge all of us who are parents. If we have our kids' attention to that degree, what are we doing with the responsibility?

Psalms 127 and 128 remind us that we need to depend continually on the Lord for help and direction if we want to build a happy home. With that in mind, I would like to suggest five principles we should prayerfully communicate and model before our children—principles that not only help them to admire us but also lead them to honor God.

1. Life's main purpose is to trust Christ and live for Him.
2. We care enough for them to protect them.
3. It's better to please God than to please people.
4. What we expect of them, they'll see in us.
5. They can't go anywhere and get more love than they get at home, not even from a boyfriend or girlfriend.

Teach your children these principles, and they'll have the best reasons to admire you.

DAVE BRANON

As the twig is bent, so grows the tree.

Ten Commandments for Parents

PSALM 127–128

*The father of a righteous child has great joy;
a man who fathers a wise son rejoices in him.*

PROVERBS 23:24

Children come without guarantees. No matter how well we take care of them, they don't always perform as we think they should. They're often hard to steer. Or they may lose their "brakes."

But this doesn't mean we as parents are without responsibility. We must help our children grow into godly people. David Wilkerson, author of *The Cross and the Switchblade*, said, "Good parents do not always produce good children, but devoted, dedicated, hardworking mothers and fathers can weigh the balance in favor of decency and moral character."

To assist in your quest to be good parents, here are ten commandments for guiding your children.

1. Teach them, using God's Word (Deuteronomy 6:4–9).
2. Tell them what's right and wrong (1 Kings 1:6).
3. See them as gifts from God (Psalm 127:3).
4. Guide them in godly ways (Proverbs 22:6).
5. Discipline them (Proverbs 29:17).
6. Love them unconditionally (Luke 15:11–32).
7. Do not provoke them to wrath (Ephesians 6:4).
8. Earn their respect by example (1 Timothy 3:4).
9. Provide for their physical needs (1 Timothy 5:8).
10. Pass your faith along to them (2 Timothy 1:5).

There are no guarantees. But we can have an edge in trying to "weigh the balance."

DAVE BRANON

**The character of your children tomorrow depends largely
on what you teach them today.**

The Right Time?

PSALM 127–128

Precious in the sight of the LORD is the death of his faithful servants.
PSALM 116:15

It was time. Not the time any of us would have chosen. Yet it was God's time. And we had gathered to accept it.

It was the day my dad would be taken from us in death. His eighty-three good years of service to his Savior and his fifty-one loyal years of family leadership were over. His strong, determined body had at last succumbed to the relentless processes of aging, disease, and the lingering effects of his World War II battle wounds.

Yet it was Christmastime. The time of bright lights, joyous songs, and talk of the birth of Jesus. It was time for anticipation, children's excitement, and peace on earth.

It was not a time, it would seem, to think about funeral arrangements and saying goodbye. How could this be the right time?

It was the right time because it was God's time. It was time for Dad to stop suffering. It was time for him to spend Christmas with Jesus. It was time for reunion with my sister in heaven—and how Dad loved family reunions!

It was the right time because God never errs. He knew that my father's work was complete, his influence would live on, and his legacy was secure. He knew what He was doing. Dad was home for Christmas. It was time—God's time.

DAVE BRANON

God's timing is perfect—even in death.

All Out of Teenagers

PSALM 128

Your children will be like olive shoots around your table.
PSALM 128:3

For more than twenty years, our home was blessed by the presence of teenagers. But when our son reached his twenties, my wife and I were all out of teenagers.

Those years were full of challenges and demands that sometimes zapped our strength and took all of our mental and emotional reserves. Along the way, we navigated the rough seas of the sudden death of one of our four teens. We also enjoyed the thrills of success and struggled through the turmoil of rebellion. As I look back on our experiment in parenting, we learned some valuable lessons:

- Some teens follow life in a straight line, while others zig-zag along life's pathway. It's best to "zig" with them in love and with courage.
- All teens need unconditional love because they live in a conditional world.
- A love of God's Word is vital to successfully transferring faith from one generation to the next.
- Teens need to develop a relationship with Christ that is based not on rules but on a deep love of Jesus.

What young people has God placed in your life? Whatever their age, love them unconditionally. Help them learn to love God's Word. Show them how to have a deep love for Jesus. And hold on!

DAVE BRANON

Don't merely spend time with your children—invest it.

It's Okay to Be Happy

PSALM 128

Rejoice in the LORD and be glad, you righteous;
sing, all you who are upright in heart!
PSALM 32:11

"Is it all right for me to be happy?" This is a question a number of people have asked—including me. It may be voiced by someone who can't erase the memory of some sinful conduct confessed and forsaken many years ago. Or a person who carelessly injured someone and caused great pain may wonder if he has any right to be happy.

Such a question may grow out of a sensitivity to the misery of others. It comes to my mind when I'm enjoying a happy evening at home while a friend is suffering intense pain in the hospital, or while hundreds are grieving over the death of dear ones in a major human tragedy. With so many people who are sick, cold, hungry, out of work, or homeless, do we have a right to be happy?

The Bible answers this troubling question with a resounding YES! Of course, we are to be sorry about our sins, and we must be concerned about the grief and pain of others. But after we have confessed and forsaken sin, we should accept God's forgiveness and rejoice in it. After we have prayed for the suffering and sorrowing and have done what we can to help, we should gratefully enjoy the good things of life. They are blessings from the gracious hand of the Lord (Psalm 128).

Yes, it's okay to be happy!

HERB VANDER LUGT

Joy is the byproduct of trusting God.

Where Saintliness Begins

PSALM 128

Wives, submit yourselves to your own husbands as you do to the Lord.
Husbands, love your wives, just as Christ loved the church. Children,
obey your parents in the Lord, for this is right.

EPHESIANS 5:22, 25; 6:1

Five-year-old Brian was impressed by the story of Simon the Stylite, a Syrian hermit who lived in the fifth century. This man was admired as a saint because he lived for more than thirty-five years on a platform atop a high pillar. Determined to follow Simon's example, Brian put the kitchen stool on the table and started his perilous climb. When his mother heard some strange sounds in the kitchen, she came in, and shouted, "Brian! Get down before you break your neck!" As the youngster obeyed, he muttered, "You can't even become a saint in your own house."

Of course, Brian didn't understand that according to the Bible every Christian is already a saint, a person set apart for God. Yet his complaint does bring up another important fact: it is difficult to be saintly at home. In Robert Frost's "The Death of the Hired Man" is a statement that may explain why. Frost wrote, "Home is the place where, when you have to go there, they have to take you in." When we go out in public, we try to appear pleasant and attractive because we desire approval, but at home we figure that our family will love us no matter how we act. We're not always saintly.

Psalm 128 portrays a God-fearing father, a fulfilled mother, and children at a well-supplied table. Saintliness starts at home.

HERB VANDER LUGT

If Christ resides in your heart, let Him also preside in your home.

No Record of Our Sins

PSALM 130

If you, LORD, kept a record of sins, Lord, who could stand?
PSALM 130:3

"Out of the depths" the psalmist cries to God (Psalm 130:1). His problem surfaces: terrible guilt for things done and undone in the past. "If You, LORD, kept a record of sins, Lord, who could stand?" (v. 3).

But, thankfully, God forgives. He does not keep an account of past sins, no matter how many or how grievous they have been. "Therefore, there is now no condemnation for those who are in Christ Jesus" (Romans 8:1). God's forgiveness then leads us to revere Him (Psalm 130:4). We worship and adore God, for grace and forgiveness cause us to love Him all the more.

But what happens if we slide back into old sins? What if sin lingers? We are to repent and "wait for the LORD" (v. 5). And we are to be patient while God works. We are not hopeless cases. We can "hope" in the One who will deliver us in His time.

We now have these two assurances: God's unfailing love—He will never leave us nor forsake us (Hebrews 13:5). And God's promise of full redemption in due time—He will redeem us from all our iniquities (Psalm 130:8) and present us before His glorious presence without fault and with great joy (Jude 24).

We're forgiven! We're free! With the psalmist, let's worship the Lord as we await His coming.

DAVID ROPER

When we're forgiven, no record is kept of our failures.

Forgiven

PSALM 130

With you there is forgiveness, so that we can, with reverence, serve you.
PSALM 130:4

God is highly dangerous. We are sinful and He is holy. Sin can no more exist in the presence of God than darkness can exist in the presence of light. To stand before Him in self-righteousness would be to invite our destruction. The psalmist wrote, "If you, LORD, kept a record of sins, Lord, who could stand?" (Psalm 130:3).

In a cemetery not far from New York City is a headstone engraved with a single word: "Forgiven." The message is simple and unembellished. There is no date of birth, no date of death, no epitaph. There is only a name and that solitary word. But that is the greatest word that could ever be applied to any man or woman, or that could be written on any gravestone.

The songwriter said, "With you there is forgiveness, so that we can, with reverence, serve you" (v. 4). That refrain echoes in both the Old and New Testaments. God is honored and worshiped because He alone can clear our record.

If God could not forgive us, we could only flee from Him in terror. Yet the God whose holiness threatens us is the God who through Christ redeems us. This dangerous God offers forgiveness for all our sins. We only need to ask Him.

Are you forgiven?

HADDON ROBINSON

Sin invites judgment; confession ensures forgiveness.

Out of the Depths

PSALM 130

*Israel, put your hope in the LORD, for with the LORD
is unfailing love and with him is full redemption.*

PSALM 130:7

Sometimes the more we do to get ourselves out of a hole we've dug, the deeper we get in. That's the way it was for a man I recently heard about.

After becoming a believer in Jesus Christ, he decided to get help for some family difficulties he had before his conversion. But when it became known that there had been child abuse, the counselor was required to report the incidents to the authorities. That led to an investigation, which resulted in his being taken out of his home. To add to his difficulties, he lost his job. But the man's newfound faith was genuine, and he continued to hope in God.

This sounds a little like the desperate situation of the writer of Psalm 130. For whatever reason, he too was in a deep hole—a hole as deep as the ocean depths. The good thing about his despair was that he knew where to turn. He said, in effect, "Lord, do something! Get me out!" (v. 2). And he expressed his awe that God was a forgiving God (vv. 3–4). But best of all, he realized that his only hope was in the Lord, and he held firmly to that confidence (vv. 5–7).

Do you feel that your situation is going from bad to worse? That you are in the depths? Cry out to God. Accept His forgiveness. Hope in Him, "for with the LORD is unfailing love" (v. 7).

DAVE BRANON

Jesus can lift you from the depths of despair.

Waiting

PSALM 130

Be joyful in hope, patient in affliction, faithful in prayer.
ROMANS 12:12

Day after day for years Harry shared with the Lord his concern for his son-in-law John, who had turned away from God. But then Harry died. A few months later, John turned back to God. When his mother-in-law Marsha told him that Harry had been praying for him every day, John replied, "I waited too long." But Marsha joyfully shared: "The Lord is still answering the prayers Harry prayed during his earthly life."

Harry's story is an encouragement to us who pray and wait. He continued "faithful in prayer" and waited patiently (Romans 12:12).

The author of Psalm 130 experienced waiting in prayer. He said, "I wait for the LORD, my whole being waits" (v. 5). He found hope in God because he knew that "with the LORD there is unfailing love and with him is full redemption" (v. 7).

Author Samuel Enyia wrote about God's timing: "God does not depend on our time. Our time is chronological and linear but God . . . is timeless. He will act at the fullness of His time. Our prayer . . . may not necessarily rush God into action, but . . . places us before Him in fellowship."

What a privilege we have to fellowship with God in prayer and to wait for the answer in the fullness of His time.

ANNE CETAS

God may delay our request, but He will never disappoint our trust.

Stop!

PSALM 131

*I have calmed and quieted myself, I am like a weaned child
with its mother; like a weaned child I am content.*

PSALM 131:2

Life is a busy enterprise. It seems there are always more things to do, places to go, and people to meet. And while none of us would want a life without meaningful things to do, the fast pace threatens to rob us of the quietness we need.

When we're driving a car, stop signs and other signs warning us to slow down are reminders that to be safe we can't have our foot on the accelerator all the time. We need those kinds of reminders in all aspects of our lives.

The psalmist clearly knew the importance of times of calm and quiet. God himself "rested" on the seventh day. And with more messages to preach and more people to heal, Jesus went apart from the crowds and rested a while (Matthew 14:13; Mark 6:31). He knew it isn't wise for us to accelerate through life with our energy gauge registering on "weary" all the time.

When was the last time you could echo the psalmist's words, "I have calmed and quieted myself"? (131:2). Put up a stop sign at the intersection of your busy life. Find a place to be alone. Turn off the distractions that keep you from listening to God's voice, and let Him speak to you as you read His Word. Stop and let Him refresh your heart and mind with the strength to live life well for His glory.

JOE STOWELL

**Stop and take a break from the busyness of life
so that you can refuel your soul.**

Getting Along

PSALM 133

How good and pleasant it is when God's people live together in unity!
PSALM 133:1

I can still remember what it was like to take our family on vacation, only to have the kids in the backseat mar the joy of it all by their bickering and complaining. Who doesn't remember the disruptive effects of "Dad, she touched me!" or "Mom, he won't give me a turn!"

If you've had that kind of experience, you can imagine how God feels when His children quarrel and complain. Getting along is important to God. Jesus prayed that we would "be one" so the world would believe He came from the Father (John 17:20–21). And to disciples who were prone to quarreling, He commanded that they love and serve one another (13:34–35; Matthew 20:20–28). It should also be noted that among the seven things God hates, He includes "one who sows discord among brethren" (Proverbs 6:19 NKJV).

So I'm not surprised that the psalmist tells us that when brothers dwell in unity, it's like "precious oil poured on the head, running down on . . . Aaron's beard, down on the collar of his robe" (Psalm 133:2). In ancient times, the oil of anointing was full of fragrant spices that graced the environment wherever the anointed one went.

May the unity that comes from our love and service to one another fragrantly grace our families, churches, and friendships!

JOE STOWELL

**Christians who get along with each other
spread the sweet aroma of Jesus.**

Encourage the Faithful

PSALM 134

*Praise the LORD, all you servants of the LORD who
minister by night in the house of the LORD.*

PSALM 134:1

I recall that in one church I attended we honored an administrative assistant for her thirty years of service. It seems fitting that those who serve God's church be encouraged in their faith and faithfulness.

There's a short psalm that gives a hint that the people of Israel encouraged those who served them in their house of worship. In Psalm 134, as the worshipers were leaving the temple after a day of praising God, they would lift their voices toward the Levites who were about to enter the temple for night duty (v. 1). The Levites and priests were responsible for burning incense, giving thanks, and praising the Lord in song (1 Chronicles 9:33; 2 Chronicles 31:2). The worshipers called on the Levites to continue praising God as they carried out their duties (Psalm 134:1).

As we go about our own activities, we sometimes forget those who labor in our churches. It takes many people to make sure that our worship experience is fruitful, our fellowship as believers is valuable, and our work together as Christians is profitable.

Following the example of the worshipers of old, let's encourage those who faithfully serve us in the church, whether we do so publicly or behind the scenes.

DAVE BRANON

**A word of encouragement can make the difference
between giving up and going on.**

A Voice in the Night

PSALM 134

Lift up your hands in the sanctuary and praise the LORD.
PSALM 134:2

Psalm 134 has only three verses, but it is proof that little things can mean a lot. The first two verses are an admonition to the priests who serve in God's house night after night. The building was dark and empty; nothing of consequence was occurring—or so it seemed. Yet these ministers were encouraged to "lift up [their] hands to the holy place and bless the LORD!" (v. 2 ESV). The third verse is a voice from the congregation calling into the darkness and loneliness of the night: "May the LORD bless you, . . . he is the Maker of heaven and earth."

I think of other servants of the Lord today—pastors and their families who serve in small churches in small places. They're often discouraged, tempted to lose heart, doing their best, serving unnoticed and unrewarded. They wonder if anyone cares what they're doing; if anyone ever thinks of them, prays for them, or considers them a part of their lives.

I would say to them—and to anyone who is feeling lonely or insignif-icant: Though your place is small, it is a holy place. The one who made and moves heaven and earth is at work in and through you. "Lift up your hands" and praise Him.

DAVID ROPER

Anyone doing God's work in God's way
is important in His sight.

Rained Out

PSALM 135:1–7

Praise the LORD. Praise the name of the LORD; praise him,
you servants of the LORD, . . . He makes clouds rise from
the ends of the earth; he sends lightning with the rain
and brings out the wind from his storehouses.

PSALM 135:1, 7

You have probably heard testimonies of how Christians prayed and the rain stopped just before an outdoor service was scheduled to begin. Or perhaps it didn't start pouring until the final "Amen." Nowhere in the Bible, however, does God promise that He will always answer in such a dramatic way.

One time I was asked to speak at an outdoor evangelistic service at a county fair in Michigan. It was to begin at 2:30 p.m. The grandstands were full. A fine Christian high school choir was in place. We had prayed for the service, even as heavy, dark clouds were gathering. Then, just as the first hymn was announced, a violent storm swept through the fairgrounds. Swirling winds and driving rain lashed the grandstand. Lightning flashed and thunder roared. It wasn't long until we were forced to cancel the service. We were rained out!

Did this mean that God had lost control of His universe? Absolutely not! Were we out of His will for trying to hold an evangelistic service? No. It simply meant that at 2:30 that afternoon in Centreville, Michigan, God had different plans.

Whether God stops the rain or lets it pour, we can be sure that He is in control and He will do what is best. And we can praise the Lord for whatever He sends our way.

DAVID EGNER

God may conceal His purposes so that
we will live on His promises.

Forever Love

PSALM 136:1–9

Give thanks to the LORD, for he is good. His love endures forever.
PSALM 136:1

You don't have to live very long in this world before it becomes painfully clear that nothing lasts forever. The car you were so proud of when you bought it is spending too much time in the shop getting fixed. Those clothes you carefully picked up on sale are now in the hand-me-down box. At home, the roof eventually leaks, the appliances break down, the carpet needs to be replaced. And relationships we think will endure often fall apart.

Nothing lasts forever—nothing but God's love, that is. Twenty-six times we are reminded of this inspiring truth in Psalm 136. Twenty-six times the writer gives us something for which to praise the Lord, and then he reminds us, "His love endures forever."

Think of what this means. When we sin and need forgiveness, His love endures forever. When our lives seem a jumbled mess that we can't control, His love endures forever. When we can't find anyone to turn to for help, God's love endures forever. When each day is a struggle because of illness, despair, or conflict, His love endures forever. Whenever life seems overwhelming, we can still praise the Lord, as the psalmist did—for God's love is always new and fresh.

No problem can outlast God's forever love!

DAVE BRANON

God's heart is always overflowing with love.

How to Carve a Duck

PSALM 137:7–8

For those God foreknew he also predestined to be conformed to the image of his Son, that he might be the firstborn among many brothers and sisters.

ROMANS 8:29

My wife, Carolyn, and I met Phipps Festus Bourne in 1995 in his shop in Mabry Hill, Virginia. Bourne, who died in 2002, was a master wood carver whose carvings are almost exact replicas of real objects. "Carving a duck is simple," he said. "You just look at a piece of wood, get in your head what a duck looks like, and then cut off everything that doesn't look like it."

So it is with God. He looks at you and me—blocks of rough wood—envisions the Christlike woman or man hidden beneath the bark, knots, and twigs and then begins to carve away everything that does not fit that image. We would be amazed if we could see how beautiful we are as finished "ducks."

But first we must accept that we are a block of wood and allow the Artist to cut, shape, and sand us where He will. This means viewing our circumstances—pleasant or unpleasant—as God's tools that shape us. He forms us, one part at a time, into the beautiful creature He envisioned in our ungainly lump of wood.

Sometimes the process is wonderful; sometimes it is painful. But in the end, all of God's tools conform us "to the image of his Son" (Romans 8:29).

Do you long for that likeness? Put yourself in the Master Carver's hands.

DAVID ROPER

Growing in Christ comes from a deepening relationship with Him.

Those Inner Flaws

PSALM 138

The LORD will vindicate me; your love, LORD, endures forever—
do not abandon the works of your hands.

PSALM 138:8

All of us have personality flaws and character weaknesses. We see sinful tendencies in ourselves such as selfishness, irritability, impatience, and vindictiveness. Yet if our defects cause us to rely more heavily on Jesus, we can see them as blessings in disguise. As we acknowledge our weakness and seek God's help, we experience His grace and strength.

This link between imperfection and improvement is all around us in nature. Take, for instance, the formation of crystals, which make up valuable minerals and precious stones. Each kind of mineral and gem has its own special shape and appearance. In addition, every one of them is made up of a great number of atoms that are stacked in perfect alignment. Occasionally, though, one of these basic particles gets out of line. Surprisingly, these "flaws" or imperfections give gems their most beautiful properties.

How do you respond to your faults and shortcomings? Don't let them get you down. Instead, be honest about them and commit them to the Lord.

The psalmist said, "The LORD will perfect that which concerns me" (138:8 NKJV). Trust Him to turn your inner flaws into beautiful character.

MART DeHAAN

Only God can transform a sin-flawed soul
into a masterpiece of grace.

Beautiful and Broken

PSALM 139:1–6

You have searched me, LORD, and you know me.
PSALM 139:1

I was walking in the woods behind my home when I saw a beautiful, red-faced Western Tanager on the ground. The small bird had been attacked by a predator and was dragging a broken wing.

I gathered the bird in my hands—rough hands it must've seemed to him. Perhaps because he feared more abuse like he had already endured, he fought me ferociously, screeching in defiance, pecking my hands until he drew blood.

But I saw beyond the fury to his fear. I felt his heart racing under my fingers, so I held him close until he calmed down. Then I tucked him under my shirt and took him to the "Bird Lady," a neighbor who is known for nursing injured birds back to health. She would know what to do.

Some people are like that bird. They lash out in fury against anyone who tries to help them. But God knows the fear and brokenness that lie underneath. We can all say with David, "You have searched me, LORD, and you know me. You are familiar with all my ways" (Psalm 139:1, 3).

Let's ask the Lord to help us be sensitive to the hurts of others. Then let's respond with love, draw them close to us, and take them to the One who can heal their broken hearts.

DAVID ROPER

**God can mend your broken heart,
but you must give Him all the pieces.**

New Birth

PSALM 139:7–16

You created my inmost being;
you knit me together in my mother's womb.

PSALM 139:13

What is it about babies that makes us smile? Many people will stop every-thing at the sight or sound of a baby and will flock to gaze at the little one. I noticed this when I visited my dad at a nursing home. Though most of the residents were wheelchair-bound and suffered from dementia, the visit of a family with a baby almost unfailingly brought a spark of joy to their eyes that—tentatively at first but then undoubtedly—became a smile. It was amazing to watch.

Perhaps babies bring a smile because of the wonder of a new life—so precious, tiny, and full of promise. Seeing a baby can remind us of our awe-some God and the great love He has for us. He loved us so much that He gave us life and formed us in our mother's womb. "You created my inmost being," the psalmist says, "You knit me together in my mother's womb" (Psalm 139:13).

Not only does He give us physical life but He also offers us spiritual rebirth through Jesus (John 3:3–8). God promises believers new bodies and life eternal when Jesus returns (1 Corinthians 15:50–52).

Physical life and spiritual rebirth—gifts to celebrate from our Father's hand.

ALYSON KIEDA

I will praise You . . . ; marvelous are Your works.
—Psalm 139:14 (NKJV)

GodAware

PSALM 139:1–10

Oh, the depth of the riches of the wisdom and knowledge of God!
ROMANS 11:33

On the FlightAware website, Kathy checked the progress of the small plane her husband Chuck was piloting to Chicago. With a few clicks, she could track when he took off, where his flight was at any moment, and exactly when he would land. A few decades earlier when Chuck was a pilot in West Africa, Kathy's only contact had been a high-frequency radio. She recalls one occasion when three days had passed before she was able to reach him. She had no way of knowing that he was safe but unable to fly because the airplane had been damaged.

But God was always aware of exactly where Chuck was and what he was doing, just as He is with us (Job 34:21). Nothing is hidden from His sight (Hebrews 4:13). He knows our thoughts and our words (1 Chronicles 28:9; Psalm 139:4). And He knows what will happen in the future (Isaiah 46:10).

God knows everything (1 John 3:20), and He knows you and me intimately (Psalm 139:1–10). He is aware of each temptation, each broken heart, each illness, each worry, each sorrow we face.

What a comfort to experience care from the One of whom it is said, "Oh, the depth of the riches of the wisdom and knowledge of God!" (Romans 11:33).

CINDY HESS KASPER

We can trust our all-knowing God.

The Runaway Bunny

PSALM 139:7–12

Where can I go from your Spirit? Where can I flee from your presence?
PSALM 139:7

Margaret Wise Brown is known for her simple yet profound books for children. One of my favorites is *The Runaway Bunny*. It's about a little bunny that tells his mother he has decided to run away.

"If you run away," says his mother, "I will run after you. For you are my little bunny." She goes on to tell him that if he becomes a fish in a trout stream, she will become a fisherman and fish for him. If he becomes a little boy, she will become a human mother and catch him in her arms and hug him. No matter what the little rabbit does, his doggedly persistent, ever-pursuing mother will not give up or go away.

"Shucks," says the bunny at last, "I might as well stay where I am and be your little bunny." "Have a carrot," his mother then says.

This story reminds me of David's words in Psalm 139:7–10, "Where can I go from your Spirit? Where can I flee from your presence? If I go up to the heavens, you are there; if I make my bed in the depths, you are there. If I rise on the wings of the dawn, if I settle on the far side of the sea, even there your hand will guide me, your right hand will hold me fast."

God is relentless in His love for us—ever-pursuing, ever-present, and ever-guiding. Amazing, isn't it!

DAVID ROPER

No matter where you go, God goes with you.

Learning to Count

PSALM 139:14–18

How precious to me are your thoughts, God!
PSALM 139:17

My son is learning to count from one to ten. He counts everything from toys to trees. He counts things I tend to overlook, like the wildflowers on his way to school or the toes on my feet.

My son is also teaching me to count again. Often I become so immersed in things I haven't finished or things I don't have that I fail to see all the good things around me. I have forgotten to count the new friends made this year and the answered prayers received, the tears of joy shed and the times of laughter with good friends.

My ten fingers are not enough to count all that God gives me day by day. "Many, LORD my God, are the wonders you have done, the things you planned for us. None can compare with you; were I to speak and tell of your deeds, they would be too many to declare" (Psalm 40:5). How can we even begin to count all the blessings of salvation, reconciliation, and eternal life?

Let us join David as he praises God for all His precious thoughts about us and all He has done for us, when he says, "How precious to me are your thoughts, God! How vast is the sum of them! Were I to count them, they would outnumber the grains of sand" (139:17–18).

Let's learn to count again!

KEILA OCHOA

Let's thank God for His countless blessings.

Flying Backwards

PSALM 139:7–16

I praise you because I am fearfully and wonderfully made;
your works are wonderful, I know that full well.

PSALM 139:14

I had read that hummingbirds can fly backwards, but the cynic in me doubted it. So when my wife mounted a hummingbird feeder by the kitchen window and filled it with sugar water, I sat down with a cup of coffee to see if it was true.

Before long, hummingbirds began to appear—a ruby-throated male and several females. I soon gave up trying to watch their wings as they flew. All I could see was a blur. I was captivated by the feisty little creatures as they darted up and down, away and back, vying for an open spot at the feeder and chasing one another away.

After a while, only one bird was left—her long, thin beak sucking up the liquid. Then, when she was finished, she flew straight backwards, then up, and finally darted out of sight among the trees.

How did she do it? God knows. Sometime on the fifth day of creation, while He was forming whales, sharks, orioles, and loons, God created the hummingbird with its amazing ability to fly backwards—a miracle of His power.

I didn't need that awesome illustration to prove the existence and brilliance of God. But it did remind me once again that I have every reason to worship God, for I too am "fearfully and wonderfully made" (Psalm 139:14).

DAVID EGNER

The beauty of creation gives us reason to sing God's praise.

God's Marvelous Creation

PSALM 139:13–16

I praise you because I am fearfully and wonderfully made.
PSALM 139:14

In his book *If I Were an Atheist*, Wilbur Nelson includes a chapter called "If I Were a Medical Doctor." He reasons that medical doctors, of all people, because they are so knowledgeable about the human body with its marvelous functions and complexities, should recognize the Creator who fashioned and made it.

Nelson then gives us a whole series of "Think of's" to ponder. Here are just a few of them: Think of the human body, composed of more than one hundred trillion cells. Think of the skin—while water penetrates the skin outwardly, it cannot penetrate it inwardly. Think of the bones—capable of carrying a load thirty times greater than brick will support. Think of the liver—it breaks up old blood cells into bile and neutralizes poisonous substances. Think of the blood—ten or twelve pints of a syrupy substance that distributes oxygen and carries away waste from tissues and organs, and also regulates the body's temperature. Think of the heart—weighing less than a pound, it's a real workhorse. On the average, it pumps 100,000 times every day, circulating 2,000 gallons of blood through 60,000 miles of arteries, capillaries, and veins.

No wonder the psalmist declared to the Lord, "I praise you because I am fearfully and wonderfully made" (Psalm 139:14). We're not here by accident or chance. We are here only through God's marvelous creation!

RICHARD DEHAAN

**God's work of creating is done;
our work of praising has just begun.**

Breath of Life

PSALM 139:13–18

The Spirit of God has made me,
and the breath of the Almighty gives me life.
JOB 33:4

In his book *Life After Heart Surgery*, David Burke recalls his close brush with death. Lying in his hospital bed after a second open-heart surgery, he found himself in incredible pain, unable to draw a full breath. Feeling that he was slipping toward eternity, he prayed one last time, trusting God and thanking Him for forgiveness of his sin.

David was thinking about seeing his dad, who had died several years earlier, when his nurse asked how he was feeling. He replied, "I'm okay now," explaining he was ready to go to heaven and meet God. "Not on my shift, buddy!" she said. Soon the doctors were opening his chest again and removing two liters of fluid. That done, David began to recover.

It's not unusual for any of us to ponder what it will be like when we face our final moments on earth. But those who "die in the Lord" have the certainty that they are "blessed" (Revelation 14:13) and that their death is "precious in the sight of the LORD" (Psalm 116:15).

God fashioned our days even before we existed (Psalm 139:16), and we exist now only because "the breath of the Almighty gives [us] life" (Job 33:4). Though we don't know how many breaths we have left—we can rest in the knowledge that He does.

CINDY HESS KASPER

From our first breath to our last, we are in God's care.

Repeat After Me

PSALM 141

Take control of what I say, O LORD, and guard my lips.
PSALM 141:3 NLT

When Rebecca stood on stage to speak at a conference, her first sentence into the microphone echoed around the room. It was a bit unsettling for her to hear her own words come back at her, and she had to adjust to the faulty sound system and try to ignore the echo of every word she spoke.

Imagine what it would be like to hear everything we say repeated! It wouldn't be so bad to hear ourselves repeat "I love you" or "I was wrong" or "Thank you, Lord" or "I'm praying for you." But not all of our words are beautiful or gentle or kind. What about those angry outbursts or demeaning comments that no one wants to hear once, let alone twice—those words that we would really rather take back?

Like the psalmist David, we long to have the Lord's control over our words. He prayed, "Take control of what I say, O LORD, and guard my lips" (Psalm 141:3 NLT). And thankfully, the Lord wants to do that. He can help us control what we say. He can guard our lips.

As we learn to adjust to our own sound system by paying careful attention to what we say and praying about the words we speak, the Lord will patiently teach us and even empower us to have self-control. And best of all, He forgives us when we fail and is pleased with our desire for His help.

ANNE CETAS

Part of self-control is mouth-control.

Cracked Lenses

PSALM 141

My eyes are fixed on you, Sovereign LORD;
in you I take refuge—do not give me over to death.
PSALM 141:8

I started wearing glasses when I was ten years old. They are still a necessity because my sixty-something eyes are losing their battle against time. When I was younger, I thought glasses were a nuisance—especially when playing sports. Once, the lenses of my glasses got cracked while I was playing softball. It took several weeks to get them replaced. In the meantime, I saw everything in a skewed and distorted way.

In life, pain often functions like cracked lenses. It creates within us a conflict between what we experience and what we believe. Pain can give us a badly distorted perspective on life—and on God. In those times, we need our God to provide us with new lenses to help us see clearly again. That clarity of sight usually begins when we turn our eyes upon the Lord. The psalmist encouraged us to do this: "My eyes are fixed on you, Sovereign LORD; in you I take refuge—do not give me over to death" (141:8). Seeing God clearly can help us see life's experiences more clearly.

As we turn our eyes to the Lord in times of pain and struggle, we will experience His comfort and hope in our daily lives. He will help us to see everything clearly again.

BILL CROWDER

Focusing on Christ puts everything in perspective.

Cries of Desperation

PSALM 142

I cry to you, LORD; I say, "You are my refuge."
PSALM 142:5

They can break your heart. They remind me of the words of the psalm-ist: "My spirit grows faint within me, . . . No one is concerned for me" (Psalm 142:3–4).

I'm talking about letters we receive here at Our Daily Bread Ministries. They come from brokenhearted people who ask us to pray for them as they struggle through life.

"I have suffered nervous breakdowns and heart problems," says one person. "I try so very hard to accept God's will in my life."

A mother writes, "I'm so burdened for my daughter. She's backslid-den, and I wonder if she was ever really born again."

And yet another says, "I just had a cancer test, and next week I have a brain scan."

In Psalm 142, David was trapped in a cave, praying for deliverance from his powerful enemies. Although our situations may be far different, we can learn from him as we pray for help against the destructive forces we face in life. We can learn that God is always there to listen (v. 1), that He knows our situation (v. 3), and that He is our refuge (v. 5).

What is your pressing need today? Cry out to God. Lean on Him completely. Wait for His help. Then, like the psalmist, you too can praise God's holy name (v. 7).

DAVE BRANON

Your problems can never exhaust God's provisions.

Cave Man

PSALM 142

Rescue me from those who pursue me, for they are too strong for me.
PSALM 142:6

David was stuck in a cave (Psalm 142). Some Bible commentators think this was when he was running from King Saul, who wanted to kill him (1 Samuel 22:1). Trouble and troublemakers hounded him. Hemmed in by his circumstances and smothered by danger, he turned to God for help.

David was frightened, so he poured out his complaint to God (v. 2).

He felt alone and uncared for, so he cried out to God (vv. 1, 4–5).

His situation was desperate, so he pleaded for rescue (v. 6).

David was trapped, so he begged for freedom (v. 7).

What cave surrounds you today? A cave of despair brought on by grief or illness? A cave of difficulties caused by your own poor decisions? Are you stuck in a cave of questions or doubts that rob you of joy and confidence?

Here's what David did when he was trapped in his cave: He asked God for mercy, he sought refuge in Him, and he promised to use his eventual freedom as a way to praise God. In the end, he looked forward to the comfort of fellow believers.

Complaint followed by faith. Desperation followed by praise. Loneliness followed by fellowship. We can learn a lot from a cave man.

DAVE BRANON

In every desert of calamity, God has an oasis of comfort.

Thoughtful Praises

PSALM 143

I remember the days of long ago;
I meditate on all your works and consider
what your hands have done.

PSALM 143:5

Most of us long to praise God more joyfully than we do. One common hindrance is that no matter how hard we try, we often don't feel like praising Him.

Bible teacher Selwyn Hughes says that God has placed within us three main functions: the will, the feelings, and the thoughts. Our will, he says, has little or no power over our feelings. You can't say, "I am going to feel different," and then accomplish it by sheer willpower. What the feelings *do* respond to are the thoughts. Quoting another source, Hughes says: "Our feelings follow our thoughts like baby ducks follow their mother." So how can we make our thoughts the leader of our feelings?

David showed us the way in Psalm 143. Feeling overwhelmed and distressed (v. 4), he took time to think about the Lord (v. 5). He remembered God's lovingkindness, trustworthiness, and guidance (v. 8); His protection and goodness (vv. 9–10); His righteousness and mercy (vv. 11–12). Once David got going, his feelings began to follow his thoughts.

Name your own blessings daily; contemplate them thoroughly; speak about them to God and to others. Gradually your concern about feelings will diminish, and you'll be praising God with joy.

JOANIE YODER

Joy thrives in the soil of praise.

Paradogs

PSALM 143:7–12

Let the morning bring me word of your unfailing love, for I have put my trust in you. Show me the way I should go, for to you I entrust my life.
PSALM 143:8

I am amazed by the story of the World War II paradogs. In preparing for D-Day (June 6, 1944), the Allied troops needed the sharp senses of dogs to sniff their way through minefields and to warn troops of approaching danger. And the only way to get these dogs to troops behind enemy lines was by parachute. But dogs are instinctively afraid of being dropped from an airplane—and let's be honest, they are not alone. Yet after weeks of training, the dogs learned to trust their masters enough to jump at their command.

I wonder if any of us trust our Master enough to do challenging things we would never instinctively do or things that might make us fearful. We may not be instinctively generous or forgiving or patient with those who annoy us. Yet Jesus commands us to trust Him enough to do things that may be difficult but that will advance His kingdom. To say, "In You do I trust; cause me to know the way in which I should walk" (Psalm 143:8 NKJV).

Paradogs often received medals for their bravery. I believe we too will someday hear "well done" because we have trusted our Master enough to jump when He said, "Go!"

JOE STOWELL

Trust Jesus to show you how you can be used by Him.

No Complaining in Our Streets

PSALM 144:9–15

Deliver me; rescue me from the hands of foreigners whose mouths are full of lies, whose right hands are deceitful. . . . There will be no breaching of walls, no going into captivity, no cry of distress in our streets.

PSALM 144:11, 14

In the concluding verses of Psalm 144, David can be heard expressing his desire for the Lord's blessing upon His people. One of the things he requests from God is that there be "no complaining in our streets." One translator renders this phrase, "no cry of distress in our streets." Another says, "that there be no cry of distress in our city squares." Still another gives it this way, "May there be an end of raids and exile and of panic in our streets."

Any one of these renditions expresses a prayer that is most appropriate for our land today. A reliance upon the Word of God and its principles would unify us and make us strong. Instead, an increasing polarization divides us and contributes to the "complaining in our streets" (v. 14 KJV).

The only thing that will help "bridge" the great chasm of polarization of our society is to turn to the Bible, the written Word of God, and to the Lord Jesus Christ, the living Word.

No matter what happens, we have the assurance that the Lord Jesus is coming again! When His kingdom is established, "the earth will be filled with the knowledge of the LORD" (Isaiah 11:9). In that day there will be peace among the nations and "no complaining in our streets."

RICHARD DEHAAN

When people ignore godly principles, they invite problems.

Attics Are for Mice

PSALM 145:1–10

My mouth will speak in praise of the LORD.
Let every creature praise his holy name for ever and ever.

PSALM 145:21

I read about a young man who flunked out of the University of Michigan. In shame, he decided to disappear. For the next four years he hid in the unused attic of a nearby church. Taking great pains to conceal himself, he quietly prowled around only at night, living off food and water from the kitchen. He never left the building or spoke to a soul. No one ever suspected he was there. One day, a slight mistake gave him away. The young recluse accidentally made some noise and the police were called. He was finally discovered.

That shamed student reminds me of many believers in Christ who are overwhelmed by a sense of failure or embarrassment. They hesitate to take a stand for the Lord and may even try to conceal the fact that they are Christians. How unlike the psalmist, who publicly praised God for His greatness and goodness (Psalm 145:21). His relationship to the Lord was so wonderful that he couldn't keep it hidden.

Do you withdraw into an "attic of silence" rather than let it be known that you are a follower of Christ? If so, confess your fearfulness to God and ask Him for the courage to tell others about the wonderful salvation He has provided.

Remember, attics are for mice, not for men and women!

MART DEHAAN

A faith worth having is a faith worth sharing.

Seeing Near and Far

PSALM 145

The LORD is near to all who call on him.

PSALM 145:18

Having two healthy eyes is not enough to see clearly. I know this from experience. After a series of eye surgeries for a torn retina, both eyes could see well but they refused to cooperate with each other. One eye saw things far away and the other saw things close up. But instead of working together, they fought for supremacy. Until I could get new prescription glasses three months later, my eyes remained unfocused.

Something similar happens in our view of God. Some people focus better on God when they see Him as "close up"—when they think of Him as intimately present in their daily life. Other Christians see God more clearly as "far away" or far beyond anything we can imagine, ruling the universe in power and majesty.

While people disagree about which view is best, the Bible works like a prescription lens helping us to see that both are correct. King David presents both views in Psalm 145: "The LORD is near to all who call on him" (v. 18) and "Great is the LORD and most worthy of praise; his greatness no one can fathom" (v. 3).

Thankfully, our Father in heaven is near to hear our prayers yet so far above us in power that He can meet every need.

JULIE ACKERMAN LINK

God is big enough to care for the smallest needs.

Grandma's Recipe

PSALM 145:1–13

Remember the days of old; consider the generations long past. Ask your father and he will tell you, your elders, and they will explain to you.

DEUTERONOMY 32:7

Many families have a secret recipe, a special way of cooking a dish that makes it especially savory. For us Hakkas (my Chinese ethnic group), we have a traditional dish called abacus beads, named for its beadlike appearance. Really, you have to try it!

Of course Grandma had the best recipe. Each Chinese New Year at the family reunion dinner we would tell ourselves, "We should really learn how to cook this." But we never got around to asking Grandma. Now she is no longer with us, and her secret recipe is gone with her.

We miss Grandma, and it's sad to lose her recipe. It would be far more tragic if we were to fail to preserve the legacy of faith entrusted to us. God intends that every generation share with the next generation about the mighty acts of God. "One generation commends [God's] works to another," said the psalmist (Psalm 145:4), echoing Moses's earlier instructions to "remember the days of old . . . . Ask your father and he will tell you, your elders, and they will explain to you" (Deuteronomy 32:7).

As we share our stories of how we received salvation and the ways the Lord has helped us face challenges, we encourage each other and honor Him. He designed us to enjoy family and community and to benefit from each other.

POH FANG CHIA

What we teach our children today will influence tomorrow's world.

In His Hand

PSALM 145:14–21

My Father, who has given them to me, is greater than all;
no one can snatch them out of my Father's hand.

JOHN 10:29

Author Henri Nouwen writes about Jean Vanier, who liked to tell a story illustrating our need for intimacy with God. Nouwen comments, "When Jean Vanier speaks about that intimate place, he often stretches out his arm and cups his hand as if it holds a small, wounded bird. He asks, 'What will happen if I open my hand fully?' We say, 'The bird will try to flutter its wings, and it will fall and die.'

"Then he asks, 'But what if I close my hand?' We say, 'The bird will be crushed and die.' Then he smiles and says, 'An intimate place is like my cupped hand, neither totally open nor totally closed. It is the space where growth can take place.'"

Certainly God's powerful hand is to be feared and respected. But for the faithful believer, God's hand is also a place of rest and refuge. When we realize that we are safe in His hand, we can enjoy the secure and untroubled calm He intends for us.

In the hollow of God's hand, we are in the place of intimacy and growth and security. God will neither crush us nor let us fall abandoned. No one—not the devil nor our enemies—can take us out of His hand (John 10:29). In the intimacy of His presence, we need not be afraid.

DAVID EGNER

When we trust God, His power is not frightening but comforting.

The Joy of Your Presence

PSALM 145:1–18

Great is the LORD and most worthy of praise;
he is to be feared above all gods.

PSALM 96:4

"Man's chief end is to glorify God and enjoy Him forever," says the Westminster Catechism. Much of Scripture calls for joyful gratitude and adoration of the living God. When we honor God, we celebrate Him as the Source from which all goodness flows.

When we praise God from our heart, we find ourselves in that joyful state for which we were created. Just as a beautiful sunset or a peaceful pastoral scene points to the majesty of the Creator, so worship draws us into a close spiritual union with Him. The psalmist says, "Great is the LORD and most worthy of praise . . . . The LORD is near to all who call on him" (Psalm 145:3, 18).

God does not need our praise, but we need to praise God. By basking in His presence we drink in the joy of His infinite love and rejoice in the One who came to redeem and restore us. "In your presence there is fullness of joy," the psalmist says. "At your right hand are pleasures forevermore" (Psalm 16:11 ESV).

DENNIS FISHER

Worship is a heart overflowing with praise to God.

Hope Restored

PSALM 145:14-21

The LORD upholds all who fall and lifts up all who are bowed down.
PSALM 145:14

We who believe in Jesus Christ have every reason to be strong in hope. But what happens when that hope grows dim? When our circumstances or our memories or our thoughts lead us into feelings of depression or even despair? God can restore our hope.

I know, because I went through a dark episode in my life. It crept up on me gradually, unawares. As I look back now, I wonder how it ever could have happened. Finally I admitted that I was "bowed down." I could see nothing to be hopeful about. Inside, I had given up. I couldn't express it in words. I could only reach out to God for help.

God came to my rescue. His help came in several forms. Friends who had no idea what I was going through sent me encouraging notes. The two or three people I risked telling about my struggle were very supportive. My family stood with me. I received gentle, firm help from a counselor. The sunlight began to peek through the dark clouds. It became brighter as I continued to work and pray and think. I found great hope in today's verse. The Lord lifted me up.

Are you bowed down? So discouraged you feel there is no hope? Call out to the Lord for help, even if you can't put it into words. He will keep His promise. In His time, and in His way, He will lift you up.

DAVID EGNER

No one is hopeless whose hope is in God.

Looking Up

PSALM 146:1–10

The LORD lifts up those who are bowed down.
PSALM 146:8

An article in *Surgical Technology International* journal says that looking down at a smart phone with your head bent forward is the equivalent of having a sixty-pound weight on your neck. When we consider that millions of people around the world spend an average of two to four hours daily reading and texting, the resulting damage to neck and spine becomes a growing health concern.

It is also easy to become spiritually bowed down by the burdens of life. How often we find ourselves discouraged by the problems we face and the needs of those we love. The psalmist understood this weight of concern yet saw hope as he wrote about "the Maker of heaven and earth, the sea, and everything in them—[who] remains faithful forever. He upholds the cause of the oppressed and gives food to the hungry. The LORD sets prisoners free, the LORD gives sight to the blind, the LORD lifts up those who are bowed down, the LORD loves the righteous" (Psalm 146:6–8).

When we consider God's care, His great power, and His loving heart, we can begin to look up and praise Him. We can walk through each day knowing that "the LORD reigns forever . . . for all generations" (v. 10).

He lifts us up when we are bowed down. Praise the Lord!

DAVID MCCASLAND

Faith in God's goodness puts a song in your heart.

Julie's Shoes

PSALM 146

Blessed are those whose help is the God of Jacob,
whose hope is in the LORD their God.

PSALM 146:5

Shoes. Nobody had thought about shoes. The hectic pace of another summer week was suddenly upon our family, and it was time for my second daughter Julie to begin her week at basketball camp. Just a few minutes before she was to leave, it suddenly dawned on my wife, Sue, that Julie didn't have any decent basketball shoes.

We weren't prepared for a $40 surprise like that. Furthermore, it was too late to do anything about it. So Julie would have to show up at the gym wearing an old pair of ill-fitting shoes that weren't meant for competitive sports. But when Sue opened the door to go out to the car, there stood Connie, our next-door neighbor. And what was in her hands? Shoes. Basketball shoes. Too small for her Erin, but just right for our Julie. Although we had not thought about shoes, Someone had.

Did you ever read through the list of reasons to praise the Lord in Psalm 146? It mentions many ways in which God has demonstrated His providential care for those who live by faith in Him. The almighty Creator of the world lovingly cares for the needs of His people.

The Lord provides what we need today too. Things like shoes. Things that keep giving us one more reason to praise Him.

DAVE BRANON

God keeps giving us more reasons to praise Him.

Help Yourself

PSALM 146

Blessed are those whose help is the God of Jacob,
whose hope is in the LORD their God.

PSALM 146:5

Recently, I saw a television ad for a restaurant chain that made a dramatic claim. At those restaurants, the ad said you could "Help Yourself to Happiness." Wouldn't it be nice if a helping of potatoes or meat or pasta or dessert would be all that was needed to provide happiness? Unfortunately, no restaurant can fulfill that promise.

Happiness is an elusive thing—as we can see in almost every area of life. Our pursuit of happiness may involve food or a host of other things, but, in the end, happiness continues to escape our grasp.

Why? In large measure it's because the things we tend to pursue do not touch the deepest needs of our hearts. Our pursuits may provide moments of enjoyment, distraction, or pleasure, but the cry of our hearts goes unheard—the cry for help and hope. That is why the psalmist points us to a better way when he says, "Blessed are those whose help is the God of Jacob, whose hope is in the LORD their God" (Psalm 146:5).

Help yourself? Yes—if we are seeking the happiness found in the Lord. It is only when we entrust ourselves to God and His care that we can find the happiness we seek. Our hope and help are found only in trusting Him.

BILL CROWDER

The one who puts God first will have happiness that lasts.

Setting Prisoners Free

PSALM 146

The LORD sets prisoners free.
PSALM 146:7

When my wife and I visited the National Museum of the Mighty Eighth Air Force near Savannah, Georgia, we were especially moved by the prisoner-of-war exhibit, with its re-creation of a German prisoner-of-war camp's barracks. Marlene's dad, Jim, served in the Eighth Air Force, the "Mighty Eighth," as they flew missions over Europe during World War II. During the war, the Eighth Air Force suffered over 47,000 injuries and more than 26,000 deaths. Jim was one of those shot down and held as a prisoner of war. As we walked through the exhibit, we recalled Jim telling about the absolute joy he and his fellow prisoners felt the day they were set free.

God's care for the oppressed and liberation of the imprisoned are declared in Psalm 146. The psalmist describes the One who "upholds the cause of the oppressed and gives food to the hungry," who "sets prisoners free" (v. 7). All of this is cause for celebration and praise. But the greatest freedom of all is freedom from our guilt and shame. No wonder Jesus said, "So if the Son sets you free, you will be free indeed" (John 8:36).

Through Christ's sacrifice, we are set free from the prison of sin to know His joy and love, and to experience the freedom that only forgiveness can bring.

BILL CROWDER

**The prison of sin cannot withstand
the power of Christ's forgiveness.**

How to Be Happy

PSALM 146

Blessed is the one who trusts in the LORD.

PROVERBS 16:20

Everyone wants to be happy. Many people have failed in their quest to find that elusive prize, however, because they have been looking in the wrong places.

According to Proverbs 16:20, "Blessed is the one who trusts in the LORD." And today's text indicates that happiness comes to those who find their help and hope in God.

The foundation for happiness is a proper relationship with the Lord. But to fully experience that happiness, we must build on that foundation in practical ways. I found this list of "Ten Rules for Happier Living," which give us some excellent guidelines.

1. Give something away (no strings attached).
2. Do a kindness (and forget it).
3. Spend time with the aged (experience is priceless).
4. Look intently into the face of a baby (and marvel).
5. Laugh often (it is life's lubricant).
6. Give thanks (a thousand times a day is not enough).
7. Pray (or you will lose the way).
8. Work (with vim and vigor).
9. Plan as though you will live forever (you will).
10. Live as though you will die tomorrow (because you will die on some tomorrow).

Those are excellent ideas for happier living. Try them. They work!

RICHARD DEHAAN

Trusting and obeying the Lord brings true happiness.

He Knows Your Name

PSALM 147:1–9

He brings out the starry host one by one
and calls forth each of them by name.

ISAIAH 40:26

How many stars are there? Astronomers don't know. They simply assure us that the cosmos contains more stars than can be numbered. Billions for sure—probably trillions!

Figures like that are hard for us to grasp. Even the idea of a million is mind-boggling. If you were counting a million $1 bills at the rate of sixty a minute for eight hours a day five days a week, it would take you nearly seven weeks to complete the task. At the same rate it would take over one hundred thirty-three years to count a billion dollars.

Scripture declares that God, the Maker of the sun and moon, "also made the stars" (Genesis 1:16). It likewise declares that He "brings out the starry host one by one and calls forth each of them by name. Because of his great power and mighty strength, not one of them is missing" (Isaiah 40:26).

So if we ever wonder whether God is able to carry us with all our burdens, let us remember that He is the sovereign of the stars. Surely He who is the guide of the galaxies can deal with our situations.

If the skies are clear tonight, look heavenward and be thankful that the God who calls each star by name knows, loves, and cares for you.

VERNON GROUNDS

The One who upholds the universe will never let you down.

Our Caring Creator

PSALM 147:1–11

He heals the brokenhearted and binds up their wounds.
PSALM 147:3

Christian astronomer David Block tells us that our Milky Way galaxy contains one hundred billion stars—and that is just one small part of the vast heavens of which our planet is but a tiny speck. Considering the utter insignificance of our earth, it is hard to believe that the Creator of the cosmos cares about what happens to the human family that has been cynically described as a semi-invisible rash on the skin of a sub-microscopic planet in a second-rate solar system.

The astonishing truth is that God does care. Long before the invention of telescopes, David asked, "When I consider your heavens, . . . what is mankind that you are mindful of them?" (Psalm 8:3–4). And God doesn't simply care, He cares for everyone as if we each were the sole object of His loving attention! Psalm 147:3–4 contrasts the star-studded sky with the hurts of a single soul: "He heals the brokenhearted and binds up their wounds. He determines the number of the stars and calls them each by name."

Mind-boggling! The wisdom and the power that sustain the whole cosmos are focused on every believer. What a source of confidence and strength when we experience weakness and doubt!

VERNON GROUNDS

**He who holds the stars in space will surely
uphold his saints on earth.**

Hearts and Stars

PSALM 147:1–11

He determines the number of the stars and calls them each by name.
PSALM 147:4

Astronomers used Australia's largest optical telescope to map 100,000 galaxies that surround our own galaxy, the Milky Way. The three-dimensional map covers five percent of the sky and allows us to see four billion light-years deep into space. The number of stars included defies our imagination, but not the knowledge of God.

How amazing to read, "He determines the number of the stars and calls them each by name. Great is our Lord and mighty in power; his understanding has no limit" (Psalm 147:4–5).

Even more amazing, though, is the psalmist's affirmation that God, who is far greater than the universe He created, cares about our sorrows. Instead of being remote and aloof, He is close at hand with love and mercy for His own. "He heals the brokenhearted and binds up their wounds," wrote the psalmist. "The LORD sustains the humble but casts the wicked down to the ground" (vv. 3, 6).

Jesus Christ, the creator of the galaxies, visited our planet to pay the penalty for our sin and open the way to friendship and fellowship with Him. Today He stands ready to bring healing and wholeness to our deeply wounded spirits. From naming stars to mending hearts, nothing is too hard for God.

DAVID McCASLAND

In creation we see God's hand; in redemption we see His heart.

By Dawn's Early Light

PSALM 148

Glorify the LORD in the dawning light.
ISAIAH 24:15 (NKJV)

Dressed for warmth and walking the path by memory, I crept through the pre-dawn darkness to sit at a quiet place in Michigan's north woods. I settled at the base of a sixty-foot white pine, got comfortable, and joined the silent forest. As day began to break, discernible shapes emerged from the darkness. Inch by inch the dawn appeared, and with it came the awakening of the forest.

Here and there birds began to sing. A flock of majestic geese flew low to the horizon, punctuating the sky with their busy conversation. A doe and her fawns moved soundlessly along the pine break. A red squirrel stared at me and flicked his tail.

How could I experience the majestic panorama of God's creation and not praise Him? Quietly I did so, but my mind was shouting glory to His name for all the angels to hear. Yet, compared with the giant beech trees, lacy cedars, whip-thin poplars, and leafy ferns, my praise seemed insignificant. What could my words add to the wonder of the perky chickadee and the fleet-footed rabbit?

The author of Psalm 148 understood that all nature reflects the Creator's power and greatness. On that cool fall day I was privileged to join creation in glorifying God by dawn's early light.

DAVID EGNER

**Creation is the canvas on which God has painted
His greatness and majesty.**

Hubble, Zoos, and Singing Children

PSALM 148

Praise him, all you shining stars.
PSALM 148:3

What do the Hubble Space Telescope, a zoo, and singing children have in common? According to the teaching of Psalm 148, we could conclude that they all point to God's magnificent creation.

The idea that God created our world is often questioned, so perhaps it's a good time for a reminder of the praise we and all creation should heap on our heavenly Father for His magnificent handiwork.

The Hubble Space Telescope can help us with that through its eye-popping pictures of our universe. Every one of those brilliant photos points to stars that focus attention on God's creative majesty. "Praise Him, all you shining stars," says verse 3.

A visit to a zoo points us to the great diversity of wildlife God created. We look at verses seven and ten and say thank you to God for sea creatures, wild animals, insects, and birds.

And a few minutes of watching little children singing uninhibited praises to God symbolizes the truth that all people of earth should lift their voices in honor of our Creator (vv. 11–13).

Stars, animals, and children: "Let them praise the name of the LORD, for his name alone is exalted" (v. 13). Let's join in saying thanks for His creation. "Praise the Lord!"

DAVE BRANON

Creation displays God's power.

Star Praises

PSALM 148

Praise him, sun and moon; praise him, all you shining stars.
PSALM 148:3

The Hubble Space Telescope has provided us with dramatic pictures of the farthest regions of the starry heavens. Photographs show clouds of interstellar hydrogen gas towering nearly six trillion miles high, illuminated by the ultraviolet radiation of stars like our sun.

The telescope revealed evidence of an enormous galactic collision that produced immense shockwaves that pushed space dust and gases together to form new stars. The Hubble lens focused on Eta Carinae, one of the brightest and most massive stars known to man, which erupts every so often with enormous bursts of energy. And it has given a glimpse of a "stellar nursery," an area in the constellation Orion where "stars are mass-produced by the dozen."

After viewing space through the Hubble Telescope, astronomers used words like awestruck, overwhelmed, and amazed to describe their reaction. These are also appropriate responses for us as we think about the One who created this marvelous universe "at his command" (Psalm 148:5).

The stars speak in eloquent praise of the Lord's creative power. And if even the stars sing God's praises, how much more should we!

DAVID EGNER

All creation bears God's autograph.

Eclipse

PSALM 148

Let them praise the name of the LORD, for his name alone is exalted;
his splendor is above the earth and the heavens.

PSALM 148:13

A friend who experienced a total solar eclipse in England described the incredible sensation of being engulfed by the rushing shadow of darkness, then being awed by the rapidly approaching dawn. Some observers saw it as merely a coincidence that the moon was in the exact position to shut out the sun's light from reaching the earth at that particular time and place. My friend, though, called it an amazing show put on by God. She saw it as evidence of God's design, order, and precise control in the universe He created.

Psalm 148 calls upon all creation to shout God's glory: "Praise him, sun and moon; praise him, all you shining stars. . . . Praise the LORD, . . . kings of the earth and all nations" (vv. 3, 7, 11).

God's creation sings His praise and reminds us of His sovereign purposes and His control of all things in our lives. We are to "praise the name of the LORD, for his name alone is exalted; his splendor is above the earth and the heavens" (v. 13).

These truths can be comforting when the sunlight of our lives is eclipsed by a time of darkness and difficulty. We can trust and praise the sovereign God, knowing that His design is perfect, His timing is exact, and He is in complete control.

DAVID MCCASLAND

Because God is in control, we have nothing to fear.

Hymns of Praise

PSALM 149

Praise the LORD. Sing to the LORD a new song,
his praise in the assembly of his faithful people.
PSALM 149:1

Music is one of those good things in life we take for granted. Good music is a blessing from the Lord. It's a soothing tonic for troubled hearts. It can motivate us to live for Christ, and through it we can lift our hearts in praise to the Lord. Without music, we would be greatly deprived.

An old Jewish legend says that after God had created the world He called the angels to himself and asked them what they thought of it. One of them said, "The only thing lacking is the sound of praise to the Creator." So God created music, and it was heard in the whisper of the wind and in the song of the birds. He also gave man the gift of song. And throughout all the ages, music has blessed multitudes of people.

Singing God's praises honors the Lord, edifies our brothers and sisters in Christ, and brings us joy. As we join with other Christians in singing, it should be with a renewed appreciation of music. So let us join voices with fellow believers and lift our hearts in hymns of praise whenever we have the privilege.

RICHARD DEHAAN

Hearts in tune with God will sing His praises.

A Lesson in Praise

PSALM 150

Praise the LORD. Praise God in his sanctuary;
praise him in his mighty heavens.

PSALM 150:1

Psalm 150 is not only a beautiful expression of praise, but it's also a lesson in praising the Lord. It tells us where to praise, why we're to praise, how we're to praise, and who should offer praise.

Where do we praise? In God's "sanctuary" and "mighty heavens" (v. 1). Wherever we are in the world is a proper place to praise the One who created all things.

Why do we praise? First, because of what God does. He performs "acts of power." Second, because of who God is. The psalmist praised Him for "his surpassing greatness" (v. 2). The all-powerful Creator is the Sustainer of the universe.

How should we praise? Loudly. Softly. Soothingly. Enthusiastically. Rhythmically. Boldly. Unexpectedly. Fearlessly. In other words, we can praise God in many ways and on many occasions (vv. 3–5).

Who should praise? "Everything that has breath" (v. 6). Young and old. Rich and poor. Weak and strong. Every living creature. God's will is for everyone to whom He gave the breath of life to use that breath to acknowledge His power and greatness.

Praise is our enthusiastic expression of gratitude to God for reigning in glory forever.

JULIE ACKERMAN LINK

Praise is the overflow of a joyful heart.

Let's Celebrate

PSALM 150

Praise him with timbrel and dancing,
praise him with the strings and pipe.
PSALM 150:4

After Ghana's Asamoah Gyan scored a goal against Germany in the 2014 World Cup, he and his teammates did a coordinated dance step. When Germany's Miroslav Klose scored a few minutes later, he did a running front flip. "Soccer celebrations are so appealing because they reveal players' personalities, values, and passions," says Clint Mathis, who scored for the US at the 2002 World Cup.

In Psalm 150, the psalmist invites "everything that has breath" to celebrate and praise the Lord in many different ways. He suggests that we use trumpets and harps, stringed instruments and pipes, cymbals and dancing. He encourages us to creatively and passionately celebrate, honor, and adore the Lord. Because the Lord is great and has performed mighty acts on behalf of His people, He is worthy of all praise. These outward expressions of praise will come from an inner wellspring overflowing with gratitude to God. "Let everything that has breath praise the LORD," the psalmist declares (150:6).

Though we may celebrate the Lord in different ways (I'm not encouraging back flips in our worship services), our praise to God always needs to be expressive and meaningful. When we think about the Lord's character and His mighty acts toward us, we cannot help but celebrate Him through our praise and worship.

MARVIN WILLIAMS

Praise is the song of a soul set free.

Prelude of Praise

PSALM 150

*Then I will ever sing in praise of your name
and fulfill my vows day after day.*
PSALM 61:8

We enter a concert hall, find our seats, and listen with anticipation as the members of the orchestra tune their instruments. The sound is discordant, not melodic. But the tuning is simply a prelude to the symphony.

C. S. Lewis suggested that's how it is with our devotional practices and even our worship services. Sometimes they sound discordant, but God hears our prayers and praises with fatherly delight. We are really preparing for participation in the glorious symphony of heaven. Now we are making a minuscule contribution to the harmonies of angelic and redeemed hosts. But our adoration, though feeble, pleases the heart of the Divine Listener more than the finest rendition of earth's greatest orchestra.

Are we eagerly awaiting our participation in heaven's symphony of praise? Are we joyfully participating in the adoration that delights the heart of God? Or do we regard devotion as more of a discipline than a delight?

Our attitudes will be transformed when we realize that praise delights God's heart. Praise helps us to tune our lives to heavenly harmonies.

Praise is an indispensable preparation for the worship that will be our eternal joy.

VERNON GROUNDS

The heart filled with praise brings pleasure to God.

Worship

PSALM 150

Let everything that has breath praise the LORD. Praise the LORD.
PSALM 150:6

Church people can get quite upset about music. Some Christians feel that God is particularly drawn to old hymns sung to the strains of a pipe organ. Others are sure that God enjoys choruses sung over and over again. Some clap their hands when they sing while others fold their arms.

Many modern Christians would be quite unsettled if they had to worship with the ancient Israelites. They might resent the loud, boisterous music. And talk about a praise band! The instruments in the orchestra—wind, string, and percussion together—sounded out their hymns to God. In the middle of the worship, people danced. Large choirs sang their anthems heralding God's greatness.

God demands our praise! That is not negotiable. He would be dishonest if He said there was something or someone in the universe more worthy of praise than himself.

Let's worship! "Let everything that has breath praise the LORD. Praise the LORD!" (Psalm 150:6).

HADDON ROBINSON

There are many ways to worship God, but only one God to worship.

OUR DAILY BREAD WRITERS

JAMES BANKS
Pastor of Peace Church in Durham, North Carolina, Dr. James Banks has written several books for Discovery House, including *Praying Together* and *Prayers for Prodigals*.

HENRY BOSCH (1914–1995)
Henry G. Bosch was the founder of *Our Daily Bread* and one of its first writers. Throughout his life, he battled illness but turned his weaknesses into spiritual encouragement for others through his devotional writing.

DAVE BRANON
An editor with Discovery House, Dave has been involved with *Our Daily Bread* since the 1980s. He has written several books, including *Beyond the Valley* and *Stand Firm*, both DH publications.

ANNE CETAS
After becoming a Christian in her late teens, Anne was introduced to *Our Daily Bread* right away and began reading it. Now she reads it for a living as managing editor of *Our Daily Bread*.

POH FANG CHIA
Like Anne Cetas, Poh Fang trusted Jesus Christ as Savior as a teenager. She is an editor and a part of the Chinese editorial review committee serving in the Our Daily Bread Ministries Singapore office.

BILL CROWDER
A former pastor who is now an associate teacher for Our Daily Bread Ministries, Bill travels extensively as a Bible conference teacher, sharing God's truths with fellow believers in Malaysia and Singapore and other places where ODB Ministries has international offices. His Discovery House books include *Windows on Easter* and *Let's Talk*.

LAWRENCE DARMANI
A noted novelist and publisher in Ghana, Lawrence is editor of *Step* magazine and CEO of Step Publishers. He and his family live in Accra, Ghana.

His book *Grief Child*, earned him the Commonwealth Writers' Prize as best first book by a writer in Africa.

DENNIS DEHAAN (1932–2014)

When Henry Bosch retired, Dennis became the second managing editor of *Our Daily Bread*. A former pastor, he loved preaching and teaching the Word of God. Dennis went to be with the Lord in 2014.

KURT DEHAAN (1953–2003)

Kurt was a vital part of the ministry founded by his grandfather Dr. M. R. DeHaan in 1938. He faithfully led *Our Daily Bread* as the managing editor for many years, and often wrote for other ministry publications until his sudden death in 2003. Kurt died of a heart attack while jogging. He and his wife Mary had four children: Katie, Anna, Claire, and Nathan.

MART DEHAAN

The former president of Our Daily Bread Ministries, Mart followed in the footsteps of his grandfather M. R. and his dad Richard in that capacity. Mart, who has long been associated with *Day of Discovery* as host of the program from Israel, is now senior content advisor for Our Daily Bread Ministries.

M. R. DEHAAN (1891–1965)

Dr. M. R. DeHaan founded this ministry in 1938 when his radio program went out over the air in Detroit, Michigan, and eventually Radio Bible Class was begun. Under his leadership, *Our Daily Bread* was first published in April 1956.

RICHARD DEHAAN (1923–2002)

Son of the founder of Our Daily Bread Ministries, Dr. M. R. DeHaan, Richard was responsible for the ministry's entrance into television. Under his leadership, *Day of Discovery* television made its debut in 1968.

DAVID EGNER

A retired Our Daily Bread Ministries editor and longtime *Our Daily Bread* writer, David was also a college professor during his working career. In fact, he was a writing instructor for both Anne Cetas and Julie Ackerman Link at Cornerstone University.

DENNIS FISHER

As a senior research editor at Our Daily Bread Ministries, Dennis uses his theological training to guarantee biblical accuracy. He is also an expert in C. S. Lewis studies.

VERNON GROUNDS (1914–2010)

A longtime college president (Denver Seminary) and board member for Our Daily Bread Ministries, Vernon's life story was told in the Discovery House book *Transformed by Love*. Dr. Grounds died in 2010 at the age of 96.

TIM GUSTAFSON

Tim writes for *Our Daily Bread* and *Our Daily Journey* and serves as an editor for Discovery Series. As the son of missionaries to Ghana, Tim has an unusual perspective on life in the West. He and his wife, Leisa, are the parents of one daughter and seven sons.

CINDY HESS KASPER

An editor for the Our Daily Bread Ministries publication *Our Daily Journey,* Cindy began writing for *Our Daily Bread* in 2006. She and her husband, Tom, have three children and seven grandchildren.

ALYSON KIEDA

Alyson Kieda has been an editor for Our Daily Bread Ministries for over a decade—and has over thirty-five years of editing experience. Alyson has loved writing since she was a child and is thrilled to be writing for *Our Daily Bread*. She is married with three adult children and a growing number of grandchildren.

RANDY KILGORE

Randy spent most of his 20-plus years in business as a senior human resource manager before returning to seminary. Since finishing his Masters in Divinity in 2000, he has served as a writer and workplace chaplain. A collection of those devotionals appears in the Discovery House book, *Made to Matter: Devotions for Working Christians*. Randy and his wife, Cheryl, and their two children live in Massachusetts.

JULIE ACKERMAN LINK (1950–2015)

A book editor by profession, Julie began writing for *Our Daily Bread* in 2000. Her books *Above All, Love* and *A Heart for God* are available through Discovery House. Julie lost her long battle with cancer in April 2015.

DAVID MCCASLAND

Living in Colorado, David enjoys the beauty of God's grandeur as displayed in the Rocky Mountains. An accomplished biographer, David has written several books, including the award-winning *Oswald Chambers: Abandoned to God*, and *Eric Liddell: Pure Gold*.

KEILA OCHOA

From her home in Mexico, Keila assists with Media Associates International, a group that trains writers around the world to write about faith. She and her husband have two young children.

AMY BOUCHER PYE

Amy is a writer, editor, and speaker. The author of *Finding Myself in Britain: Our Search for Faith, Home, and True Identity*, she runs the Woman Alive book club in the UK and enjoys life with her family in their English vicarage.

HADDON ROBINSON

Haddon, a renowned expert on preaching, served many years as a seminary professor. He wrote numerous books and hundreds of magazine articles. For a number of years he was a panelist on Our Daily Bread Ministries' radio program *Discover the Word*.

DAVID ROPER

David Roper lives in Idaho, where he takes advantage of the natural beauty of his state. He has been writing for *Our Daily Bread* since 2000, and he has published several successful books with Discovery House, including *Out of the Ordinary* and *Teach Us to Number Our Days*.

JENNIFER BENSON SCHULDT

Chicagoan Jennifer Schuldt writes from the perspective of a mom of a growing family. She has written for *Our Daily Bread* since 2010, and she also pens articles for another Our Daily Bread Ministries publication: *Our Daily Journey*.

JOE STOWELL

As president of Cornerstone University, Joe stays connected to today's young adults in a leadership role. A popular speaker and a former pastor, Joe has written a number of books over the years, including *Strength for the Journey* and *Jesus Nation*.

MARION STROUD (1940-2015)

After a battle with cancer, Marion went to be with her Savior in August 2015. Marion began writing devotional articles for *Our Daily Bread* in 2014. Two of her popular books of prayers, *Dear God, It's Me and It's Urgent* and *It's Just You and Me, Lord* were published by Discovery House.

HERB VANDER LUGT (1920-2006)

For many years, Herb was senior research editor at Our Daily Bread Ministries, responsible for checking the biblical accuracy of the booklets published by ODB Ministries. A World War II veteran, Herb spent several years as a pastor before his ODB tenure began. Herb went to be with his Lord and Savior in 2006.

PAUL VAN GORDER (1921-2009)

A writer for *Our Daily Bread* in the 1980s and 1990s, Paul was a noted pastor and Bible teacher—both in the Atlanta area where he lived and through the *Day of Discovery* TV program. Paul's earthly journey ended in 2009.

JOANIE YODER (1934-2004)

For 10 years, until her death in 2004, Joanie wrote for *Our Daily Bread*. In addition, she published the book *God Alone* with Discovery House.

MARVIN WILLIAMS

Marvin's first foray into Our Daily Bread Ministries came as a writer for *Our Daily Journey*. In 2007, he penned his first *Our Daily Bread* article. Marvin is senior teaching pastor at a church in Lansing, Michigan. His book *Radical Generosity* is available from Discovery House.